9

MEXICAN WORKERS

AND THE STATE

From the Porfiriato to NAFTA

MEXICAN WORKERS

AND THE STATE

From the Porfiriato to NAFTA

By
Norman Caulfield

TEXAS CHRISTIAN UNIVERSITY PRESS / FORT WORTH

Library of Congress Cataloging-in-Publication Data

Caulfield, Norman.
      Mexican workers and the state : from the Porfiriato to NAFTA / by Norman Caulfield
         p. c.m.
      Includes bibliographical references and index.
      ISBN 0-87565-192-5 (alk. Paper)
      1. Labor movement—Mexico—History—20th century. 2. Labor policy—Mexico—
History—20th century. I. Title.
HD8114.C3 1998
332'.2'0972—dc21
98-16392
CIP

Cover and text design by Bill Maize; Duo Design Group

for
María Elena Esquivel Caulfield
and Margarita Caulfield

CONTENTS

ACKNOWLEDGMENTS

Conceptualization of this book began many years ago, studying Latin American history at the University of Houston under the tutelage of Professors John Mason Hart and Thomas F. O'Brien. I owe much gratitude to them as mentors who were always available to give me direction and valued advice. Above all, I thank them for sifting through earlier versions of this book and offering insightful criticism. I have tried to emulate their demanding yet friendly style when working with students.

Of course, many people and institutions share responsibility for enabling me to complete this project. Professor William Beezley's support of this work is greatly appreciated. I also thank James Kirby Martin for his patience in helping a raw and overanxious graduate student to think and to write. Raymond Wilson, friend and colleague in the history department at Fort Hays State University, was persistent in encouraging me to plug away and complete this work. Mark Roller, art major and history student, was instrumental for the illustration stage of the manuscript. Fort Hays State University provided me with a sabbatical, which contributed immensely to the writing of this book. I also wish to thank the *International Review of Social History* and Cambridge University Press for allowing me to reprint reworked versions of my articles, "Wobblies and Mexican Workers in Mining and Petroleum, 1905-1924" (volume 40, 1995), and "Mexican State Development Policy and Labor Internationalism, 1945-1958," (volume 42, 1997). Information culled from *Mexican Labor News and Analysis* was crucial in bringing the last chapter up to date. Dan La Botz and the United Electrical Workers (UE) provide an excellent resource on labor news. Readers can access the UE's international web site at www.igc.apc.org/unitedelect/ or communicate with La Botz directly at 103144.2651@compuserve.com. Special thanks goes to the staff at TCU Press, especially Tracy Row, whose timely assistance and gentle pushing helped generate the final product.

My immediate and extended families offered encouragement as well. My father, Robert Caulfield, always cognizant of his working-class roots, along with my brothers and sisters, let me know that they cared about this project. My daughter, Margarita, and my loving wife, María Elena, deserve the real credit. Especially important was their patience and sense of humor, which always seemed to make the bumps along the road tolerable. Finally, I thank all of those salt-of-the-earth people who toiled alongside me during my "unlettered years," which always served as a reference point while working on this book.

Norman Caulfield
LaCrosse, Kansas

GLOBALISM AND REVOLUTION REVISITED

Ricardo Flores Magón, Mexican revolutionary, anarchist, labor organizer, and long considered one of the important precursors of the Mexican Revolution, challenged the prevailing social order in both Mexico and the United States in his "Manifesto to the Workers of the World." Issued in November 1914, it described the Mexican Revolution as economic and called upon workers in the United States to act in solidarity with Mexicans as they fought to shake off the yoke of capitalism. He added that the Mexican workers' fight was not a national one, but universal, because the cause of the "wage slave" has no frontiers. Magón also warned the American worker of the dire consequences if the revolution failed.[1] If Mexico's workers lost, Flores Magón predicted, the nation would become an ideal land for business because of low salaries, and American workers would find their firms and factories there instead of the United States because it would be more profitable to employ Mexicans.[2]

Although international in scope, Magón's message had strong nationalistic overtones. He and his followers opposed what anarchists called economic despotism, exploitation, material privilege; and they identified capitalism as a form of theft. Because many Mexican workers toiled for foreign employers, their protests over low wages, long hours and poor conditions evolved into a larger struggle that viewed foreigners as parasitic outsiders with no legitimate claim to the nation's resources, labor and economic infrastructure. These struggles produced a working-class nationalism, the essence of which was the "Mexicanization" of foreign-owned enterprises under the aegis of workers' self-management. Although the anarchism of Ricardo Flores Magón represented a strong ideological current within working-class nationalism, he and his close associates remained in self-imposed exile in the United States, while members of the Mexican Liberal Party (PLM) united social classes around a more narrow form of nationalism.[3]

This group of disgruntled intellectuals representing the intermediate classes increasingly received support from sectors of the politically sophisticated elite of northern Mexico who viewed the growing national government and American domination of their region as an economic and political threat. By 1910 these forces had joined a cross-class alliance that called not only for armed struggle against Porfirio Díaz, but also for agrarian and labor reform. In 1911 this coalition of classes united around Francisco Madero's program of "Effective Suffrage, No Re-election," and overthrew the Díaz regime.

As an intellectual and elite member of northern provincial society, Madero (whose education included studies at universities in Europe and the United States) had fallen under the influence of antipositivist philosopher Karl Christian Krause (1781-1832), a contemporary of positivist philosopher Auguste Comte. While not rejecting the crucial components of positivist philosophy, namely order and progress, Krausism aimed at transforming society with a redemptive moral aspect. Thus Madero's moralism focused exclusively on political change, believing that socioeconomic adjustments would result from reforming the Porfirian process and system. Madero's concentration on politics denied the reality of the gross material inequities in Mexican society. Accordingly, he lacked the conviction to remedy the problems of the nation's workers and peasants.[4]

While Madero balked at enacting genuine labor and agrarian reform, the PLM split ranks over revolutionary strategy and tactics. The *magonista* faction promoted the mobilization of workers and peasants through the 1911 PLM program, which among other things, called for a war to the death against private property and existing political authority. Others in the PLM dissented by embracing reform socialism and collaborating with the *maderista* mainstream of the revolution, hoping to gradually implement the PLM program through peaceful means.

On September 22, 1912, PLM members played an active role in founding the Casa del Obrero Mundial (House of the World Worker). Although the Casa functioned as an open forum for the debate of a myriad of political tendencies, anarchosyndicalism (loosely defined as a doctrine in which workers take control of the economy by radical means such as a strike) represented its strongest ideological current. The Casa's growth, combined with continuing revolutionary turmoil, resulted in Madero's murder and downfall, spawning the emergence of a new government led by a group of revolutionary generals calling themselves the Constitutionalists. Representing a third position between capital and labor, it took over the prevailing ideology of the Revolution, which was agrarian, nationalist and proletarian. Immediately, this elite group established an intermediate and shaky regime that maintained itself by playing off the interests of capital and labor, both foreign and domestic.[5]

The first example of this occurred in 1915, when the Casa signed a pact to take up arms with General Alvaro Obregón and the Constitutionalists against the forces of Pancho Villa's Division of the North and Zapata's Army of the South. Casa leaders had hoped that the defeat of the peasantry would· set the stage for a proletarian explosion. Instead, the head of the Constitutionalist cause, Venustiano Carranza, permanently suppressed the Casa in the aftermath of a failed general strike of Mexico City in August 1916. Besides decapitating the independent working-class movement, the Casa's defeat also created an equilibrium between social classes, which the revolutionary generals were able to rise above in the role of moderator.

The 1917 Constitution reflected this new set of conditions and demonstrated that the Mexican state was attempting to transcend class interests. Article 27 declared the nation's ownership of all minerals and oil deposits in the subsoil, and Article 123 ensured the right of workers to organize and strike. While Articles 27 and 123 reflected the political strength of working-class nationalism, the Constitution also provided ideological coherence and consensus for an emerging elite nationalism. Having been grounded in the protection of private property and development within the capitalist framework, the elite nationalism that emerged with the writing of the Constitution was an ideological amalgam that not only incorporated working-class demands, but also the slogan that united all social classes during the Revolution, "Mexico for the Mexicans." The Constitution established a stable basis for rule and allowed the victorious elite to emerge as state builders, creating political institutions that incorporated the subordinate participation of workers and other social groups defeated during the Revolution.

Despite the establishment of what Italian revolutionary Antonio Gramsci called the "hegemony of ruling ideas," the elite struggled to limit the expression of workers' demands, repress rank-and-file militancy, and convert labor unions into completely passive instruments of the state.[6] In the aftermath of the Revolution and the decades that followed, the state-building upper classes never established total ideological hegemony. Their forced co-existence with organized labor produced political space for ideas and values that were "counter-hegemonic," and in opposition to elite nationalism. As Gramsci writes, "worldviews are rarely consistent; they typically involve a contradictory amalgam of ideas."[7] Following Gramsci's analysis, working-class and elite nationalism can be seen as dividing, merging, agreeing, and conflicting, in a continuing and varied dynamic.

Fundamental to this process was the continued foreign domination of the Mexican economy. As foreign-owned enterprises violated Article 123 with impunity, workers followed anarchosyndicalist leaders in demanding higher wages, better conditions, union recognition and the self-management of nationalized industries. Caught between working-class nationalism and a weakness in the face of foreign capital, the post-revolutionary politicians searched for a sophisticated response to Mexico's social problems. The result was the state's backing of the *Confederación Regional Obrera Mexicana* (CROM), which accommodated workers' demands while limiting the scope of change by defeating radical unionism. This intersected with the labor movement in the United States and involved the direct participation of the reformist American Federation of Labor (AFL) and the revolutionary Industrial Workers of the World (IWW), or "Wobblies."

The AFL endorsed the official relationship between the CROM and the Mexican government, partially to neutralize the activities of its chief rival, the IWW. Fearing the influence of IWW internationalism, Samuel Gompers, AFL president, promoted the concept of "business unionism" for Mexico's workers. He described business unionism as trade unionism "pure and simple," a struggle for higher wages and benefits that excludes the notion that workers form a class with widely shared interests.[8]

Gregg Andrews, in his study of the AFL and the Mexican Revolution, writes that the AFL's response to the conflict forged the beginnings of tripartite structures designed to maintain U.S. hegemony in Latin America.[9] The AFL consistently sought a consensus of big business, labor and government, which involved its "labor aristocracy" membership receiving higher wages in exchange for supporting the expansion of corporate interests and opposing radicalism at home and abroad.[10] Because Mexico's workers represented a potential market for manufactured goods, Samuel Gompers and the AFL ardently supported their right to organize and earn a better wage. Accordingly, the AFL opposed working-class nationalism because it threatened to remove Mexico from the geopolitical orbit of the United States. Gompers was insistent that Mexican workers, like their North American counterparts, accept the capitalist framework and labor's subordinate position within the system. Prosperity would be achieved through mediation and conciliation, thus unions and employers would work out their problems through evolutionary rather than revolutionary processes.[11] The AFL's mission was the promotion of a rational strategy of cooperation and goodwill, which in the process would eradicate the emotional European radicalism found in Mexico, which stemmed from Spanish roots.[12]

The AFL's support of the establishment of business unionism and its desires to moderate revolutionary nationalism clashed with the IWW, which had organized Mexican workers on both sides of the border since the early days of the Revolution. Although numerous works on the AFL's involvement in the Mexican Revolution exist, a thorough examination of IWW activities south of the border has yet to be explored. The IWW's presence in Mexico resulted from shared levels of industrial development among regional economies that straddled the international border. Uniting the two economies initiated a cross-border flow of Mexican migrants, laborers who joined American workers to protest the abusive practices of turn-of-the-century North American capitalist management. As the Revolution unfolded, the interaction between Mexican workers, their organizations, and the U.S. labor movement intensified. This was especially true for Mexican workers in mining and petroleum, where workplace organization and the quest for immediate gains took on revolutionary significance.

Like the Casa, the IWW advocated anarchosyndicalism, which—among other things—called for the building of a labor movement through a series of strikes around immediate demands for better pay and conditions. Bread-and-butter issues, combined with the objective of future workers' self-management, struck a responsive chord among laborers caught up in a nationalist revolution. Mexican workers sought to regain control from foreigners the nation's natural resources, productive systems and economic infrastructure. The IWW's early organization of Mexican miners in the U.S. and its willingness to confront American corporate management on both sides of the border bolstered its credibility among Mexican workers. And, because its ideological orientation corresponded to the Mexican labor movement's deeply rooted anarchosyndicalist traditions, it found acceptance among Mexican workers within the context of Mexican nationalism and the Revolution.

During the late 1910s and the early 1920s, the Wobblies cooperated with remnants of the Casa and other radical labor groups and agitated among petroleum workers, especially in the Tampico region. As a result, they became central to the tension that developed between foreign-owned petroleum companies and the Mexican government. Because the IWW's presence was so pervasive in strategic profit-making industries like mining and petroleum, its activities help to explain the shifting diplomatic, economic and political interests of foreigners and Mexicans and the role that organized labor played during the Revolution. The IWW was central to the interplay between the forces of revolutionary nationalism, labor internationalism as represented by the AFL, and prerogatives of foreign capital in Mexico.

Along with the *Confederación General de Trabajadores* (CGT) and other radical labor groups, the IWW combated the growing CROM-AFL partnership.

Although the Wobblies and their allies presented formidable opposition to the AFL, the CROM, and the government, they ultimately failed to stop the spread of reform unionism. Their defeat resulted from a number of factors. First, the CROM strengthened its control over arbitration and conciliation boards (created by Article 123) and punished its militant rivals by securing decisions favorable toward its own organizing activities. More importantly, however, the CROM and the government worked in tandem to win ideological consent to their domination and rule. Because Mexican working-class experiences involved resistance to foreign exploitation and domination, they embraced an implicit nationalistic worldview. In defeating the anarchosyndicalists, the CROM skillfully drew out and systematized the worldview that was implicit in working-class practices of resistance. By attacking ideologies such as communism and anarchosyndicalism as a foreign discourse, the CROM and the government portrayed radical unionism as anti-Mexican; conspiracies designed in places like Bolshevik Russia. Working-class leaders who championed "foreign ideologies" were attempting to destroy the Revolution and the developing "organic link" between organized labor and the emerging revolutionary party of generals and bureaucrats.

The CROM's promotion of "workers' cooperatives" as a substitute for self-management in expropriated industries complemented the government's deportation of "internationalist" radicals and "pernicious" foreigners. Through the further systemic development of elite nationalism, state-builders and their labor allies thwarted the counter hegemony posed by the IWW, the CGT and other radical groups. As a capstone to establishing a "hegemony of ruling ideas," the state constructed a political party that effectively subordinated working-class organization to the interests of the "whole nation."

Although effectively suppressed on an organizational level by the mid-1920s, anarchosyndicalism was not purged entirely. Because the CROM and the government failed to confront the power of foreign-owned enterprises, labor unrest continued. The CROM's promotion of a political consensus revolving around elite nationalism had degenerated into a bureaucratically managed collaboration between capital and labor, both foreign and domestic. The governments of Alvaro Obregón (1920-1924) and Plutarco Elías Calles (1924-1928) failed in their efforts to establish a margin of economic independence from foreign capital as they reached financial accommodations with the United States. While this occurred, workers in foreign-dominated enterprises, especially in mining and petroleum, organized independent trade unions and remained outside of government tutelage and

CROM control. The increased labor militancy unleashed by the Great Depression further exposed the inherent contradictions of elite nationalism and its compromise with foreign economic interests. The government reacted to the crisis by withdrawing its long-time support for the CROM and searching for ways to direct the insurgent working-class nationalism. The result was the July 1931 passage of the Federal Labor Code, giving the government the power to recognize unions, legitimate strikes and intervene in labor conflicts. The law paved the way for a new labor-state alliance and the creation of the *Confederación de Trabajadores de México* (CTM) to replace the corrupt and discredited CROM. President Lázaro Cárdenas encouraged labor mobilization through the CTM with the hope of institutionalizing worker discontent.

A renewed political consensus fusing working-class and elite nationalism occurred, and it facilitated Cárdenas' ability to stand up to foreign economic pressures and enforce the provisions of Article 27. The expropriation of the foreign-owned oil companies and landholdings bolstered the country's political and economic independence and raised organized labor's expectations of workers' self-management of the nationalized industries. The consensus unraveled when rank-and-file clashed with government within the framework of production politics. The CTM collaborated with the government in suppressing workers' control in large industries like petroleum and promoting state-run experiments with worker self-management on the railroads and in small- and medium-sized enterprises. Militant workers advocating self-management of the petroleum industry were called "traitors" and "agents" of foreign governments and oil companies.

In his book on American enterprise in Latin America, Thomas F. O'Brien writes that the oil nationalization defined *Cardenismo*. Obregón and Calles failed not only to create a margin of economic independence but also faltered in their efforts to forge a partnership with foreign capital as well. By striking out at a major symbol of foreign corporate power, Cárdenas successfully garnered universal support within Mexican society, which enabled politicians to reassert their claim as heir to the nationalist traditions of the Mexican Revolution. This allowed Cárdenas to rein in militant workers in other economic sectors controlled by foreigners, harmonizing relations between capital and labor, thus balancing the interests of foreign capital (necessary for Mexico's modernization) and the nationalistic Mexican masses.[13]

Like the revolutionary and reconstruction periods, organized labor from the U.S. played a key role in suppressing working-class nationalism. Aiding the CTM and the state to formulate policy was the newly formed

7

Congress of Industrial Organizations (CIO) from the United States. The CIO gave tacit support for the oil nationalization, and the CTM skillfully manipulated it to suppress workers' self-management in the new state-run industry. As in the 1920s, political leaders had established a "hegemony of ruling ideas" that found support among broad sectors of the Mexican working class, which welcomed government control of nationalized industries as preferable to the chaos of industrial democracy. The effective suppression of the demand for workers' self-management paralleled the increased subordination of working-class organization to the goal of state development policy within the capitalist framework.

During the administrations of Manuel Avila Camacho (1940-1946) and Miguel Alemán (1946-1952) this process accelerated. Because the Mexican economy received such a boost from the demand generated by the Second World War, the Avila Camacho government and the CTM implemented a labor peace, which included a no-strike pledge and a major modification of the nation's labor code. The changes gave more power to arbitration boards and severe penalties for workers carrying out illegal strikes.

The CTM cooperated with the government because its principal leaders, especially the Marxist Vicente Lombardo Toledano, believed in the progressive character of the state's economic development project of "accelerated industrialization." Like other Marxists of his time, Lombardo had hoped that the development of "productive forces" in Mexico would ripen conditions for an eventual confrontation between the bourgeoisie and proletariat. Meanwhile, Lombardo asserted, organized labor should stand with the "whole nation," as an underdeveloped Mexico struggled against economically advanced countries like the United States. According to Lombardo, "excessive" demands by workers jeopardized this strategy. At the end of the Second World War, the CTM and the government continued to press for minimizing labor conflict and maximizing production.

The quest for "class peace" failed. Despite more changes in the law that imposed severe penalties on unions for conducting work stoppages, strikes by major industrial unions increased in number and intensity. The growth of insurgent factions within CTM unions was responsible. Calling themselves *depuradas* (purified unions), they rallied worker support by demanding higher wages, union autonomy and defending the rights won by Mexican labor during the Revolution. By 1948 the CTM suffered from major defections within its ranks. In addition to the withdrawal of the petroleum, railroad and mining unions was the emergence of several new federations declaring their independence of the government.

The Alemán administration reacted to the groundswell by crushing the powerful independent unions and installing *charros* (leaders who followed government policy and used violence against their opponents). In the process, Alemán embraced the anticommunism of the Cold War, further opened the Mexican economy to foreign capital and deepened the country's relationship with the United States. As the nation speeded ahead with what historian Barry Carr calls the "Frenesí of Developmentalism," the power of foreign capital increased while the living standards of the working class deteriorated.[14] By the early 1950s, with the assistance and escalated involvement of organized labor from the United States, charros had captured control of most major unions. The historiography of Mexican labor lacks a detailed study of the important role that the U.S. labor movement exercised in helping the Mexican state and its CTM allies to consolidate the *charro* system. As Gregg Andrews writes, AFL activities in Mexico during the Gompers era provided U.S officials and businessmen with a framework to preserve the long-range strategic and economic policy toward Mexico through financial diplomacy and less confrontational means. After World War II, the AFL's early labor diplomacy became more significant, when international bankers, multinational corporations, and U.S. officials conceded a more aggressive role for organized labor in foreign policy.[15]

The strategy to promote capitalist-oriented trade unions in Mexico and elsewhere in Latin America by American labor, business and government officials intensified in the post-war era to protect the growing informal empire of the United States. As U.S. investment poured into the country, blunting radical unionism became a central feature of the American government's policy toward Mexico. Besides attaching labor experts to the American embassy to monitor trade-union activities, the U.S. State Department acted as a liaison between union leaders of both countries. The objective was to steer Mexican labor away from working-class nationalism and foster an acceptance of the increased presence of American capital in Mexico. Through the distribution of propaganda and dollars to the CTM and its affiliates, American unions participated as key players in the removal of "independents" and "communists" from union posts and in the entrenchment of charro leaders.

Charro domination paralleled the transformation of the elite social structure and the Mexican state. Since 1940 the business sector has increased its influence within the state bureaucracy while working-class organization has gradually weakened and labor's share of national income has declined. While elite and working-class nationalism merged and divided during the 1910s, 1920s and 1930s, since 1940 the Mexican state has veered toward domestic and foreign capital and gradually has abandoned labor as a base of social support. Meanwhile, rank-and-file workers have been backed into a corner, struggling to defend their rights won during the Revolution and outlined in the 1917 Constitution.

Despite the state's development of more sophisticated methods of repression and co-optation, its hegemony over organized labor has never been complete. Elements of the working class continue to resist top-down control of their unions and seek organizational autonomy. The government's suppression of the 1958-1959 railroaders' rebellion against *charrismo* and the emergence of independent unions in the last two decades, reflects the on-going contradictions between the working class, the bureaucracy and its increasing accommodation of foreign economic interests. The 1968 student rebellion also exposed these contradictions. It represented a broad-based social movement that demanded that the Mexican state live up to the 1917 Constitution, democratize the system and invite popular participation in government.

The implementation of the North American Free Trade Agreement (NAFTA) and the increasing presence of direct U.S. investment in Mexico verifies the prediction made by Ricardo Flores Magón in his 1914 "Manifesto to the Workers of the World." Mexico's struggle to maintain control over the nation's economic infrastructure, resources and production systems demonstrates the limits of nationalism in the increasingly dynamic and inclusive world economic system of the late-twentieth century. In modern Mexico, these conditions have determined the nature of the conflict between workers and the state and their allies, both external and internal.

Finally, as the Mexican government of the 1990s pursues an economic development strategy to promote the nation as a haven for low-wage export manufacturing and makes further accommodations to foreign economic interests, the future of state-labor relations has yet to be answered. Will working-class nationalism re-emerge to challenge these policies? Will organized labor in the U.S. and Mexico initiate the practice of a labor internationalism that Ricardo Flores Magón had hoped for nearly a century ago? What follows is a history of state-labor relations that should provoke discourse on an increasingly important subject affecting our times.

CHAPTER ONE

A REVOLUTION FRAGMENTS

In the aftermath of a miners' uprising in 1906, the pro-Díaz newspaper *El Imparcial* complained that anarchists, socialists and nihilists had captured and subverted the labor movement by brainwashing the gullible working-man. That same year, *El Imparcial* noted that the nation had embraced the slogan "Mexico for the Mexicans" and that workers were responsible for it.[1] In 1916 and 1917 management of the foreign-owned oil companies at Tampico lamented that radical labor agitators badgered "good" Mexican workers into striking. For the next several years many U.S. diplomats openly expressed fears that radicalism among workers threatened to bring Bolshevism to Mexico. What were the origins of this labor unrest?

Almost immediately after its formation, the Mexican working class participated as part of a revolutionary storm that included peasants, a politically disillusioned middle class, intelligentsia, and provincial and local elites. This coalition unified around nationalism and protested foreign-control over the nation's basic resources and economic structure. This broad-based, cross-class alliance viewed the Mexican state as its adversary, claiming that the government acted as a subordinate ally of foreign capital in its efforts to acquire massive quantities of raw materials, inexpensive labor and new consumers.

In the process of opposing foreign capital and the regime that served it, Mexican workers developed a myriad of ideologies, such as reform socialism, anarchism and syndicalism. Almost simultaneously these ideological tendencies converged to create a working-class nationalism that was widespread among labor organizations. These groups called for wage equity with foreigners, decent living standards, an end to dictatorial rule and workers' control of foreign-owned enterprises. In 1911 they formed part of a nationalistic multi-class coalition that overthrew the Díaz regime. But the nationalism that emerged during the Revolution and provided the "unifying" ideology for all social classes fragmented along class lines.

The nationalism espoused by the middle strata and local and provincial elites that protected private property and the profit system contrasted with working-class nationalism. Because anarchosyndicalists looked on capitalism as their fundamental enemy and represented the best-organized ideological tendency within the working-class, the elites were unwilling to permit the organized labor movement to develop independently. To counter this tendency and control the direction of organized labor, the state began its long history of enlisting the support of the U.S.-based AFL. The elite promotion of a reformist labor policy had a decisive impact on the working-class movement and produced divisions within the ranks of organized labor.

Anarchosyndicalists and reform socialists split ranks over the question of cooperation with post-revolutionary governments. The rupture within the working-class movement first became apparent in 1915, when the Casa del Obrero Mundial took up arms with the Constitutionalists and defeated the agrarian forces led by Pancho Villa and Emiliano Zapata. Although the Casa experienced a crushing defeat in the 1916 Mexico City general strike, the 1917 Constitution reflected the agrarian, nationalist and proletarian ideology of the Revolution. In theory, the document merged working-class and elite nationalism, but in practice it neither mended the divisions within the working-class movement, nor did it reconcile Mexican nationalism with foreign economic interests.

Foreigners continued to dominate the Mexican economy, and in most cases, refused to comply with Mexican law. The result was enduring anarchosyndicalist organization in the nation's industrial periphery, where the IWW and Casa remnants organized workers around the immediate demands of higher wages, better conditions and union recognition. The co-optation and repression employed by the state against the anarchosyndicalists subdued them only temporarily, because enforcement of the 1917 Constitution was too slow to satisfy the expectations of a nationalistic working class. This condition not only generated an intense ideological debate within the working-class movement, but also sharpened the contradictions among the state-building elite, organized labor and foreign economic interests.

THE IDEOLOGY OF AN INTERRUPTED REVOLUTION

Workers emerged as an important social class during the closing decades of the nineteenth century when Mexico experienced rapid social and economic change. Peasants migrated from the countryside and worked in an expanding network of industries in cities and towns. Under the impact of favorable government policies toward foreign investors, thousands of peasants lost their land and earned their livelihoods in the manufacturing, mining, construction, service and transportation sectors of the economy. Another large group joined their ranks as day laborers when the traditional peasant economy had been pushed aside in favor of privately owned estates. Although Mexico's industrial workers comprised only sixteen percent of the nation's economically active population, they existed in highly concentrated pockets. By 1900 Mexican workers were already showing signs of volatility and propensity for collective action. Factory groups mounted the first large-scale strikes and less than a decade later workers led upheavals that decisively challenged the regime.

Although the ideological character of the working-class challenge to the regime was nationalistic, it also incorporated anarchosyndicalism. Any attempt to conceptualize Mexican anarchosyndicalism must examine how modern industry changed the culture of peasants and artisans as well as the inner structure of life and work characteristic of the pre-Díaz era. Mexican peasants and artisans carried their preindustrial attitudes toward religion, marriage, family, child-rearing, recreation and community to the mines, railroads, oil fields and factories. Their preindustrial customs and traditions shaped their responses to industrialism and facilitated their attempts to recreate stable communities in an alien environment.

Anarchosyndicalism acted as a catalyst in providing the apparatuses that created a new world that satisfied the expectations and forms of security which peasants and artisans carried from their past. Anarchosyndicalism represented a transitional form of labor-movement activity between earlier craft industry and modern-day factory production by calling for workers' control of the wealth created by the wage-labor system. Often misinterpreted as a backward-looking movement to restore a pre-capitalist society of peasant and artisan producers, anarchosyndicalism advocated the decentralization of society run by groups of workers from the workshop floor.[2] Accordingly, anarchosyndicalists developed strategies to organize workers at the point of production rather than through a political party or parliamentary politics. And, since their anti-political stance reflected the view that state institutions abetted the advance of capitalism and political centralization, anarchosyndicalists sought to build organizations independent of government control and tutelage.

The Porfirian government used force and co-optation to stifle anarchosyndicalist organization and promote an environment for industrial development and class peace. From the mid-1880s to 1900, strong labor discipline combined with effective means of co-optation provided "industrial peace" for the foreign investors and the Porfirian regime.[3] The Porfirian state's labor policy remained effective because workers had experienced a slight increase in real wages.[4] By 1900, however, world prices for Mexico's precious metals and export commodities began to fall along with workers' wages, and the fifteen years of "industrial peace" unraveled.

The economic crisis also lowered middle-class expectations and closed the doors to upward social mobility. Witnessing the deterioration of their own social position and a government overwhelmed by foreign economic invasion, the middle classes grew frustrated with the dictatorship. After 1900 the increasing ties between the regime and foreign capital alienated the nation's elite groups, especially northern provincial society, where a large influx of American colonists claimed title to land and resources. Although some members of the northern elite profited from their connections with foreigners, ultimately the failure of the Porfirian political system to address progress and its problems effectively generated an elite crisis. Political modernization did not accompany economic growth and the abrupt erosion of elite political autonomy forced the upper class into action.[5] By 1910 alienation had turned into violent resistance against state authority as the provincial aristocracy joined workers, peasants and the middle classes in open rebellion against the regime. Initially, the excluded social groups used the Mexican Liberal Party (PLM) to oppose the foreign intruders, the regime and its policies.

Founded in the city of San Luis Potosí on February 5, 1901, the PLM adopted a broad program that included land redistribution, social betterment of the masses, and an end to foreign domination of the economy. The PLM's membership, comprised of shopkeepers, local manufacturers, artisans, industrial workers, and village elites, consisted of approximately fifty clubs scattered over the northern half of Mexico. The PLM enjoyed support there and in the industrial areas of the south such as Puebla and Orizaba, where foreign economic interests were overwhelming and radicalism among the workers was on the rise.[6]

Ricardo and Enrique Flores Magón represented the more radical elements within the PLM's leadership. The youths had attended law school at the National University in Mexico City and had become involved in the anti-Díaz student movement. By 1900 they had adopted the anarchist and syndicalist views of Mexico's radical workers and began publishing a resistance newspaper, *Regeneración*, which attacked the government as a tool of foreign interests. When PLM clubs proliferated to over 150 chapters, the regime reacted by closing the paper and jailing the editors in Belem prison. After their release, the Flores Magón brothers and other PLM activists continued to agitate against the government. After three years of constant arrests and intimidation, the Flores Magón brothers and their close associates chose self-imposed exile across the border in the United States.

While in the United States, the *magonistas* continued to publish *Regeneración*, which eventually reached a monthly circulation of 20,000. The ideas that appeared in the pages of *Regeneración* reflected the growing radicalism of the magonistas, who, after moving to the United States, came into contact with American radicals. Through their abandonment of liberalism and their openly declared anarchism, the magonistas committed themselves to organizing the Mexican working class, especially Mexican miners who worked the vast mineral regions that stretched across the American West into northern Mexico. PLM clubs flourished in the mining communities of Sonora and Arizona, like those started by Lázaro Gutiérrez de Lara in Cananea, Sonora, and Praxedis Guerrero's *Obreros Libres* in Morenci, Arizona. Many Mexican miners were already members of the Western Federation of Miners (WFM), a union that had organized Mexican laborers since 1903. By 1906 many WFM organizers had become IWW members and had established ties with the PLM inside Mexico at the Rockefeller-controlled mining complex at Cananea.[7]

The complex at Cananea was part of a vast pool of precious mineral resources that extended north throughout the western United States, where bitter worker-employer relations had emerged. Many Mexicans who had crossed the border and worked in the United States became participants in the intense industrial battles waged in the mining regions of the American West. The veterans of those struggles carried back the organizational methods and strategies of their North-American experience and ultimately contributed to the unrest among miners in northern Mexico.[8]

Miners responded to radical union propaganda because it addressed many of their urgent problems. These included falling wages, the increasing concentration of capitalist industrial power and the consequences of technological change, which, in the mining industry resulted in the displacement or downgrading of craft skills to semi-skilled and unskilled status. With the traditional bargaining strength of skilled labor diminishing, a growing number of miners looked to the joint organization of skilled, semi-skilled and unskilled in one industrial union. The gap between job control and the anarchosyndicalist emphasis on workers' control narrowed as economic grievances mounted and technological dislocation increased. In addition, Mexican miners at Cananea had seen their wages slashed in the face of a fifty percent peso devaluation. Management used discrimination to justify low wages for the Mexican workers, who often received only one-third as much pay as ther American counterparts.[9]

The worsening conditions led to a militant outburst on June 1, 1906. Mexican workers at Cananea demanded equal pay, access to better jobs, an eight-hour day and the dismissal of two abusive American foremen. The Díaz government rejected the Cananea workers' pleas and sent in troops, including 275 Arizona Rangers, to shoot strikers down. Cananea copper management blamed the WFM for the outbreak of the strike, and, fearing the WFM's influence, attempted to get rid of its non-Mexican workforce—about forty percent of the miners. By the end of 1907, more than a year after the uprising, the percentage of non-Mexicans working at the complex had been reduced to twenty-eight.[10]

The Cananea uprising and the Díaz regime's use of force to crush the workers had long-range consequences. The PLM and WFM's work among the miners demonstrated that apart from a small cadre of worker-intellectuals, there existed a far larger group of literate workers. These workers formed the core of a new lower-class reading public for whom the written word increasingly became the dominant means of articulating social values and developing consciousness. The printed word was the principal form of communication in the factory, the mining camp and the city. In the streets, shops and places of work, announcements, signs, newspapers and books, beckoned those who were able to read. Increased worker literacy produced a growing class consciousness, and along with it, a stronger propensity for direct action.

This was evident in the foreign-owned textile industry where PLM activists joined groups of worker-intellectuals and formed the Gran Círculo de Obreros Libres at Orizaba, Veracruz. In 1907 the Gran Círculo initiated militant strikes at Río Blanco that soon spread to the factories at Puebla. Like Cananea a year earlier, the government brutally crushed the rebellion and blamed "outside agitators" and "anarchistic propaganda" for the unrest, which continued at the La Hormiga and La Magdalena textile factories near Mexico City. There workers protested dismissals of militants, as well as wage reductions and longer hours. Once again, the government and the owners blamed "anarchistic propaganda" for the strikes and used armed force, while the strikers pointed to abusive management practices and wage cuts as the causes.[11] Labor unrest acted as a catalyst in building a cross-class alliance that advocated the overthrow of the regime. Nationalism united elites, peasants, workers and the middle classes against the foreigners and the regime that openly favored them. The coalition of these discontented social forces ripened conditions for revolution.

The leadership of the Revolution fell to Francisco Madero, a wealthy landowner and industrialist. Madero represented the provincial elite who had struggled with the regime over the issues of autonomy, an open political system and the disbursement of local economic opportunities. Believing that the most pressing problem for Mexico was an outdated political structure, Madero's ideas appealed to members of the upper and middle classes whose interest was in preserving the social structure while breaking down the rigidity of the political system.[12] But to overthrow Díaz, Madero needed the support of the working class and the peasantry. He attempted to gain backing by issuing the plan of San Luis Potosí, which offered industrial workers the right to organize freely and peasants the opportunity to reclaim usurped land. By the end of May 1911, workers and peasants who followed northern provincial leaders had seized the border city of Ciudad Juárez, and Díaz had abdicated and fled to Europe. When leaving Mexico, Díaz warned that "Madero had unleashed a tiger, now let us see if he can control it."[13]

TAMING THE TIGER

The tiger Díaz had referred to was the integration of workers and peasants into one armed struggle. This was especially important when considering the increasing organizational development of Mexico City's working class. Recent unrest in Mexico City had generated an effort to unite all active labor organizations into a single national confederation that would recruit peasants and workers alike. The result was the organization of the anarchosyndicalist-dominated Casa del Obrero Mundial.

Madero reacted to the Casa's growth by creating a department of labor and actively supporting the Gran Liga Obrera de la República Mexicana as an alternative. He also enlisted the support of AFL leaders who increasingly had seen Mexican workers on both sides of the border look to their chief rival, the IWW, to improve their material conditions. While the AFL cooperated with employers, the IWW's program resembled that of the Casa's, which rejected class collaboration and promoted workers' self-management. In October 1912, United Mine Workers of America (UMWA) Vice-President Frank J. Hayes, WFM representative J.D. Cannon, and Mary "Mother" Jones met with Madero in Mexico City, where he invited the Americans to organize workers with government support.[14]

Madero's promises rested upon his ability to face mounting challenges to his power and authority. His unwillingness to act on peasant, worker and middle-class demands coupled with his insistence on maintaining the political and economic institutions of the deposed Porfirian regime, left his supporters demoralized and confused. The Gran Liga failed to attract workers and the Casa won a series of well-publicized strikes and sit-ins in the Mexico City area, mostly against foreign-owned enterprises. Even railroad workers, who had fallen under the influence of the AFL railroad unions, rejected the Gran Liga.[15] By mid-1913, the Gran Liga had been reduced to a paper organization and the unionism offered by the Americans never had a chance to get off the ground. As peasants continued to seize land and attack foreign-owned properties, investors, industrialists, landowners and the army officer corps grew increasingly hostile to Madero's weak rule. In February 1913 ex-Porfirian army officer, General Victoriano Huerta, overthrew the Madero government.

Occupied with other matters, such as putting down Zapata's peasant insurgency and U.S. President Woodrow Wilson's disapproval of his rule, Huerta did not challenge the labor movement immediately. The Casa seized the opportunity and organized new unions. It also staged Mexico's first large May Day parade honoring the fallen anarchist martyrs of the 1886 Haymarket Riot in the United States. By late 1913 the Casa had begun to use the strike to win higher wages, better conditions and organize workers around the long-term objective of self-management. The Casa affiliated with the Anarchist International Association of Workers in Amsterdam and nominally joined the worldwide anarchosyndicalist movement.

Huerta and the Casa clashed after his campaign had failed to crush the Zapatista peasant movement in the south and contain the rebellion of *maderista* governors who opposed his rule in the north. In late May 1913 Huerta moved against the urban working-class after more than 8,000 marchers rallied in Mexico City and listened to speeches by anarchosyndicalists denouncing "military dictatorship." After the demonstrations, police raided Casa headquarters, arresting some of its leaders and later deporting three Casa organizers as "undesirable" aliens.

Huerta finally fell from power in 1914 when the Constitutionalists, led by a Sonoran, Alvaro Obregón, who was loyal to the revolution's "first chief," Coahuilan hacendado Venustiano Carranza entered the capital.

As they occupied Mexico City, the Constitutionalists moved quickly to cultivate urban working-class support. Having witnessed labor unrest in his home state of Sonora and the important military contributions of workers in the battle against Huerta, Obregón realized that a new government would require working-class support. Accordingly, Obregón provided churches and convents for use as union headquarters and allowed the Casa to reopen in the historic House of Tiles. With government approval, the Casa proceeded with an intense organizing drive in the factories and shops of Mexico City, Guadalajara and Tampico.[16] The urban radicals, however, failed to unite with the peasantry, which numerically constituted the nation's largest social class. This strengthened the revolutionary generals' political position as they carried out propaganda and urged the urban workers to support the Constitutionalist cause.[17]

Standing out among the revolutionary generals was Obregón, who combined a wide range of talents, including the ability to act as a liaison between workers, peasants, middle-echelon intelligentsia, urban radicals, businessmen, foreigners and the autocratic Carranza.[18] Obregón used these attributes to develop a close relationship with some Casa leaders, such as the famous painter, Geraldo Murillo (alias Dr. Atl). In the early months of 1915, the Casa and the Constitutionalists tested their alliance. Continued political and economic instability caused by the revolution had led to runaway inflation and unemployment. The situation produced a number of Casa-directed strikes, most of which were aimed at foreign-owned enterprises. The Casa's strike leadership increasingly mixed anarchosyndicalist rhetoric with Mexican nationalism. The Constitutionalist government recognized the political value of the nationalistic message delivered by Casa leaders when it supported a strike against, and later a seizure of the Swedish-owned Ericcson Telephone Company. The government's actions impressed Casa leaders who began to call openly for collaboration with "progressive" sectors of the elite to better the position of the working class.

Rejecting what "Dr. Atl" identified as the impossibility of the peasants' religiosity and their narrow agrarian and provincial view of the revolution, Casa delegates listened attentively to a passionate speech delivered by Murillo in early February 1915. He called for Mexican workers to come to the aid of "The Revolution" and oppose the "reactionary" peasant armies of Villa and Zapata. After three days of heated debate, the Casa directorate convened a general assembly of the membership and approved the organization's participation in the armed struggle against the "reactionary" peasant forces. In exchange, the Constitutionalists promised the Casa assistance in establishing branches in newly conquered areas and the enactment of future labor reforms.[19]

Although the Casa leadership fostered no illusions about "bourgeois alliances," the pact divided the Mexican working-class movement into two distinct camps: reform socialist and anarchosyndicalist. Reform socialists sought legislative solutions to working-class problems as a gradual means to acquire power. By joining forces with the Constitutionalists, Casa leaders had hoped to strengthen their numbers first and later to confront the bourgeoisie. In contrast, the anarchosyndicalists opposed petitioning the state and relied exclusively on direct action to better the lot of the working-class and prepare it for the "final confrontation" with capital.

Beginning in March 1915, Casa leaders began organizing the Red Battalions, which initially involved between 7,000 to 10,000 persons, including the wives and children of the Mexico City Casa members.[20] The Casa also sent representatives to other areas of the country to augment the Red forces. But not all sectors of the Mexican working class responded enthusiastically, especially those in outlying industrial areas. Textile workers in Puebla and oil workers in Tampico and Veracruz adamantly opposed the pact and armed worker participation.[21] From the U.S., Enrique Flores Magón wrote in *Mother Earth*, published by anarchist Emma Goldman, that Carranza had duped the Casa and acted as a radical because he needed working-class support.[22] Pedro Coria wrote in *El Rebelde*, the Los Angeles Mexican IWW Local #602 newspaper, that the armies of Villa, Zapata and Carranza were "criminal." As an alternative, Coria advocated Mexican worker solidarity on both sides of the border.[23]

While the anarchosyndicalists condemned the alliance, the Constitutionalist forces and the Red Battalions received support from American military and civilian advisers, which included John Murray, a representative of the AFL. While working as a reporter for the socialist *New York Call*, Murray acted as a liaison between reform socialist Casa leaders and the Constitutionalists. Re-equipped with arms the Americans had left during their occupation of Veracruz and aided by a U.S. embargo against the Villista forces on the border and by sea, the Constitutionalists, with the help of the Red Battalions, defeated the peasant armies.[24] The effective removal of the peasantry from the revolutionary equation sharpened the contradictions between the Constitutionalists and the Casa, as well as among the workers themselves.

While organized workers expected material rewards for their contribution, the protracted fighting had taken its toll on the economy. The Casa fought joblessness and runaway inflation through the organization's newspaper, *Ariete*, which carried articles from IWW publications in the United States, such as *Solidarity*, *El Rebelde* and the *Industrial Worker*.

As continuing hardships and unemployment mounted, the Casa sponsored street demonstrations to demand price controls, higher wages and jobs. The Carranza government reacted by disbanding the Red Battalions, closing

At left, Spanish-language propoganda from from the Industrial Workers of the World; below a Mexican IWW membership card (both in the author's collection).

the House of Tiles headquarters, and rounding up Casa leaders.[25] Labor groups in Tampico and Veracruz responded immediately with street demonstrations that led state governors of the areas to declare a "state of siege" to regain control of the volatile situation.[26]

In May 1916 the unrest evolved into a general strike on Mexico City. Strikers demanded the replacement of the hated script that obliged workers to purchase basic necessities at inflated prices in company-run stores. In a bold nationalistic move, the government required the foreign-owned enterprises to replace scrip with valid Mexican currency and mandated back pay for the strikers to cover the time lost during the work stoppage. Besides standing up to foreign economic interests, the government also identified cooperative leaders such as Luis Morones, a signatory of the agreement. The government's nationalistic posture and its newfound allies were a perfect formula for institutionalizing class conflict. In the decades that followed the alliance became a powerful instrument for the government and its trade-union partners to smother working-class protest against government policies.

In August 1916, however, the formula had only produced a short-lived peace as the new currency quickly became worthless. Bankers, commercial houses, industrialists and the government set the peso at one-fiftieth the value of the older gold-based currency.[27] As the situation worsened, the Casa petitioned government and business leaders to revalue the peso. Their refusal to act triggered another general strike, during which a committee of strikers demanded payment of salaries in gold or its currency equivalent.[28] Carranza called the strike committee "traitors to the nation," ordered their immediate arrest and declared martial law. As authorities rounded up Casa leaders and restored electrical power to the city, a new strike committee met and voted to recess the Casa.[29] The government had demonstrated working-class organizational weakness, but the action did nothing to change Mexico's dependence on foreign capital. The state's inability to deliver higher wages and better conditions to workers toiling in foreign-owned enterprises energized anarchosyndicalist organization, especially in outlying industrial areas.

OIL WORKERS AND THE CRISIS OF MEXICAN NATIONALISM

In Tampico, the foreign-owned oil companies' overwhelming presence and abusive management practices bolstered working-class nationalism and reflected the peculiar nature of the region's political, social and economic development. Local patriarchs and the social elite, religious leaders, landowners and merchants, were almost non-existent in Tampico. These classes constituted the backbone of the Porfirian society and usually represented political power. When the Tampico area became politically and economically important, the omnipresent power of the foreign-owned petroleum companies swallowed up the principal members of the region's tiny upper class. Some ended up working as lawyers, accountants and managers for the oil companies.[30] The absence of a traditional elite social structure and the emergence of the petroleum companies as the most powerful agents in the community produced a strident Mexican nationalism and reinforced anarchosyndicalist organization.

Anarchosyndicalists began organizing Tampico workers in 1915 when representatives of the Mexico City Casa established a branch there. One year later, the IWW joined Casa organizers when the Marine Transport Workers' Union (MTW) arrived in Tampico on the *C.A. Canfield* from Philadelphia. Many MTW sailors spoke Spanish and originated from either Spain or other Latin American countries. The Spanish-speaking sailors joined the IWW by the hundreds when they had been refused entry into the AFL's International Seamen's Union because of its policy of not organizing foreign-born workers.

Although the U.S. government successfully crushed most IWW unions during the hysteria surrounding World War I, the MTW remained intact because of the international scope of its activities. Throughout the 1920s the MTW's influence grew in Latin America, where local chapters emerged in Mexico, Chile, Ecuador, Uruguay and Argentina. In Chile, the MTW and the IWW played crucial roles in the early organization of stevedores, dock workers and textile factory workers. In 1919 the MTW established a regional Latin American headquarters in Buenos Aires, and in 1924 it conducted an international conference of union seamen in Montevideo, Uruguay.[31]

IWW activities in Mexico began with the publication and distribution of Spanish-language newspapers and literature across the border in the United States. By 1911 two Spanish language IWW papers had appeared in the United States: *La Unión Industrial,* published in Phoenix, Arizona; and *Huelga General,* printed in Los Angeles. The newspapers spread radical ideas to Mexicans working on both sides of the border and especially influenced workers in the mining and smelting districts of northern Mexico. By 1912, the IWW had extended its activities throughout northern Mexico and had established five metal workers' locals in Torreón.[32] In Tampico, the IWW and the Casa shared the same building, conducted meetings together, and jointly distributed syndicalist propaganda that eventually resulted in the organization of hundreds of workers. They issued demands for higher wages, better conditions, union recognition and advocated workers' control.[33]

Tampico workers joined Casa and IWW unions because living and working conditions in the area prompted them to search for an alternative that would help them remedy their wretched existence. The young, single men who migrated to Tampico arrived without customary kinship support structures and confronted problems with housing, sanitation, working conditions and a high cost of living.[34] These conditions forced them to build new patterns of social interaction. The old customs and social relationships that aided their integration into local society were redefined and shaped to suit their new environment. As French historian and philosopher George Rudé suggests, "traditional beliefs, instead of becoming abandoned, are transformed and adopted to meet new needs."[35] This certainly applied to Tampico, where the majority of workers used a reference point from their past—collective resistance and action—to confront problems in their new industrial environment. The anarchosyndicalist union, with its program of "direct action" and workers' self-management, offered Tampico's workers a vehicle for confronting and challenging the institutions that controlled their lives.

Collective action began with protesting Tampico's inadequate housing, which resulted from a number of factors. In 1910 Tampico was a moderately sized provincial commercial city of 23,500. A demographic avalanche swept the area shortly after, however, when migrants responded to the labor demands of the region's booming petroleum industry. Tampico became the major administrative, refining and export center for the petroleum business in Mexico because of its proximity to the oil-producing zones. Located near the mouth of the Pañuco River on the Gulf of Mexico, it was already an important port by 1910 as a result of the earlier completion of a pair of river jetties and two railroad lines. Between 1910 and 1921 the population of Tampico and its surroundings increased to 150,000.[36] This put enormous pressure on living space because Tampico's geographical juxtaposition allowed less than 1.5 square miles for workers' housing.[37]

Compounding the problems of overcrowding was the landlords' refusal to improve the physical conditions of workers' housing. New construction centered on providing accommodations for high-level foreign managers and technicians employed by the petroleum companies.[38] Tampico workers spent an increasing percentage of their income on rent for dwellings where 200 people might live in fewer than 30 rooms. Most residents did not have access to potable water, toilets and sewage; and where these necessities existed, they were often deficient.[39] Former peasants and artisans used reference points from their past and began carrying out collective actions to resolve the housing problem. Group action stopped landlords' threats of eviction, and residents organized themselves into work units responsible for cleaning common areas.[40]

The relatively minor role the Catholic Church played in the development of Tampico social life also contributed to the workers' rejection of traditional authority. The Church presence in the region had always been limited, even after years of population growth. In 1918, when the area's population reached over 100,000, only one Catholic parish existed, and daily attendance in the main square church averaged between 50 and 100 persons.[41] The revolution accelerated anti-clerical feelings throughout Mexico, and in Tampico it blunted the Catholic church's growth. The spread of anarchosyndicalism with its fierce anti-clericalism also inhibited the influence of the church. The Casa and the IWW denounced the Unión de Obreros Católicos, which they claimed was an attempt to shield the worker from socialism and the dangers of radical unionism.[42]

The Catholic unions followed the teachings of Pope Leo XIII's papal encyclical, *Rerum Novarum*, and called for a minimum wage, an end to child labor, accident insurance, decent housing and compulsory arbitration of industrial disputes. The short-term demands issued by the Catholic unions attracted support from many Mexican workers, and by 1916 the unions boasted a membership of over 15,000.[43] In Tampico, however, due to the historical weakness of the Church and the region's unique social and economic development, the unions never established a foothold.[44]

The anarchosyndicalists organized workers by attacking working conditions in the petroleum industry. When the petroleum companies set up their Tampico operations they homogenized professional categories to classify work operations. The foreign-owned petroleum companies espoused the modern industrial practice of placing more emphasis and value on the skills and know-how of supervisory personnel who controlled the pace and direction of production rather than on the workers themselves. These companies, like other modern industrial enterprises that penetrated Mexico, relied upon supervisory staffs and personnel departments to determine the criteria for measuring the competence and pay of the work force.[45]

In April 1916 the first mass protest against conditions occurred when IWW leaders sent ultimatums to the petroleum and shipping companies. They demanded an eight-hour day and a minimum wage for all workers based on gold to be paid at the highest rate of exchange.[46] The workers supported the IWW's actions because inflation and the declining value of the national currency continued to eat away at their standard of living. When the companies refused to meet the demands, hundreds of workers responded to the IWW's call for a strike.[47] The first day witnessed the shut down of most of the oil companies and public facilities, and hundreds of Tampico residents looting stores in the central business district. General Emiliano P. Nafarette, the local military commander, sent detachments of infantry and mounted troops to disperse labor meetings, clear the streets and arrest strike leaders. Several confrontations occurred between strikers and soldiers that resulted in the death of one striking worker.[48]

The next day General Nafarette hoped to diffuse the situation by calling for a conference of employers and labor representatives. During the meeting he insisted that the IWW leaders drop their demands and declared that public order would be maintained at any cost. He demanded that the strikers return to work the next morning and added that, only if this condition was met, would he accept a list of grievances for submission to the employers within the next ten days. Ricardo Treviño, representing the IWW and the workers, called off the strike and accepted Nafarette's terms.[49]

Inflation continued, however, and it bolstered radical organizing. In late 1916 Mexican IWW leader Pedro Coria arrived in Tampico from Arizona, where he had been organizing miners and distributing IWW literature. In January 1917 Coria helped establish Tampico IWW union, MTW Local #100.[50] Now better organized, the IWW and the Casa pressed their demands by insisting that the companies pay workers in gold instead of the worthless paper currency issued by the government. On April 23, 1917, the IWW led employees of the British-owned El Aguila Petroleum Company out on strike. They demanded payment of a minimum wage in gold and boldly called for the company to take immediate action or face the "consequences." When company officials refused to meet with a strike committee, strikers assaulted supervisors and officials when they tried to run operations.[51]

When the British consul petitioned authorities to arrest the leaders, workers shut down the American-owned Pierce Oil Corporation, assaulted company officials and drove off supervisory personnel.[52] The strike then spread to the docks as stevedores, longshoremen and boatmen prevented tankers from loading and unloading their cargo.[53] Claude Dawson, the American consul, demanded protection for the American companies from the local military commander. Dissatisfied with the slow response, he then requested military protection from the USS *Annapolis* stationed offshore in the Gulf of Mexico.[54]

Meanwhile, American diplomats urged Mexican officials to pressure the Tampico military commander to take immediate action and protect

American lives and property.[55] After the Americans moved more naval vessels to Tampico, Mexican forces were finally put on alert. With American ships offshore and Mexican military forces poised for an attack on the strikers, tensions rose. On May 1, hundreds of strikers filled the streets and public services ground to a halt. IWW leaders Ramón Parreno and Francisco Gamallo made speeches in the city's central plaza that called for an end to "workers' exploitation."[56]

On the same day the strike spread to the Standard Oil and Texas companies, and the leadership demanded more salary increases.[57] The IWW asked for a fifty percent increase in wages and payment of salaries in Mexican gold or United States money at the government rate of exchange. As more workers became strikers, pickets armed themselves with clubs and physically prevented management and supervisory personnel from entering company facilities. The strikers were further emboldened when the American steamship *Mexicana* remained in Tampico's harbor because the ship's crew refused to cross their picket line.[58] In June the strike spread to the Huasteca Petroleum Company, and labor leaders began to threaten a general strike if their demands for salary payment in gold or U.S. currency were not met.[59]

On July 16, maritime workers, boatmen and dockworkers joined the strike when employers rejected the IWW's demands for higher pay. The strikers immediately paralyzed operations by shutting down three American-owned dredging vessels. Six days later, a general strike of the Tampico area commenced when over 15,000 workers stopped all petroleum production. The vice-president of Pierce Oil Corporation, Eben Richards, asked the United States government to protect company property and American lives. Meanwhile, workers in all Tampico refineries had walked off their jobs in sympathy with the maritime employees striking on the Pañuco River. The U.S. State Department assured Richards that steps already had been taken by Mexican officials to control the situation.[60]

The general strike in the petroleum and shipping industries soon affected the entire Tampico community as street-car workers suspended service and ice-factories and electric light plants closed. Public speeches became more frequent in the city's central plaza where Casa and IWW leaders attacked the Mexican government and the foreign companies. As the crisis deepened, the foreign-owned firms and the American consul blamed foreign agitators for precipitating the strike. They specifically identified the IWW and claimed that its leaders intimidated "good" Mexican workers by threatening them with violence if they did not join the strike.[61] The Mexican Petroleum Company manager, George Paddleford, attempted to divide the strikers. He said that he would meet and negotiate with a committee of "regular workers" and not representatives of the IWW, whom he called "outside agitators." Paddleford also refused to negotiate with any team of workers until they complied with state Governor Alfredo Ricaut's proclamation that ordered them back on the job. Strikers ignored Ricaut and Paddleford; the shutdown continued.[62]

Responding to American company pressures and reacting to the strikers' refusal to quit, authorities ordered 300 troops to Tampico from the provincial capital, Ciudad Victoria. The troops arrived in Tampico on July 24, and company officials and the state governor arranged a meeting for the following day. Upon arrival, an American navy officer, Captain Louis C. Richardson, met with the region's new military commander, General Francisco Guerre, and the two discussed the IWW. Richardson informed Guerre that the IWW did not respect his or the governor's authority and described it as an organization bent on the destruction of private property. He added further that "good" labor unions in the United States opposed the IWW and its tactics. Richardson, when referring to the "good" labor unions in the United States, did not specifically mention the AFL. It can be assumed, however, that this is what he meant because the AFL had cooperated with the American government's persecution of the IWW during the period. He also urged Guerre that he should relate this information to the state governor at their meeting the next morning.[63]

When the three parties arrived for the meeting the next day, they discovered that several IWW leaders were already in the office, and that a crowd of angry strikers had surrounded the building. The company representatives repeated that they would meet only with a committee of what they called regular workers. They refused to discuss a July 12, 1917, letter sent to them by IWW leaders Francisco Gamallo and Ramón Parreno, which demanded immediate wage increases and union recognition. Company officials also insisted that they would not meet with any committee until all strikers had returned to work. After company officials left, Governor Ricaut attempted to defuse the situation by scheduling another meeting with strikers the next morning.[64] But shortly after the meeting broke up and the crowd outside dispersed, Ricaut had Commander Guerre order his troops to surround IWW headquarters and arrest the strike's leaders. Soldiers apprehended seventeen IWW members in all, leaving the strike's leadership decimated. By the end of the month, all workers had returned to their jobs. The oil companies expressed their appreciation to the United States Department of State and praised Governor Ricaut's handling of the volatile situation.[65]

Months later, the Wobblies had regrouped and called for a general strike on November 15, 1917, to win the release of three organizers jailed during the previous wave of persecution. Once again, Governor Ricaut intervened and threatened the IWW with more arrests if the strike continued. When the IWW refused, 200 troops arrived in Tampico from Ciudad Victoria and guarded the foreign-owned company's property with machine guns. Ricaut then declared martial law and prohibited demonstrations from taking place on Tampico's streets. He also ordered the arrest of two prominent IWW leaders and had troops surround Wobbly headquarters. He then forbade the organization from holding any public meetings in the Tampico area.[66]

The constant repression prompted an attempt by the anarchosyndicalists to unite all radical working-class organizations during a Tampico Casa-sponsored Second National Labor Congress, which convened on October 13, 1917. The Tampico Casa issued invitations to all unions in Mexico and to Mexican IWW Local #602 in Los Angeles, which supported the principles of the Congress. Congress organizers hoped to unite all Mexican labor groups in one union affiliated with a workers' international federation.[67] Delegates also included Luis Morones, who claimed to represent the syndicates from Mexico City and the state of Hidalgo. Morones, head of the Mexico City electricians' union, advocated cooperation with the government. The IWW, represented by Pedro Coria and Rafael Zamudio from Tampico and Andrés de León from Torreón, joined Spanish-born Tampico Casa leader Jorge D. Borrán in opposing Morones.[68]

Morones controlled a small majority of delegates and gained the support of Tampico IWW defector Ricardo Treviño, when heated debate over the content of the Congress began. Borrán called for an anti-political declaration that entailed organizational autonomy and the support of an anarchosyndicalist program. Morones argued against the Borrán proposal, stressing the success of earlier cooperation with the government and pointing to recent failures the labor movement had experienced by confronting it. His arguments won the support of the majority of delegates who gave his faction the votes needed to defeat Borrán's program. The Congress also passed a ten-point resolution that provided for whatever type of political organization the workers' movement deemed necessary. As a token to the anarchosyndicalists, the resolutions also called for the creation of a regional labor federation that would become part of a world-wide labor organization.[69]

Morones and his followers planned to build a movement around the nationalistic provisions outlined in the 1917 Constitution. Article 27 declared state ownership of all subsoil wealth, while Article 123 guaranteed the right to unionize, a minimum wage, an eight-hour day and equal treatment for Mexican and foreign workers. Article 123 represented most of the short-term demands expressed in the labor manifestos issued since the 1870s but failed to grant workers control over production through self-management.[70] Article 123 also provided foreign-owned companies a loophole in its enforcement. It gave jurisdiction over labor legislation to the states, which were to adopt regulating laws within the general outline of the article.[71] The provision allowed foreign companies to claim special local conditions for noncompliance of payment of the minimum wage, improving job conditions and union recognition.

The Constitution became the framework for social order. It combined revolutionary idealism and nationalism with realpolitik to achieve legitimized political stability. It appealed to many in the working-class movement who viewed it as a peaceful vehicle to fulfill the promise of a complete social revolution. For the elite it was an attempt to draw out and systematize the worldview of Mexico's workers—revolutionary nationalism. Through Article 123, state-builders established a "hegemony of ruling ideas" and a social program for labor that entailed state control over labor relations. It laid a legal foundation for workers' rights and the limits of those rights in a capitalist economy.

CHAPTER TWO

FOREIGN INTERESTS, ELITES AND ORGANIZED LABOR IN TRANSITION

Despite the convergence of working-class and elite nationalism in the Constitution, the unresolved conflicts that involved the bureaucracy, foreign economic interests and the masses of wage laborers sharpened between 1917 and 1924. Almost wholesale non-compliance with Article 123 by foreign capitalists generated more unrest from a nationalistic working-class that demanded higher wages, better conditions and union recognition. As a result, those working for foreign companies followed anarchosyndicalist leaders who advocated self-management among other basic issues. The state reacted by creating organizational alternatives and political institutions that incorporated labor as a subordinate group. At the center were the IWW and the AFL. The AFL was instrumental in establishing the Confederación Regional Obrera Mexicana (CROM) as a subordinate ally of the state in the enforcement of its anti-anarchosyndicalist and anti-independent labor organization policy. The AFL served not only the interests of the Obregón government (which sought an accommodation with foreign capital and an eradication of radical ideologies within the working-class movement), but also foreign business in Mexico, which was willing to accept a reformist unionism to shield workers from radicalism.

Although the CROM and the government used violence and co-optation to defeat the anarchosyndicalists, they also worked in tandem to win ideological consent. Besides deporting foreign-born labor organizers who advocated "anti-Mexican" ideologies, the state expropriated small- and medium-sized industries and experimented with workers' cooperatives. Through these actions the state and the CROM created the illusion of building socialism to oppose foreign capital while simultaneously accommodating business interests. CROM tactics demoralized and confused radical opponents, whose ideological divisions weakened their ability to challenge government labor policies. CROM control of the arbitration and conciliation boards gave it power to limit the workers' right to organize and to award its own unions favorable agreements with employers. The Confederación's actions forced the working-class movement away from anarchosyndicalism and toward reformist trade unionism, as reflected in the petroleum workers' signing collective bargaining agreements with their employers. The emergence of trade unionism effectively made labor subordinate to elite nationalism.

Despite the marginal role of the radicals, the CROM's ascendance facilitated the growth of working-class organization overall, and it represented an important power bloc in the revolutionary government. Yet, it had not satisfied the short-term demands of industrial workers laboring in foreign-owned enterprises; the process was incomplete and unresolved.

WOBBLIES AND MEXICAN MINERS IN THE BORDERLANDS

North of the border, the IWW's influence among Mexican miners had grown since the advent of the Spanish-language IWW press in the United States. Newspapers such as *La Unión Industrial, Huelga General* and *El Rebelde* had spread the ideas of anarchosyndicalism, and the union's joint organizational activities with the Casa in Tampico helped to strengthen the IWW's legitimacy. By 1917 over 5,000 Mexicans belonged to IWW mining locals in the United States.[1] The IWW's influence grew in the mining camps of the American Southwest because it confronted falling wages, poor living and working conditions and a management system that discriminated against Hispanics.

Early in January 1917, a thousand Mexican, Indian and Anglo workers struck mining operations in Ajo, Arizona. They demanded higher wages and refused to accept an agreement negotiated by the AFL's International Union of Mine, Mill, and Smelter Workers (IUMMSW). The workers rejected the agreement with the mining companies because it provided a sliding scale between $1.50 to $2.50 per day for miners working underground and on the surface. Mexican miners considered the wage increases paltry and discriminatory. Local authorities received the cooperation of the IUMMSW's leadership when they arrested twenty-six miners, whom the union leadership and local press called "outside agitators."[2]

Despite the repression, Mexican miners continued to organize for higher wages, better conditions and bolt the IUMMSW because of the union's refusal to back their demands. Mexican miners at Clifton-Morenci, Arizona, also voted to withdraw from the IUMMSW's predecessor, the WFM, after that union had failed to back a walkout in 1916. The increasingly cautious position of the Western Federation of Miners, which led to the creation of the IUMMSW, was largely due to the policies of the union's president, Charles H. Moyer.

Moyer was an ex-IWW leader and one of the founders of the WFM. But he adopted a cautious strategy toward organizing workers after authorities released him and IWW leader "Big" Bill Haywood from prison. Haywood and Moyer languished in jail during their trial for the murder of Idaho Governor Frank Steunenberg. Although the jury found both men not guilty, the jail experience radicalized Haywood and steered Moyer toward reformism. While Haywood continued in the IWW, Moyer joined the AFL. In February 1917 he revoked the Arizona AFL's IUMMSW charter, claiming that the district's attitudes were "too radical and independent."[3] Afterward, miners joined the IWW's Metal and Mine Workers' Industrial Union #800. By May 1917 most Mexicans had abandoned the AFL and had joined the IWW.[4]

Between June 15 and 17, 1917, Industrial Union #800 held its first statewide convention in Bisbee, Arizona, and discussed strategy to confront the copper companies. The 500 members in attendance called for the abolition of the physical examination, two men to work on each machine, two men to work on raises, discontinuing of all blasting during a shift change, abolition of all bonus and construction work, replacement of the sliding scale of wages with a flat daily rate of $6 for all underground work and no discrimination against members of any organization.[5]

The demands reflected a desire among miners to exercise control of their work environment and their communities. As in Tampico, large North American enterprises exercised power over the entire community. In Arizona, Phelps-Dodge Corporation owned the state's largest mining operation (the Copper Queen at Bisbee) as well as the local hotel, hospital, department store, library, newspaper and a host of other smaller enterprises. The Mexican miners' fight against the power of Phelps-Dodge evolved into a struggle that encompassed the entire communities where they lived and worked.

In Jerome, Arizona, Mexican miners established a Metal and Mine Workers' Local after the IUMMSW failed to back their demands for higher wages and better conditions. When the United States entered the war in Europe, the IUMMSW fell completely out of favor with the miners after its parent affiliate, the AFL, pledged not to strike for the remainder of the conflict.[6] On July 5, 1917, the IWW called a strike and demanded $6 for a six-hour day. While the IUMMSW called the demands "absurd," "unpatriotic," "disloyal," and "disruptive" to the war effort, both Mexican and Anglo miners supported them and stopped working. Since 1914, the beginning of the European war, orders for strategic minerals had been pouring in from the Allies, particularly Britain. To fill them, management ordered twenty-four-hour production and froze wages at pre-war levels. As working conditions deteriorated and the owners' profits soared, miners were in no mood to compromise their right to strike or to follow the dictates of the IUMMSW.[7]

The management at Jerome shared the sentiments of the IUMMSW and those of L.C. Shattuck, general manager of the Shattuck Arizona Company in Bisbee. A month earlier he had called the demands of the IWW a "conspiracy by enemies of the United States government to restrict or cut off the copper output required to prosecute the war."[8] On July 10, 1917, five days after a strike began in Jerome, authorities and vigilantes apprehended sixty-seven "suspected leaders" of the walkout and deported them to Needles, California. In Bisbee on July 12, local law enforcement officials and vigilantes responded to strike activity violently. Besides deporting many Mexicans back to their homeland, they rounded up almost 1,200 strikers, put them on a train and dumped them in the middle of the New Mexico desert with neither food nor water. The miners were prohibited from returning to Bisbee.[9] Outraged by the vigilantism, radical miners in the Globe-Miami and Clifton-Morenci districts lodged vehement protests to the governor.[10]

Morenci miners responded quickly to the Bisbee and Jerome deportations because they had already experienced harassment from the federal government in their battle against the management of the Arizona Copper Company, a Phelps-Dodge subsidiary. Abelardo Ordoñez, an IWW organizer, speaking before miners on May 4, 1917, at an open-air meeting on company property, cursed United States Department of Justice agents for trying to intimidate the men in the camp from striking.[11] In Globe-Miami, Julio Blanco and José Rodríguez had also made speeches attacking the American government. After the Jerome and Bisbee deportations, Pedro Coria of Tampico IWW Local #100, Tomás Martínez, and B. Negreira, members of Los Angeles Local #602, joined the Globe-Miami leadership. Together they condemned the deportations and spread propaganda through public appearances and through the IWW newspaper, *El Rebelde.* As repression escalated within the context of U.S. domestic wartime hysteria, tensions heightened between the authorities, the copper companies and the miners.[12]

On the heels of the Jerome deportation, the IWW leaders made frequent speeches that called on workers to resist the "authoritarianism" of the companies and the officials of local, state and national government. On

July 6, 1917, José Rodríguez had spoken before a Globe-Miami crowd of over 300 and railed that American corporations and the United States government had made Mexican workers "slaves."[13] He urged Mexicans to join the IWW and claimed that it was the only organization prepared to unite workers the world over, regardless of their national origin. Rodríguez boasted that the U.S. government did not have enough bayonets to suppress or stop the IWW. Speaking to the same audience, Julio Blanco called the American flag the "banner of oppression" and proclaimed that the red flag, the "banner of the workers of the world," belonged to them. In the same speech he also pledged that the companies would not get one pound of copper for the war effort and that Mexican miners should view their fight for better wages and conditions as part of a worldwide battle against a class that "slaughtered" their brothers on the battlefields of Europe.[14]

Blanco and Rodríguez escalated their attacks against the American government after the lynching of IWW miner and organizer Frank Little in the mining region of Butte, Montana. Addressing crowds of 1,200, they directed their remarks at President Woodrow Wilson, calling him a man dedicated to the "enslavement" of the working class.[15] Wilson viewed the IWW as an anarchistic organization that refused to compromise with capital. Accordingly, he believed its activities had to be checked by assuring that no grievances existed within the armies of working people.[16] For Wilson, the reformist AFL was well suited to carry out his ideas. Little's murder and the deportations at Jerome and Bisbee, however, served as an organizational catalyst for the IWW in the Globe-Miami region. Weekly meetings began to attract over 1,000 miners and smelter workers. As workers regularly met at a place known as "Wobbly Hill," the IWW enlisted the support of Italians, Finns, Poles and Anglos, in addition to the Mexicans, who constituted the union's leadership core.[17] By September 1917, when the IWW local at Globe-Miami struck for better wages and conditions, the union had grown to over 700 dues-paying members. United States military intelligence personnel targeted forty-two Mexican miners as the leading agitators of the strike.[18]

The IWW's Spanish-language press exercised a key role in educating the workers and triggering the strikes. Mexican organizers Julio Castillo, Tomás Martínez and Pedro Coria all contributed articles. Through distribution of *El Rebelde*, they established closer ties between Mexican workers in the United States, the northern mining regions of Mexico and the oil-producing region of Tampico.[19] Because of their activities, Martínez and other IWW leaders faced arrest by U.S. Justice Department officials and local police.

On the afternoon of March 22, 1918, authorities apprehended Martínez and B. Negreira, members of Los Angeles IWW Local #602 and frequent contributors to *El Rebelde*. Justice department officials simultaneously shut down the paper and arrested editor Aurelio Azuara.[20] Although *El Rebelde's* forced closing dealt a severe blow to the IWW's propaganda machine, José Vásquez, a Spanish anarchist and close friend of Negreira, began distributing *El Hombre Libre*, an anarchist paper printed in Spain and distributed in Mexico.[21]

Mexican miners in Arizona never recovered from the repression, which reached its apex on October 6, 1918, when the United States Congress passed the Alien Act.[22] In effect, the legislation sanctioned the Bisbee and Jerome deportations, the arrests of Martínez and others, and the subsequent expulsions of hundreds of foreigners suspected of subversive activity. The passage of the Alien Act and its strict enforcement meant that Mexican miners had to accept war-time production conditions or face deportation. In addition, the federal government sanctioned IUMMSW contracts with the copper companies that pledged not to interfere with the war effort by stopping production. The agreements also contained a provision that stated "no employment should be made available for IWW members or for other persons who had been guilty of disloyal utterances against the United States."[23]

The IUMMSW praised the agreement and threatened to cancel the charter of any local that did not accept it.[24] After the strikers returned to work and peace prevailed in the mining camps, the companies stretched the agreement and refused to recall anyone "whose employment for any reason is contrary to the best interests of the operations."[25] Management then refused to employ any man who belonged to a union, even the IUMMSW, and proceeded to operate the mines as open shops. Inside Mexico, however, the IWW and its anarchosyndicalist allies presented problems for a government that sought to build a reformist labor movement. To achieve this goal, the Mexican government increasingly looked to the IWW's chief rival, the AFL.

BUSINESS UNIONISM CONFRONTS WORKING-CLASS NATIONALISM

The interest of the U.S. government and the AFL in the affairs of the Mexican labor movement resulted from the emergence of the United States as a world industrial and military power at the turn of the century. As American businessmen sought new markets, outlets for capital investment, and access to raw materials, the AFL joined them in a partnership to promote the growth of an informal economic empire.

The AFL leadership entered the alliance for a number of reasons. At home it emphasized bread-and-butter issues, while its rival, the IWW, advocated goals similar to those of the Mexican anarchosyndicalists. Samuel Gompers, AFL president, especially feared the influence of the IWW in Mexico since it had already established a foothold among Mexican miners working in the American Southwest. In addition, he believed that U.S. expansion would bring greater material benefits for American workers because the affected countries would become lucrative markets for goods made by American workers. The extension of AFL-style unionism into Mexico meant higher wages and democratic rights for the nation's workers; at the same time it insulated them from radical or revolutionary theories, ensuring the hegemony of U.S. economic interests.[26]

Attempts to reorganize Mexican labor around AFL-style unionism began when the governor of Coahuila, Gustavo Espinosa Mireles, called a labor conference in Saltillo for May 1, 1918. While receiving the full support of Carranza and Alvaro Obregón, the organizers hoped to create a semi-official labor organization from the proceedings, which over 120 delegates from throughout Mexico attended. It was at Saltillo that delegates voted to organize the Confederación Regional Obrera Mexicana and elected Luis Morones as its general secretary.[27] But it was not without debate from the anarchosyndicalists.

The controversy centered on the question of whether the working class should use combined (multiple action) action—the use of the strike and political participation—instead of the anarchosyndicalist concept of direct action, which exclusively focused on the organization of workers at the point of production. Because Morones controlled the majority of delegates and enjoyed the support of two former Wobblies—Ricardo Treviño, one-time oil worker, and J. Marcos Tristán, leader of the Coahuilan coal miners—the conference voted for the adoption of multiple action. Although the radicals rejected the platform and refused to participate, the Confederación's statutes contained anarchosyndicalist language that declared the organization "regional," as part of a worldwide working-class movement against capitalism.[28] The radical rhetoric attracted the support of many delegates who increasingly looked to the government to deliver short-term gains, such as wages, conditions and union recognition.

Almost immediately afterward, a three-man AFL delegation—John Murray, Santiago Iglesias (a trade-union Socialist and AFL organizer from Puerto Rico) and James Lord (head of the AFL Mining Department)—visited Saltillo and Mexico City. They met with labor and government officials and promoted the idea of a hemispheric labor federation based on a partnership of equals. Meanwhile, within the CROM debate raged over the AFL question, which resulted in the withdrawal of five unions and the creation of the Gran Cuerpo Central de Trabajadores (GCCT).[29] Fearing more defections within its ranks, the CROM engaged in radical posturing during its meeting with AFL leaders. Luis Morones and others questioned the AFL's complicity in the American government's persecution of the IWW. Despite disagreements, the AFL delegates established official ties with Morones and finalized plans for a joint labor conference to be held in Laredo, Texas, on November 13, 1918.[30]

While Morones' unilateral decision to open relations with the AFL came under attack from the CROM rank and filers, Lord, Iglesias and Murray returned to the United States and reported that several Mexican senators from mining and industrial states had promised their cooperation. They also stated that the American-dominated mining management had complained to AFL officials about the unstable conditions in the mines. They blamed the instability on the strong influence of anarchosyndicalism among miners and mill workers. To ensure industrial peace and eradicate radical unionism, management would bargain with an AFL-style union, if one could be established. The AFL leaders further emphasized that many Mexican labor leaders were disillusioned with radicalism and wanted to organize around basic issues.[31]

The efforts to strengthen reform unionism moved ahead at the Laredo, Texas, meeting where CROM and AFL leaders established the Pan-American Federation of Labor (PAFL). Despite general agreement on principles, the Confederación delegates raised questions that irritated the AFL participants, especially Gompers, who sought support for President Woodrow Wilson's peace proposals. Ignoring the Gompers political agenda, the Mexican delegates instead issued a program that included calls to improve conditions for Mexican workers in the United States, the release of IWW members who were jailed during the war and a resolution to avoid a vote on U.S. foreign policy matters.[32] The AFL delegates openly resented charges that their unions practiced discrimination against Mexicans, and Gompers went into a tirade against the IWW, calling it the equivalent of the "Bolsheviki in Russia." Although Luis Morones complained that a "blanket endorsement" of the AFL's views would open him and the CROM to attacks by left-wing unionists in Mexico, the PAFL delegates established the basis for future cooperation.[33]

While Morones and the CROM established ties with the AFL, the GCCT attempted to address the pressing needs of Mexican workers and force foreign employers to comply with Article 123. Since the Revolution, the cost of living had risen eighty percent while workers received wages between seventy-five centavos and one peso per workday—typically nine to fourteen hours.[34] Beginning in March 1919 the GCCT led a series of strikes protesting the deteriorating economic situation. Bakers, textile workers and miners in northern Mexico struck for higher wages and shorter hours. In Aguascalientes, the nation's most important railroad center, workers walked off their jobs and demanded wage increases and the dismissal of abusive foremen.[35] The strike spread to San Luis Potosí, Monterrey, Saltillo, Durango and the Balbuena car shop in Mexico City. As the protest moved into May and included Mexico City teachers, the government reacted by sending in armed troops, closing union halls and arresting strike leaders. The actions decimated the GCCT's rank and file as management fired the strikers.[36] Repression also resulted in a serious decline of CROM membership. While boasting 38,000 dues-paying members at the time of its founding, by June 1919 CROM participation had dwindled to less than 7,000 when Luis Morones attended the AFL convention in the United States.[37]

Although Morones and other CROM delegates went to the convention at the expense of the Mexican government, the proceedings commenced in the context of a deteriorating relationship between Venustiano Carranza and organized labor.[38] Pointed discussions over a number of issues developed against the backdrop of increasing friction between the Carranza regime and Washington. Many American businessmen had grown frustrated with Mexican nationalism and now advocated armed intervention to protect their interests south of the border.[39] While not allowed to speak at the meeting, Jorge D. Borrán of the Tampico Casa del Obrero Mundial attacked the CROM and the AFL in the IWW's new paper, *La Nueva Solidaridad*. Stating that the laboring people of the Western Hemisphere "had nothing in common with the AFL," he accused the PAFL of being an "organization composed not of working people, but of lawyers, parasites, and members of the bourgeoisie." He also defended the IWW and called for the release of Wobbly prisoners held in U.S. jails.[40] Meanwhile, Luis Morones accepted the AFL's policy that supported restricting Mexican immigration into the United States.

In Mexico employers went on the offensive against the CROM in its Orizaba stronghold. Textile factory owners had forced workers to sign yellow-dog contracts, which prohibited the signatories from joining a union. Beginning in June 1919, protests, strikes and lockouts followed at the Santa Rosa textile mill in Orizaba. Unrest spread to Puebla, Mexico City and Tlaxcala and soon involved railroad and streetcar workers in daily demonstrations of over 8,000 marchers. Besides demonstrating in the streets, strikers stoned scabs and sabotaged machinery.[41]

The number of violent incidents increased as the unrest continued for several months. In Puebla, where a lockout had occurred at the San Juan de Amatlán mill in February 1920, workers protested police arrests by chanting: "Long Live Free Russia," "Long Live the World Revolution," "Death to the Government," and "Death to the Gachupines."[42] Hoping to diffuse the radicalism, CROM leaders and Plutarco Elías Calles, minister of industry, demanded that local authorities release the jailed millhands and that the owners open the factories. The decision to release the jailed workers and incarcerate a factory foreman infuriated the owners of the mills. One French owner complained by saying, "the matter is extremely grave not only because of the absurd position against capital ... but also because of the eloquent demonstration of Bolshevism, which tramples without any scruples, the principle of authority."[43] Finally, in March 1920, factory management across the textile region agreed to end the practice of yellow-dog contracts and to take no reprisals. The CROM claimed credit for the victory and emphasized that continued cooperation with the government meant greater material benefits for the workers.[44]

The settlement of the Orizaba strike prompted Morones and other CROM leaders to place more emphasis on political action. Convinced that Carranza's policies toward labor had grown too conservative, they signed a secret pact with Obregón and backed his bid for the presidency against Ignacio Bonillas, Carranza's hand-picked successor. To promote Obregón's candidacy, Morones and other CROM officials formed the Partido Laborista Mexicano—Mexican Labor party. Morones also gained control of the Mexican Socialist party, which, along with the Labor party, supported Obregón during the military coup that toppled Carranza in the spring of 1920.[45]

Despite CROM support, the Obregón-backed government of Adolfo de la Huerta encountered new labor unrest. Miners, oil and textile workers, as well as cigar makers went on strike for higher wages, shorter hours and union recognition. While Morones offered labor government support through political participation, poor conditions continued to push the rank and file toward anarchosyndicalism. A weak economy that produced falling wages and inflated prices for basic necessities led to anarchosyndicalist-directed strikes against foreign-owned companies. To counter the radicals, the Mexican government worked more closely with the AFL, which believed that Obregón would give the CROM more clout and be more flexible on the 1917 Constitution's Article 27.[46] While helping to guarantee social stability at home, the CROM worked with the AFL to enable the government to ease tensions with Washington, both of which were essential for national reconstruction.

RADICALS, REFORMISTS AND WORKING-CLASS NATIONALISM

The anarchosyndicalists responded to the growing cooperation between the CROM, the AFL, and the government by attempting to forge a new organizational unity. The IWW, which had scattered its efforts throughout the Mexican north and south to Tampico, established a national headquarters in Mexico City. Initially led by José Refugio Rodríguez, a carpenter, and Linn A.E. Gale, an American draft dodger, the organization published *El Obrero Industrial*, and worked closely with the newly formed Mexican Communist party.[47] In 1919 increasing labor strife in foreign-owned industries had produced a shift in IWW organizing strategy. The Wobblies purged Gale for advocating political action through his *Gale's Magazine*. The purified Mexican IWW also broke from the Communist Party and outlined a program for organizing Mexico's workers exclusively along industrial lines. M. Paley joined Refugio Rodríguez in leading the Wobblies and maintaining *El Obrero Industrial*. They planned to agitate and organize among Tampico oil workers and the nation's miners.[48]

Almost immediately, the IWW's message of better wages and conditions and workers' self-management reached miners and smelter workers in Guanajuato, Hidalgo, Coahuila, Chihuahua and Sonora. In July 1920 at Pachuca, management at the American-owned United States Smelting, Refining, and Mining Company complained about the widespread distribution of IWW literature, which they blamed for a recent strike by 4,000 workers demanding wage increases and the dismissal of an American foreman.[49] In November 1920, foreign-owned mining companies in Chihuahua reported that the region had been overrun by radical labor agitators. Management called them "Arizona-Mexicans," IWW members and veterans of strikes that had swept the border region since 1900.[50] Because Arizona-Mexicans had been paid twice as much in the United States, they demanded the same wages in Mexico and an end to abusive management practices.[51]

Many mine operators in Mexico claimed they could not afford to comply with Article 123 because their properties contained only low-grade ore.[52] Employers established wages, hours and conditions outside the framework of the Constitution, claiming that local conditions made it difficult to run at a profit. Since enforcement of Article 123 was left to the states, it enabled many foreign companies to avoid compliance with its provisions, which provided for an eight-hour day, a minimum wage and the right to unionize. Knowing that the export of minerals generated needed foreign exchange, rarely did the state or federal governments pressure the mining companies to comply with the provisions of Article 123.[53] The relaxation of enforcement resulted in sharp conflict between miners, smelter workers and their foreign employers. In 1920 the Mexican government reacted, using a combination of tactics to quell labor unrest in the mining industry. In a series of strikes in Coahuila, Chihuahua and Sonora the Mexican government used arbitration, expropriation and repression to establish peace.

The major cause of discord in the mining industry was low wages. In 1920 daily wages for an unskilled Mexican miner ranged from between $1 and $1.25 in Mexican currency when they worked near a railroad. When working long distances from a railroad, they received $1.50 to $2.50 Mexican currency per day, while skilled mechanics, carpenters, bricklayers and machinists made between $7 to $12 Mexican currency a shift. With the constant devaluations of the peso, wages for miners barely paid for basic necessities imported from the outside.[54]

On October 5, 1920, under the leadership of Wobbly organizer Antonio C. Ramírez, miners struck the Cananea Consolidated Copper Company to protest the company's non-compliance with a 1916 state labor law and to demand the dismissal of abusive American foremen. Cananea Copper agreed to place the maximum length of a shift in a mine at seven hours but refused to pay the miners for eight hours work. The walkout of nearly three weeks turned violent when the acting governor of Sonora, A.M. Sánchez, sent in 250 troops after the shooting of an American supervisor.[55]

While the government used arbitration to settle the Cananea dispute, it refused to stop a seven-week-long lockout by Guggenheim management in the Santa Barbara district near Parral, Chihuahua. The lockout was a response to an IWW miners' strike led by Wobbly organizers Alfredo Lugo and Albert Fodor, former editors of the *Arizona Labor Gazette*. With government troops guarding the mines, company officials imported replacement workers, despite the fact that some soldiers threw down their weapons and joined the strikers. When the companies found enough men to operate, they made non-wage concessions while the authorities drove the IWW organizers from the area.[56]

On October 11, 1920, the unrest continued in the Sabinas Basin of Coahuila where coal miners struck the foreign-owned companies. A hundred percent pay increase topped the list of demands, which also included free housing, medical insurance, payment of pensions to widows and recognition of their union.[57] As in Santa Barbara, some of the soldiers guarding the mines sided with the strikers and joined them in a march where demonstrators, carrying red and black flags, jeered the foreign owners.[58] Since the strike affected railroads and other crucial areas of the economy, the government finally intervened. By mid-November, former IWW member and now CROM union official J. Marcos Tristán presented the strikers with an offer of a twenty percent pay hike. After heated debate, miners at Esperanzas, Minor and Palau, accepted the raise and returned to work. Meanwhile, miners at Agujita and Cloete faced a lockout when company officials refused to comply with the negotiated settlement. Boldly, the government confiscated the Agujita and Cloete operations and guaranteed the twenty percent pay increase.[59]

The government's expropriation of foreign-owned properties combined with the CROM's negotiated settlement illustrated the power of linking ideology and practice in the course of establishing a "hegemony of ruling ideas." The CROM employed the rhetoric and language of working-class nationalism to move gradually toward a policy of cooperation—instead of confrontation—with employers. The nationalization of the defiant foreign-owned coal companies provided the CROM another weapon in its propaganda arsenal that advocated close cooperation with the government.

The events in Coahuila were difficult to duplicate elsewhere, however, especially in Tampico where the anarchosyndicalists still wielded a strong influence. There the IWW had organized Petroleum Workers' Local Union #230 and Construction Workers' Local Union #310. The locals conducted weekly meetings in the small industrial village of Doña Cecilia on the Pañuco River. Wobblies Víctor Martínez, Ramón Cornejo and José Zapata, cooperated with remnants of the Tampico Casa who published *El Pequeño Grande*.[60] Together they sparked a July 1920 general strike of 10,000 oil workers. Like the mining industry, the issues were wage increases and better working conditions. Tampico's workers had been encouraged after oil workers in Minatitlán, Veracruz, won wage concessions from the British-owned El Aguila Oil Company.[61] Although the Tampico strike failed, it alarmed American authorities. The local American consul blamed the discord on the ambivalent attitude of the Mexican government and called for government officials to exercise a more interventionist role in labor relations, claiming that such a strategy would guarantee the protection of American economic interests.[62]

RADICALS, REFORM UNIONISTS AND LABOR DIPLOMACY

The protection of American corporate interests in Mexico remained a priority for U.S. officials. As a result the U.S. withheld full diplomatic relations with the Obregón government. In order to gain favor, Obregón had to diffuse the nation's intense social conflict and stabilize the country. Fearful that the new American administration would side with U.S. oil companies that openly called for military intervention, Obregón desperately worked through Samuel Gompers to secure diplomatic recognition. Obregón sent Luis Morones to AFL headquarters to arrange a meeting in the White House to assure bureaucrats that his new government did not threaten American interests. The Mexican president also hoped that the upcoming PAFL convention in January 1921 would serve as a useful beginning to accomplish his objectives of labor peace and U.S. diplomatic recognition.[63] Instead, the January meeting revealed the deep ideological differences that divided Mexican labor. Pressured by CROM members to engage in radical posturing, Morones asked the convention to adopt a resolution calling for the release of IWW prisoners held in U.S. jails. An irritated Samuel Gompers insisted that the IWW did not exist in the United States. The delegates then rephrased the resolution to acknowledge the presence of "enemy" labor organizations.[64] AFL delegate John Frey referred to the IWW as an organization bent on destroying the trade union movement.[65]

To settle the question, Gompers suggested that Mary "Mother" Jones, a long-time supporter of the Mexican Revolution, address the delegates. She called for unity, stressing that the bickering within the Mexican labor movement would end only when workers chose the path of the AFL. Pointing to AFL delegates James Lord and Daniel Tobin, she remarked, "you couldn't get truer, better men than they are."[66] She told the Mexicans to trust their government leaders, saying that she had "studied them all" and found them to be "noble men."[67] Unity between CROM and the AFL finally prevailed when the convention adopted a resolution that supported Article 123 of the 1917 Mexican Constitution.[68]

On February 15, 1921, anarchosyndicalists organized the General Confederation of Workers (CGT) to combat the AFL-CROM alliance. The new group included fifty unions claiming a membership of 36,000. Rodolfo Aguirre, head of the 4,000-member transit workers' union in Mexico City, served as the CGT's general secretary. While former Casa members dominated the organization, the CGT accepted the participation of the Communist Party and the Juventud Comunista, directed by José Valadés, one of the labor movement's youngest and most talented leaders. The CGT accepted the idea of a workers' state exercised by the workers themselves and not by a political party.[69] Two of the leaders, Spaniards José Rubio and Sebastían San Vicente, led a new faction of workers and called themselves anarcho-communists. Rubio and San Vicente had entered Mexico as members

Samuel Gompers, Plutarco Elías Calles and Mary "Mother" Jones at the San Angel Inn, Mexico City, 1921 (reproduced from Salazar and Escobedo, *Las pugnas de la gleba, 1907-1922*, Mexico City: Comisión Nacional Editorial, 1972).

of the IWW's MTW Local #510 of Philadelphia.[70] Wobblies M. Paley, Refugio Rodríguez and Wenceslao Espinoza all attended the convention and argued for a centrally controlled organization exercising tight restraints over the industrial union affiliates. Instead the delegates chose a loosely structured federal organization with each local group exercising autonomy. Unwilling to compromise, the IWW withdrew.[71]

Three days after the CGT's creation, the Confederación de Sociedades Ferrocarrileras (Confederation of Railroad Societies) began a strike for union recognition and for a voice in the management of the government-run railroad. Francisco Pérez, director of the railroads, had previously financed the organization of a company union—the Union of Conductors, Machinists, Brakemen, and Wagonmen. When 12,000 workers struck, Pérez ran the railroads with 15,000 replacements but forced them to join the company union as a condition for employment. Soldiers occupied railway terminals to protect the replacements and to ensure continuing commerce. As the walk-out went on, strikers spread propaganda among the scabs, called for the removal of Pérez, held street demonstrations and engaged in sabotage that successfully hindered operations. The government reacted by arresting workers and conducting trials for those accused of sabotage. As the courts sentenced to death those convicted of sabotage, the CGT and the CROM engaged in a battle to win over the rank and file.[72] While the CGT planned a general strike to support the workers, the CROM recommended government mediation. Instead of confronting the military and facing more arbitrary dismissals, the strikers' leadership opted for negotiation. In a compromise move the government recognized the union and removed Pérez. The railroad workers' acceptance of a negotiated settlement was a clear indication that the government had outmaneuvered and neutralized the CGT.

The CROM's successful promotion of negotiation in place of direct action united the radicals under the banner of the Moscow-based Communist Third International. In March 1921 José Valadés, José Rubio, Frank Seaman, Felipe Lejia Paz (a young CROM dissident) and M. Paley from the IWW, met with the foreign Communist delegation visiting Mexico and formed the Bureau Mexicano de la Internacional Roja de Sindicatos y Uniones de Trabajadores. The Third International's success in uniting the Mexican radicals resulted from the growing stability of the Bolshevik Revolution in Russia and the financial resources behind it. The radicals used the funds to publish *El Trabajador*, edited by Seaman and Valadés.[73]

Relying on the resources of the Bureau, the radicals initiated a series of trips to organize workers in outlying industrial areas. Paley and Rubio went to Tampico and Monterrey, San Vicente to Atlixco, and a new arrival from Peru, José Fernández Oca, organized a strong local federation in Veracruz, where he published *Solidaridad*.[74] At the 1921 May Day celebration in Mexico City, CGT and IWW leaders announced an alliance and made rousing speeches denouncing the government as a tool of the foreign capitalists who "ruthlessly exploited" Mexican workers.

Alarmed at the growing unity among labor's radical factions, Obregón commented that "all of these actions are Bolshevik in character, provoked by socialist anarchy, and they will be suffocated energetically by the government."[75] Using Article 33 of the Mexican Constitution—which gave the president power to deport "pernicious foreigners"—Obregón began with the most vulnerable member of the radical community, Linn A.E. Gale. Authorities arrested Gale and turned him over to American agents at the U.S. border where he renounced his radical ideology.[76]

Following Gale's arrest, authorities apprehended Paley and Rubio in Monterrey, where they had been organizing textile workers. The government also arrested Frank Seaman along with IWW members Walter Fortmeyer and A. Sortmary and José Allen, an undercover agent for the United States Department of Justice. Despite the repression, the IWW pressed forward in Nuevo León, where it had managed to organize a local of nearly sixty men and women textile workers in Villa de Santiago. At the request of textile factory management, authorities incarcerated Ramón Cornejo, head of IWW Local #410. Nuevo León Governor J.N. García then ordered police to raid the IWW's office in Monterrey, where they arrested four members and confiscated union literature.[77]

CGT stevedores in Veracruz and Tampico Wobblies protested the government's repression by conducting two-hour work stoppages and holding mass meetings in their respective cities, In Tampico soldiers attacked the meetings and arrested several IWW leaders. On June 5, the IWW, the National Association of Molders and Helpers and the Federation of Port Workers led workers on a general strike to protest the recent deportations and violence.[78] American petroleum companies petitioned the U.S. State Department for protection of American lives and property. Two U.S. naval vessels soon arrived in the area, and the companies lodged protests against the Mexican government's recent new tax increase levied against them. Reacting to the labor unrest, the companies locked out 20,000 workers. In an effort to defuse the situation, government authorities offered Tampico's workers free tickets for passage to other areas of the republic. Thousands of workers left Tampico and never returned. The lockout was the beginning of a permanent work force reduction by the companies.[79] Despite the government's open collaboration with foreign companies, the CROM met for its annual convention on July 1, 1921, and called for closer cooperation with the state.[80]

The problems the radicals encountered with foreign companies, the CROM and government officials were exacerbated by divisions within their own organizations. The CGT debated the Bolshevik Revolution's increasing persecution of anarchosyndicalists and the communist strategy of "boring within" the CROM unions. The radical majority condemned the authoritarian shift in Bolshevik Russia and opposed cooperation with CROM unions. The result was the withdrawal of the minority faction represented by the Federation of Young Communists, which included some of the most active and brilliant of Mexico's young labor organizers.[81] Meanwhile, the CROM and the government grew closer when Ricardo Treviño, former IWW member and part of the CROM's inner circle of decision makers, *Grupo Acción*, became head of the Department of Labor, Commerce, and Industry.

THE AFL AND AMERICAN RECOGNITION

The Obregón government courted the CROM because an important precondition for U.S. recognition depended on its ability to harness the labor movement and expel its radical elements. Recognition from the U.S. government—which increasingly expressed fears and concerns of growing Bolshevism in Mexico—meant much needed financial aid and manufactured products, such as machinery and capital goods, important for the rebuilding of a nation devastated by years of revolutionary fighting. The CROM offered Obregón the opportunity to stabilize an unsettled social environment and, perhaps more importantly, provided the means to achieve U.S. diplomatic recognition. Obregón hoped to exploit the CROM's relationship with the AFL to convince Washington that his government did not jeopardize U.S. economic interests.[82]

Obregón also turned to the AFL because other efforts to win diplomatic recognition from the U.S. had failed. By 1922, the Mexican Supreme Court had issued five consecutive rulings in favor of U.S. petroleum companies, while the government had negotiated an agreement with the International Bankers Committee on Mexico to renew service on the debt. But U.S. officials still withheld diplomatic recognition and expressed concern about the spread of radicalism in the Mexican labor movement.[83]

Obregón initiated a two-track policy. First, he cooperated more closely with AFL officials working inside Mexico, especially with members of the

International Association of Machinists (IAM). The IAM had negotiated an agreement with the Mexican government that promised the exclusive purchase of American goods carrying the AFL union label. The accord was a ploy to strengthen the AFL's domestic bargaining position with the Warren G. Harding administration. Harding also had hoped to work through the AFL to influence the Mexican government's policy toward U.S. business.[84] Secondly, Obregón wanted to use the CROM to help purge radicals from the labor movement and institutionalize an industrial relations system.

In January 1923 the government policy went into effect against the CGT in Mexico City where transit workers were on strike for higher wages and an end to abusive management. Before the walkout, the CROM had failed in its attempts to gain control of the union, which had grown up as a Casa affiliate. Determined to break the power of the CGT, the government sanctioned a new CROM union to negotiate with the company. Authorities released common criminals from Mexico City jails to serve as strikebreakers and to build the CROM unions. The army guarded the property and protected the ex-prisoners from the increasingly hostile and violent CGT strikers. On February 1, 1923, an hour-long street battle between armed CGT strikers and soldiers resulted in injury and death. Two days later, Obregón deported four Spaniards who had been active transit strike leaders. In all, authorities arrested over 100 CGT members. Although Adolfo de la Huerta negotiated their release, the CROM had dislodged the CGT and now controlled the powerful transit unions.[85]

The government used the same tactics in June 1923 at Orizaba textile mills where employers continued to resist compliance with the 1917 Constitution and had failed to abide by agreements that outlawed the introduction of piece work. After the CGT called a general strike, the owners locked the factories and authorities sent in soldiers to protect the foreign-owned property. Meanwhile, CROM leaders received government authorization to open some of the smaller factories and run them as cooperatives. When workers joined the cooperatives, the larger mills negotiated contracts with the CROM and operated their factories as closed CROM shops. The CROM and the government employed the same tactics in Atlixco, where owners also encouraged strikes, locked out workers and negotiated closed-shop agreements.[86] In textiles, printing and transportation, the CROM secured long-term collective bargaining agreements and established joint government-labor commissions that gave workers a voice in management.[87]

The AFL and its representative, Robert Haberman, worked closely with the Obregón government in its maneuvering against the CGT and the deportations of foreign-born radicals.[88] The offensive against the CGT and other radical unions paved the way for U.S. recognition of the Obregón government. The U.S. State Department dismissed reports from American consuls in Mexico that claimed that radicals in the labor movement still enjoyed government support. Formal recognition of Obregón's government came on August 15, 1923, when the Mexican president approved the Bucareli Accords by giving the U.S. verbal assurances that Article 27 would not be retroactive. Almost immediately afterward Samuel Gompers and AFL leaders received official thanks from the state department, Obregón, CROM leaders and American businessmen operating in Mexico.[89] Although American officials acknowledged Obregón's success in creating a more stable social and political climate, some long-time observers noted that Mexican "workers and peasants still threatened strikes and general lawlessness."[90] The situation also worried Obregón, and he remained on the offensive.

The continuing anxiety produced a turbulent struggle to determine Obregón's successor in 1924. While Obregón and the CROM hierarchy favored Calles, railroad workers and elements of the CGT joined disaffected CROM affiliates and backed Adolfo de la Huerta for president. Many wealthy landowners and conservative elements who feared a more radical drift under Calles, also supported de la Huerta, who by December 7, 1923, had decided that a military revolt was necessary to stop the "imposition" of Calles. Despite pleas from American officials in Mexico who opposed Obregón's "Bolshevik" government because they claimed that it threatened American business interests there, Washington supported him with substantial military aid. The American support contributed to the *de la huertista* rebels' defeat.[91]

Also instrumental in the Obregón-Calles victory was the AFL arms embargo against the rebels. De la Huerta, headquartered in Veracruz, became the victim of the International Seamen's Union embargo imposed on the port city from the United States. Meanwhile, the International Association of Machinists effectively monitored the border and ensured that northern de la huertistas received no war matériel across the Rio Grande.[92] Although the defeat of the rebels strengthened the AFL- and CROM-government alliance and assured the election of Calles, the anarchosyndicalists continued to organize, especially in the nation's industrial periphery.

WOBBLIES AND MEXICAN MINERS IN CHIHUAHUA

In Chihuahua, the IWW's organizational strength reflected its long-time success organizing miners in the Mexican north and across the border in the

United States. Wobbly organizers focused their efforts on employees of the Guggenheim-owned American Smelting and Refining Company (ASARCO) and the El Potosí Mining Company. The IWW campaign began at the ASARCO complexes in Santa Barbara where management had been promoting unions of "free workers."[93] The Wobblies, led by Eduardo Modesto Flores, countered management by establishing Metal Miners' Industrial #210.[94] Their organizational efforts resulted from the distribution of their newspaper, *Solidaridad*. Printed in Chicago, the newspaper reported a rapid increase in circulation during 1923 and 1924 when thousands of Mexicans trekked northward to take jobs in American industry.[95] Central to the paper's effectiveness as a tool of agitation was the news it carried about Mexican political prisoners in the United States.[96] On May 1, 1923, at the American consulate in Chihuahua, railroad unionists held a mass rally demanding the release of sixty-one Mexican prisoners held in American jails. While remembering the 1886 Haymarket anarchist martyrs, the union leaders attacked "free" workers' associations and Catholic unions, both of which had been used by management to forestall radical worker organization. Rafael Gómez, president of the local executive committee of the Federation of Railway Unions of the Republic of Mexico read an open letter to American President Warren G. Harding. He demanded the release of Mexican IWW members Aurelio Azuara (former editor of *El Rebelde*), Manuel Rey, Tomás Martínez and Félix Cedeño, all former fellows of Mexican IWW Local #602 in Los Angeles, California.[97]

Solidaridad built upon the earlier work of the Spanish-language IWW press. Supported by other Mexican unions, IWW organizers employed *Solidaridad* to organize Mexican miners around immediate demands like higher wages, better conditions and an end to abusive management practices. Besides earning meager wages, which averaged around $1 a day, miners and smelter workers had to buy their necessities in company stores at inflated prices. To protest the conditions and the firing of two of its members, IWW Local #210 called for a strike at the El Potosí Mining Company in Santa Eulalia. Employees responded and the strike quickly spread to Avalos and eventually involved 5,000 miners and smelter hands. The strikers then demanded an end to all piece work, a minimum wage of $2.50 per day and the dismissal of two foremen.[98]

The IWW held public meetings throughout the mining districts of Chihuahua that eventually attracted hundreds of workers. Company officials pleaded with local authorities to break up the meetings and force the strikers back to work. Local authorities finally acted on May 11, 1924, when a contingent of thirty mounted rural guards charged a gathering of strikers at Santa Eulalia. During the scuffle police injured twelve demonstrators and apprehended seven. Immediately, the IWW organized a march of several hundred men to Chihuahua City to demand the freedom of the three arrested strike leaders. The next day, Governor Reynaldo Talavera released Francisco Morales, Enrique Castillo and Francisco Nuñez, all of whom had been principal leaders.[99]

The strikers then received help from the IWW's international office in Chicago. While the North American IWW conducted a fund-raising campaign to help sustain them, Tampico construction workers and meat cutters also sent help to Chihuahua. Just when it appeared that the strikers had captured the initiative, local officials and company management wielded the instruments of co-optation and repression. On May 27, 1924, a group of "free" workers signed an agreement with ASARCO and the El Potosí Mining Company. It contained a number of concessions, including the minimum wage and Sundays off. Piecework provisions remained, however, and management fired known IWW members and required all workers to sign contracts that prevented them from joining the union. Most of the workers returned to their jobs, but a minority remained on strike.[100]

When the IWW chartered two new locals in Los Lamentos, authorities escalated their attacks on Wobbly meetings and demonstrations. During June 1924, police repeatedly attacked crowds, beating demonstrators with clubs and pistols. On June 30 they fired on strikers at an open-air meeting and killed IWW leader Marcos Martínez. At the same meeting police severely beat Pascual Díaz, secretary of Local #210, and arrested IWW members Jesús González and Basilio Pedroza.[101] While destroying the IWW, management looked for business-like union organizations to help stabilize production and win worker approval for standardized conditions.[102] The anarchosyndicalists had suffered another defeat and the working-class movement was in transition to a more accommodating organizational mode that satisfied foreign and domestic employers alike.

RADICAL LABOR IN TRANSITION

Tampico had long been the scene of bitter relations between Mexican workers and their foreign employers. In 1924 it intensified when electricians at the British-owned Tampico Light and Power Company walked off their jobs, protesting the firing of union members. After the company refused to settle the dispute through state and federal arbitration, the government deported the plant's general manager and the strikers seized the property. Watching the developments closely, foreign oil company management viewed the actions as the first step toward government expropriation of their properties.[103]

As tensions rose, clashes between armed workers, government troops and company "white guards" escalated. The situation reached a crisis when Mexican troops began aiding strikers in their battles against the white guards. Hoping to diffuse the situation, the government intervened and attempted in part to meet the strikers' demands. The company rejected government mediation and the strike spread to El Aguila Petroleum company where 2,000 workers walked off their jobs. Unions in the area supported the strikers by collecting weekly cash contributions. Meat cutters donated eighteen steers and community businesses donated food and other provisions for the strikers' families.[104]

The conflict at El Aguila soon evolved into a general strike against the foreign-owned companies. Workers at Pierce, Transcontinental, Huasteca, Mexican Gulf and Corona oil companies, all walked off their jobs. Daily disturbances occurring at picket lines resulted in the deaths of two strikers and the wounding of eleven others. As workers protested and shut down other businesses, a concerned government rushed CROM leader Luis Morones in to mediate. Although the strikers rejected the CROM's intervention, Tamaulipas Senator Emilio Portes Gil succeeded in persuading the strikers to negotiate with the foreign companies and sign collective bargaining agreements.

The oil workers' acceptance of collective bargaining agreements signaled an important turning point in Mexican labor relations. Tampico had long been an anarchosyndicalist stronghold that had opposed reform unionism. While workers had rejected CROM and had opted for union autonomy, in the process they had embraced the trade-union principle of negotiation. Hoping to capitalize on this trend, Plutarco Elías Calles sought to strengthen ties among the AFL, the CROM and the government. In November he extended an invitation to AFL delegates attending their annual convention in El Paso, Texas, to come to his inauguration in Mexico City on December 1, 1924.

The AFL convention featured a number of speakers, including Antonio Díaz Soto y Gama, president of the Partido Nacional Agrarista—National Agrarian party, the rural counterpart of Morones' Labor party. Díaz Soto y Gama claimed that the need for violent revolution was over, because Mexico's government now represented workers and peasants, and everyone cooperated to make the country "safe" and "hospitable" to foreign investment.[105] The AFL delegates cheered Díaz Soto y Gama's declarations.

Mexican prosperity meant jobs for American workers. Better wages for Mexico's producing classes made them consumers of American-made products. The AFL reasoned that as long as Mexican workers produced raw materials and foodstuffs for exports, they would not compete against American workers.

But some AFL leaders openly worried that continued divisions within Mexican labor would lead to disaster. They specifically referred to the demand by some workers' groups for ownership of the factories and mines.[106] At his inauguration, Calles calmed the AFL's fears when he announced the government's desire to work with the CROM. He told AFL leaders that "the trade unions of today are in charge of limiting capitalism's absolute power, serving at times to protect it from possible attacks which might destroy it."[107] CROM leaders agreed, saying that "foreign capital would always be welcome by organized labor in Mexico, which will provide it with all kinds of facilities for investment ... and thus further the policy of the national government."[108]

CHAPTER THREE

WORKING-CLASS NATIONALISM AND THE POLITICS OF PRODUCTION

The Confederación Regional Obrera Mexicana's rise to the top of the labor movement by the mid-1920s failed to reconcile the contradictions between Mexican workers and their foreign employers. Worker protest over low wages and poor conditions exposed the weakness of the CROM versus foreign capital. By decade's end, the Mexican government had distanced itself from the CROM as escalating labor unrest resulting from the Great Depression led to a groundswell of support for the creation of a new labor federation. To control the situation, the state enacted a Federal Labor Code in 1931, which effectively curtailed the existence of an independent labor movement.

The emergence of the Confederación de Trabajadores de México (CTM) during the administration of Lázaro Cárdenas (1934-1940) provided for the further growth of the labor movement under government tutelage. The Cárdenas government encouraged labor mobilization and supported strikes by workers against foreign-owned companies. By attaching the government to the nationalistic struggles of the workers, Cárdenas distanced himself from his predecessors, who failed in their efforts to establish a margin of economic independence from foreign capital. Through the expropriation of foreign-owned oil companies and landholdings, Cárdenas established a degree of economic independence for Mexico and raised the expectations of workers in their search for self-management. When the government embraced working-class nationalism, the move generated a battle of production politics, in which organized labor became subordinated to the state-building elite's on-going program of capitalist development. Experiments in workers' self-management, combined with a propaganda offensive against "anti-Mexican" forces, stabilized elite nationalism and effectively suppressed counter hegemonies that emerged from elements within organized labor.

Central to this process was the continuing presence of organized labor from the United States in Mexican state-labor relations. The Cárdenas government skillfully exploited the ideological divisions in the 1930s U.S. labor movement to gain tacit support for Mexican economic independence and to reinforce reform unionism in organized labor. In the 1930s, like the revolutionary period and the reconstruction decade of the 1920s, organized labor in the U.S. exercised its role in the balance of power between foreign economic interests, Mexican workers and the state.

THE CONFEDERACIÓN REGIONAL OBRERA MEXICANA CRASHES DOWN

The beginning of the Calles presidency marked an important turning point in government efforts to formalize legal control over labor unions. The appointment of Luis Morones as minister of commerce, industry, and labor insured the CROM's active and powerful support against rival unions. Through the right to declare the legality of strikes, the CROM arbitrarily incorporated unorganized workers and independent unions that previously had resisted government tutelage. Rival unions and employers that fought the CROM's encroachment found themselves confronting the government. With government support, the CROM grew corrupt, and the union's collaboration with many employers increasingly alienated the working man. The CROM strategy to organize competing unions where independents existed also served to alienate workers. In 1925 the CROM organized the Alliance of Workers and Employees of Buses and Streetcars to replace the anarchosyndicalist union of the Street Railway Company (a subsidiary of the foreign-owned Mexican Light and Power Company). Aided by the government, the CROM asked the company manager, R.G. Conway, to recognize the new minority union. When he refused, President Calles intervened and threatened to expropriate the company if it did not recognize the "legality of association," a Mexican law. Facing government hostility, the company recognized the CROM union and signed a long-term contract that guaranteed wage increases, disability and death benefits and the establishment of grievance procedures. Once again, reform unionism had been established among workers who had long been anarchosyndicalists.[1]

Because the CROM had failed to organize the petroleum workers at the El Aguila refinery in Minatitlán, it sought other methods to manipulate oil workers who had organized independently. On January 28, 1925, the Mexican Supreme Court ruled that the El Aguila company compensate strikers with back pay for time lost during a 1924 dispute. Secretary of Commerce, Industry, and Labor Luis Morones appropriated 1.6 million pesos of the back pay promised to the El Aguila strikers. At the same time, Morones made no effort to secure the reinstatement of 700 blacklisted strikers. Instead, hired company guns had either assassinated dissidents or management had fired them. The Minatitlán union did not recover until almost a decade later.[2]

CROM and rival unions also clashed during a dispute on the railroads where the CROM had attempted to undermine independent organization. On the Isthmus Railroad, workers called a strike to force the rehiring of a discharged employee who had been organizing for the independent National Federation of Railwaymen. Morones declared the strike "illegal," and the government mobilized strikebreakers to crush the walkout. In December 1926, Morones declared a strike by the Mexican Union of Mechanics for wage increases and better conditions "illegal." When the government furnished the CROM with strikebreakers and federal troops, strikers engaged them in a pitched battle, which resulted in a number of casualties on both sides. Afterward, police attacked demonstrators who supported the strikers and jailed Hernán Laborde, leader of the independent Confederation of Railway Societies. In February 1927, the national railways and the government declared that it would no longer bargain with the Confederation of Railway Societies. Instead they would negotiate with individual CROM unions.[3]

The CROM and the government also united to oppose independent unionism in the mining industry. In August 1927 at the American-owned Amparo Mining Company in Jalisco, miners demanded wage increases, safety precautions and recognition of their independent union. Rather than bargain with the miners, management negotiated with the CROM and its affiliate, the Amparo Miners' Alliance. Management also received support from the federal government, which dispatched troops to help the Confederación union take control of the mines.

The independent union countered by accusing the company of asking protection from the United States government, implying that the CROM acted as an agent for the protection of the foreign-owned enterprise. In response to the miners' nationalism, Margarito Ramírez, Jalisco governor, sent state troops to protect them. The potential confrontation forced the federal government to back down and agree to let Ramírez arbitrate the dispute. Since the CROM union only represented 340 of approximately 1,100 workers, the radical union easily won recognition in arbitration-board-sponsored elections. The company granted most of the strikers' demands.[4]

Increasingly, workers grew disillusioned with the CROM's corrupt leadership. As the CROM struggled to organize and to control discord among workers toiling in foreign-owned enterprises, the government also had begun to distance itself from the Confederación. In 1928 the problems between the

CROM and the government reached a climax when the press accused Luis Morones as the "intellectual author" of the assassination of president-elect Alvaro Obregón. As early as 1927 Morones had openly aspired to the presidency. When the issue caused considerable debate among the rank and file, the state withdrew its official support. Without government protection, the CROM began to disintegrate.

Luis Morones about 1918 (from Araiza, *Historia del movimiento obrero mexicano*, Tomo 4, Mexico City: Ediciones Casa del Obrero Mundial, 1975).

Again the CROM faltered. Its mission to incorporate working-class organizations into the National Revolutionary Party (PNR) fell short. Although the PNR drew together rival parties—military officers, leaders of both the agrarian and labor movements as well as state bureaucrats—and tried to unite them around the legacy of the 1910 Revolution there was no true coalition.

Calles and others viewed the PNR as a means of consolidating different classes and class factions to stabilize Mexican society. The establishment of the National Revolutionary Party coincided with the interim presidency of Emilio Portes Gil, a long-time and active opponent of the CROM. This further weakened the CROM, and unions began to defect on a regular basis. First, the Federation of Federal District Workers (FSTDF) withdrew. Led by Fidel Velázquez, Fernando Amilpa, Jesús Yuren, Alfonso Sánchez Madriaga and Luis Quintero, the Federal District union represented urban transport, municipal and hotel workers, and laborers in menial, low-paying jobs employed in the Federal District. As president, Portes Gil awarded the five leaders control of the arbitration and conciliation boards. The labor leaders capitalized on the workers' opposition to Morones' excessive authoritarianism and corruption. The discontent, combined with the resentment, frustrations and the hardships of unemployment brought on by the Great Depression, prompted workers to look elsewhere for leadership and organization.[5]

LABOR UNREST, THE GREAT DEPRESSION AND A NEW LABOR CODE

Between 1929 and 1933 the number of documented "labor conflicts" tripled.[6] While 245,000 out of 800,000 industrial workers faced unemployment, those who remained on the job protested wage cuts and shorter working days mandated by foreign-owned companies. Despite the 1917 Constitution's nationalistic content, the power and presence of foreign capital in the Mexican economy had increased dramatically. U.S. investment in Mexico had grown from $185 million in 1900 to over $695 million in 1931, while overall foreign investment had reached $2.18 billion.[7]

Business and government leaders reacted by initiating discussions for the codification of Article 123. The business sector, led by industrialists from Monterrey, had pushed for a uniform labor code as early as 1925.[8] Since the Revolution the Monterrey clique had expanded its commercial, financial and industrial activities.[9] They believed that a uniform national labor code presented the possibility of absolute control and predictability in the operation of their enterprises. Moreover, their participation in the writing of a national labor code provided the opportunity to enhance their prestige compared to other fractions in Mexican society, especially organized labor.

The Monterrey private sector hoped to spread its management system of labor-employer cooperation and paternalistic practices to include all of Mexico. They argued that strikes, boycotts and picket lines by organized labor undermined the nation's goal of economic reconstruction. Mexican nationalism required harmony between the classes and the ultimate reliance on the entrepreneur as the agent of progress and the guardian of the nation's welfare. They followed the scientific management practices of their North American counterparts, which involved total control of the factory shopfloor. "Like parts in a machine," the Monterrey industrialists believed, "workers required regular fixing to render good, loyal service."[10]

For the Monterrey elite, control over the codification of Article 123 corresponded to their theory that the government's primary responsibility was maintaining order, and that the meddlesome presence of the state in labor affairs threatened the progress and economic welfare of the nation. In the codification debate that raged between 1929 and 1931, the Monterrey businessmen considered management's control of the collective bargaining system as fundamental as its right to hire and fire employees and make decisions about the future of their enterprises. Throughout the debate they asserted that the government's attempts to control the codification process infringed upon those rights.[11]

The impact of the worldwide depression on the Mexican economy bolstered the northern industrialists' arguments against government control of the codification process. They emphasized that the passage of the proposed labor law would prevent the nation's recovery and contribute to the worsening of the economy. Foreign business leaders joined the Monterrey elite in the desire to write the labor code because they hoped to retain local enforcement of Article 123, which allowed enterprises to claim adverse local conditions as a justification for non-compliance. Henry Ford, for example, threatened to remove his auto plant from Mexico if the proposed code became law.[12]

Despite opposition to the proposed labor code, the Calles-controlled Ortiz-Rubio administration passed the bill on August 5, 1931. The government used the legislation to exert authority and control over the increasing working-class protest sweeping the country. Besides assuring the state's right to declare strikes "legal," "illegal" or "nonexistent," the law also gave the government the right to recognize or ignore the elections and direction over labor unions. In the midst of renewed labor insurgency, the code centralized state power in labor matters.

"PURIFYING" THE CROM AND A NEW LABOR-STATE ALLIANCE

To help the state enforce the new code, government leaders looked for a renewed alliance with labor. The PNR won support from Alfredo Pérez Medina, the head of the powerful Federation of Workers' Unions of the Federal District (FSODF). In 1932 the government backed Pérez Medina in a struggle with Luis Morones for control of the CROM. Although the fight left Morones in control, Pérez Medina had pulled the federal federation unions out of the CROM, resulting in the decimation of its membership. Morones replaced Pérez Medina as head of the remaining federal federation unions

Luis Morones from the proletarian's perspective (from Salazar and Escobedo, *Las pugnas de la gleba, 1907-1922*, Mexico City: Comisión Nacional Editorial, 1972).

with Vicente Lombardo Toledano, who had climbed the CROM's ranks through his leadership of the 12,500-member teachers' unions in the Federal District. Despite his open Marxism, Lombardo had worked closely with Morones throughout the 1920s. Morones considered his service to the CROM invaluable, because his essays and books on worker education, political economy and foreign policy provided the CROM the legitimacy it needed to present itself as a true social movement.[13]

Lombardo moved to take control of the CROM when he published a plan calling for the democratization of the existing CROM unions. The program advocated regular union meetings and elections of officers, the reduction of the arbitrary power exercised by local union officials and the financing of a central strike fund. Lombardo believed that success depended upon his newly created Karl Marx Workers' Schools and their ability to educate the workers about class interests. The schools developed from Lombardo's experiences in administrating the 1917 workers' and artisans' People's University and the National Preparatory School in 1922. A clash with Morones was inevitable.

It erupted on September 18, 1932, at a federal federation meeting where Morones made insulting remarks about Lombardo's background and education. Immediately, Lombardo and his followers bolted the federation, and on March 11, 1933, they organized a "purified" CROM. The group issued a manifesto that called for the "Mexicanization" of the nation's foreign-owned resources and industries, as well as workers' self-management. Rather than promoting independent labor organization, the "purified" CROM looked to the state and its enforcement of the 1931 Labor Code as the arbiter of class conflict.[14]

While Lombardo's CROM attempted to curry government favor, it competed with Pérez Medina's Cámara Nacional del Trabajo (National Chamber of Labor or CNT), which received strong support from powerful government bureaucrats. The CNT attempted to ally with the nominally anarchosyndicalist CGT, which had degenerated into a reformist organization that also courted state backing. Better organized, the Lombardo association successfully united many of the unions into the General Confederation of Workers and Peasants of Mexico (CGOCM). Immediately, the CGOCM sought and received government support to win a July 1934 general strike of Mexico City. The crucial backing built the foundation for the incorporation of Lombardo's group into the ruling party.[15]

Within the context of renewed working-class nationalism, President Lázaro Cárdenas implemented a revised PNR six-year plan that called for reducing the nation's dependency on foreign markets, agrarian reform and the development of national industries. Pressure to initiate the PNR's nationalistic program mounted when a wave of strikes erupted at foreign-owned enterprises during 1935, Cárdenas' first year as president. Workers in petroleum, transportation and communications all went on strike to protest wage cuts. None of the strikers belonged to the general confederation, however, and this presented problems for the ruling party, which hoped to restructure the relationship between the state, foreign interests and the working-class. Ultimately, the strategy depended on gaining control over the organized labor movement in major foreign-dominated industries.

The key was the Cárdenas government's open support of workers' unionization through strikes. In 1935 the number of officially recognized strikes had jumped to 642 from just eleven in 1931. The increase resulted from the Cárdenas administration's assistance to the CGOCM in winning a number of juridical decisions against foreign industries. Favorable government decisions toward workers in conflict with their foreign employers encouraged more nationalistic actions, which swelled the general confederation's ranks.[16]

While Cárdenas encouraged worker organization and strikes, other elements within the ruling party feared that the situation invited social instability and threatened the established political order. Leading the opposition to Cárdenas was former President Calles. He denounced all strikers as "unpatriotic" and challenged the president to restore order or "suffer" the consequences. His remarks initiated a political offensive that many feared could lead to civil war, because the former president still had a tight grip on some elements within the military. But Cárdenas also had climbed the party's ranks through his role as a military leader, and since becoming president he had taken significant measures to cultivate military support. As insurance, Cárdenas relied on worker and peasant organization, particularly armed militias, thus leaving Calles isolated when the two started on a collision course for control of the Mexican state.

Cárdenas' support solidified when the general confederation, railroad, streetcar and miners' unions met on June 15, 1935, and agreed to form the National Committee of Proletarian Defense (CNDP). While supporting Cárdenas against Calles, the labor unions agreed in principle to create a single national labor confederation. Its more immediate task, however, was the defense of the government against *callista* attacks. Action culminated on December 22, 1935, when 80,000 workers marched through the streets of Mexico City in support of Cárdenas. The event, along with demonstrations organized in other parts of the country, isolated Calles and his shrinking supporters, which included the CROM and Luis Morones. The Cárdenas victory clearly indicated that the CNDP constituted the shell in which the regime would build its alliance with organized labor and pursue its strategy for national development within a capitalist framework.[17]

But the CNDP's strength rested largely on the powerful independent unions: miners, electricians, petroleum and railroad workers, all of which had remained outside the general confederation ranks. When the CNDP announced plans to merge formally at a convention in February 1936, Lombardo realized the necessity of organizing other industrial workers to counter the large, independent industrial unions. The struggle to organize industrial workers was crucial for enhancing Lombardo's position within the new confederation and solidifying government backing. Efforts focused on Monterrey, where intransigent industrialists had succeeded in establishing well-entrenched company unions.[18]

Lombardo had decided in early 1935 to target the Vidriera, a huge glass works controlled by the powerful Garza-Sada family.[19] He chose the Vidriera for its recent history of labor unrest and because its sophisticated technology made it vulnerable to skilled workers' demands. The plant manufactured bottles for soft drinks and alcoholic beverages and had made a quick recovery from the Depression, largely due to the repeal of Prohibition in the United States. Despite the lead in the city's industrial recovery, management still insisted on Depression-level wages and forced overtime. The plant was ripe for union organization.[20]

Early in 1936 management's fight to prevent union organization suffered a severe setback. A decision by the federal arbitration board outlawed company unions, paving the way for the organization of the Vidriera workers. When foundry workers at the glass complex went on strike in January 1936, the federal arbitration board declared the strike legal and ruled against the company union in a representation election. Business leaders closed ranks and prepared to confront labor and the Cárdenas regime.[21]

On February 6, 1936, the Monterrey elite shut down all commerce in the city. Besides showing resourcefulness and strength by successfully halting the city's economic activity, local businessmen also appealed to the country's fervent nationalism. Hoping to weaken organized labor's efforts among Monterrey workers, the elite fomented fears of communism. They directed their attacks against Lombardo, who had recently returned from a trip to the Soviet Union. By calling him an agent of the Soviet Union, the Monterrey elite put the labor leader on the defensive, while portraying themselves as defenders of the *patria* and *mexicanismo*.[22]

Cárdenas, meanwhile, attempted to persuade the businessmen that a unified labor movement meant stable labor-employer relations. He argued that a strong, centralized labor movement presented fewer problems for management because it would be easier to control. Insistent on their desire to control labor through top-down, patronal-type management—that had functioned well in Monterrey for decades—the industrialists rejected Cárdenas' overtures. The president responded by calling for labor-state cooperation, the preeminence of government and the necessity for organized labor to unify into a single federation. He also endorsed the strike at the Vidriera foundry and threatened the expropriation of industries that remained hostile toward organized workers and national laws that protected them.[23]

Encouraged by Cárdenas' declarations in Monterrey, labor leaders convened in Mexico City during February 1936 and formed the Confederación Trabajadores de México. Convinced that the president's statements about worker-controlled industries and "unpatriotic" employers were basic components of a new state policy toward labor, major industrial unions that had been independent since their conception joined the CTM. The miners, railroad, petroleum and electrical workers' unions helped swell the ranks of the CTM to over 600,000 members. Calling "for a society without classes" and identifying itself as a "positively free autonomous grouping of workers' unions with ideological and organizational independence," the CTM's rhetoric struck a responsive chord with rank-and-file workers, who allied themselves with Cárdenas and the Mexican state.[24] Although the CTM's effort to organize Monterrey's industrial workers ultimately failed, threats of government expropriation reinforced the president's pro-labor image.

While CTM leaders Lombardo, Fidel Velázquez and Valentín Campa all advocated "workers' democracy," they did so within the context of the Cárdenas regime's plan for national development. Although recent government policy weighed heavily in favor of workers, the alliance with the CTM's bureaucracy placed it in a better position to limit the demands of workers for higher wages, better conditions and organizational autonomy. Much like the CROM of the 1920s, the CTM simultaneously accelerated the growth of organized labor and authoritarian tendencies within the working-class movement. But the rank and file, particularly in major industrial unions, resisted top-down control and continued to push a militant agenda. They demanded the right to strike as guaranteed in the 1917 Constitution and sporadically called for workers' self-management. Conflict followed.

The first confrontation occurred when the newly created Sindicato de Trabajadores Ferrocarriles de la República Mexicana—railroad workers' union

65

or STFRM—attempted to negotiate its contract with the state-owned Ferrocarriles Nacional de México (Mexican National Railway). Workers demanded enforcement of a February 18, 1936, presidential decree that gave them a paid holiday for every six days worked, something already agreed to by private railroad companies. When the national-railroad management refused to comply, 45,000 members went on strike. On May 18, 1936, two hours after the strike began, the committee of conciliation and arbitration declared the walkout "illegal" and ordered the strikers back on the job within twenty-four hours.[25]

The Mexican army used airplanes to drop thousands of copies of the committee's decision over railroad terminals where strikers walked the picket lines. Fearful that a prolonged strike would involve replacement workers and the federal army to protect them, union leadership suspended the walkout. The rank and file, however, demanded that the CTM use its power to call for a national solidarity strike. Shouted down by strikers at meetings, the CTM leadership compromised and called for a symbolic half-hour national strike. In doing so, the CTM avoided a confrontation with both angry workers and the Cárdenas government.[26] The national railroad crisis of May 1936 represented the first of many conflicts among the rank and file, the CTM leadership and the government over wages, shop conditions and the issue of union autonomy in state-controlled industries. Throughout 1936 and 1937, the demands for organizational autonomy and higher pay included calls by electrical, railroad and petroleum union members for national control of foreign-owned enterprises under the aegis of workers' self-management.

Representative of independent working-class insurgency was a militant strike waged by electrical workers against Mexican Light, a British-Canadian enterprise. Attempting to renegotiate contracts with the company for wage increases, the Sindicato Mexicano de Electricistas (Electrical Workers' Union or SME) defended their right to strike, staged street demonstrations and built a broad nationalist coalition among the Mexican population to oppose the foreign-owned company. Instead of relying on the government bureaucracy, the union organized a mass demonstration to mobilize popular support. With electricity provided only to the National Palace, Radio Chapultepec, fire stations and hospitals, and with over 3,000 strikers and their supporters in the streets, the government declared the electrical workers' action "legal."[27]

The decision encouraged the strikers to demand that the CTM call a general strike instead of relying on arbitration to settle the dispute.[28] When the strike committee rejected CTM mediation, President Cárdenas personally intervened and forced the company to accept the strikers' demands. While ultimately relying on the power of the state to settle the dispute, the electrical workers defended their right to strike and maintained their organizational autonomy. Other unions, such as the petroleum workers, followed the example and challenged the power of foreign-owned enterprises. Their actions led to what some scholars have argued was the climax of the 1910 Revolution.

OIL EXPROPRIATION: THE APEX OF WORKING-CLASS NATIONALISM

Petroleum workers had been encouraged to unionize by Lázaro Cárdenas during his campaign for the presidency in 1934. While the union movement among oil workers began in the 1920s with the organization of Tampico and Veracruz workers, it had proceeded unevenly and slowly throughout the industry for the rest of the decade. The drive toward unionization came to a halt during the early years of the Depression, but it experienced a surge around 1934 when economic situations improved. Workers organized in Mexico City, as well as at Nanchital, Las Choapas and Agua Dulce, where they joined the Federation of Workers' Unions of the Oil and By-Products Industry of Veracruz.

In 1935, after a series of successful strikes supported by the government, Tampico unions joined the others and called for the creation of a national union and a standard contract. The government encouraged the idea of a national union through the use of the committee of conciliation and arbitration, the secretary of labor, and the president. After local union representatives met and formed the Sindicato de Trabajadores Petroleros de la República Mexicana—Petroleum Workers' Union (STPRM)—the organization received government backing and joined the CTM.

While the CTM and petroleum union leadership talked contract, the rank and file seized the initiative. Workers carried out strikes in the oil fields and refineries at Tampico, El Ebano, Cerro Azul, Mata Redonda, Ciudad Madero, Nanchital and Las Choapas.[29] Nurtured on revolutionary syndicalism, laborers demonstrated their historical propensity to solve disputes with the foreign companies through direct action rather than a legal framework. Their actions forced union planning committees to call an "official" one-day strike on November 25, 1936.

The union demanded a forty-hour week, guaranteed sick pay, paid holidays, workers' housing and a minimum wage for unskilled labor. Fearful that the militancy of the oil workers could grow to uncontrollable proportions, President Cárdenas intervened and convinced the union leadership to postpone strike activity for 120 days. After months of deadlocked negotiations, a strike erupted on May 28, 1937. When the government declared the strike "legal," the oil companies claimed that they could not meet the union's demands because of the existing financial state of the industry. They then submitted a request to the Committee of Conciliation and Arbitration and asked that the strike be declared a "conflict of an economic order."

With the committee's recognition of the strike as a "conflict of economic order," and its promise to investigate the companies' ability to meet the union's demands, strikers returned to their jobs. The investigation documented the history of the foreign companies' relationship with Mexican workers, and the ensuing report mandated that the companies pay the workers $26 million pesos. The report also claimed that the situation for oil workers had not changed since the early 1920s when former President Calles toured Tampico and found deplorable living and working conditions.[30]

Although the companies rejected the report and refused to comply, the committee ordered them to implement the decision by January 1, 1938. Encouraged by the government's support, workers in Tampico continued the strike from October through December. The companies refused to give in and sought an injunction (*amparo*) from the Mexican Supreme Court. The court ruling and the subsequent expropriation of the companies bolstered the government's credibility with the oil workers and the Mexican people. Both the oil workers and the Mexican population viewed the struggle as one between foreign domination of their country and the nation's economic self-determination upheld by the Cárdenas government. The oil workers escalated the struggle a step further when they seized the fields, refineries and the offices of the foreign companies. Conflict soon broke out over the issues of worker administration, improvements in wages, working conditions and benefits.

WORKERS' SELF-MANAGEMENT IN CRISIS

Oil workers in the new Poza Rica region in Veracruz led the fight for employee control and government compliance with the demands made against foreign companies. Besides workers' self-management, the Poza Rica union (Local #30) called for the equalization of pay rates because their salaries remained considerably lower than those of the old petroleum-producing Northern Zone of the Gulf Coast, which included Tampico and Ciudad Madero.[31]

Like the Tampico oil workers of the 1920s, those at Poza Rica took the lead in the struggle for organizational autonomy. As in Tampico a decade earlier, the workforce was a mix of skilled roughnecks and roustabouts and country peasants. Culturally, the peasants—largely unskilled migrants from the southern Sierra Madre—found themselves in an unusual situation.[32] The Poza Rica region lacked the traditional authority figures that were commonplace in Mexican society: the influence of the Catholic Church was weak, and the Masonic Lodge and the unions substituted as the institutions that gave the community a sense of cohesiveness. At Poza Rica, company managers divided the skilled and unskilled workers by pay difference. Both groups, however, faced deplorable living and working conditions, leading to resistance to the abusive management practices of the oil companies and strident nationalism among workers, small business people and some government officials.[33] The working-class nationalism developed by the Poza Rica workers soon clashed with the Cárdenas administration's efforts to subordinate workers' self-management to the "national interest." Although the government initially supported self-management at the local level because it depended on workers to insure continued production, state officials soon sought to centralize the operations with limited worker participation. A principal feature of this strategy was an attempt to use Local #30 President Eduardo Pérez Castañeda to arbitrarily select the directors of the local administrations. The rank and file opposed the measure and insisted that each department democratically elect their own directors.[34]

When the Poza Rica local and the national petroleum union rejected centralization, the Cárdenas government maneuvered to discredit the oil workers' demands. The federal government worked with the national union leaders to convince the rank and file outside the Poza Rica region of the pitfalls of worker administration. At the petroleum workers' union second national convention in 1939, Local #5 leaders from the Azcapotzalco refinery in Mexico City argued that worker administration was not possible while the Cárdenas government negotiated with the foreign companies over the issue of compensation.

The Mexican oil industry faced enormous difficulties. Production levels had fallen and sales had slumped after an international boycott of Mexican crude by the British government. With the national union's refusal to back worker control, President Cárdenas issued his "Fourteen Points," based on calls for layoffs, wage cuts and greater management power on the job. Meanwhile, Mexican newspapers and other unions, such as the miners and textile workers, called the oil workers "traitors to the country" and demanded that they put aside their interests for the "good of the nation."[35]

As tensions rose between Cárdenas, the foreign companies and their governments, arguments for workers' self-management lost credibility. By invoking the concept of protecting national interests, the government and the CTM rallied support from other sectors of Mexican society and isolated rank and file who advocated workers' self-management of the industry. Because the petroleum workers' union was a CTM affiliate, pressure began to build within its own ranks to follow Cárdenas.

The political right also threatened oil workers. The National Sinarquista Union, founded in 1938 to combat growing communism in Mexico and the Cárdenas government's pro-labor policy, attacked union meetings with the support of powerful Mexican industrialists. Lombardo maneuvered the CTM to support the government against the perceived imperialist threat abroad and the growing fascist menace at home.[36] Without the CTM's support, the rank and file stood alone in the fight for oil workers' self-management.

Having solidified a formidable alliance, the government formed Petróleos Mexicanos (PEMEX) and gave the new company's president powers to name all directive personnel.[37] But the Poza Rica workers refused to accept the order, claiming that it nullified workers' power in administration.[38] To defuse Local #30 militancy, the government settled long-standing wage disputes between the Poza Rica rank and filers and the El Aguila Company. Next, it appointed local union officials as superintendents of PEMEX.[39] As with the CROM during the 1920s, the government moved to establish stronger ties with trade-union leaders and convert them into state functionaries.

After the government selected union officials to assist in the management of PEMEX, Poza Rica workers demanded a clear explanation of their role in the company's administration. Specifically, the rank and file asked whether they were "government employees," "cooperative partners," "co-owners" of the new company, or "new paupers."[40] To establish their role in PEMEX, Local #30 members called for a special convention of the national petroleum union. They issued a document that outlined "workers' administration" and criticized the government's refusal to consider worker control.[41] Cárdenas—insisting that workers were not "technically fit for management"—followed his long-standing principles on the subject while he attempted to put the oil-company operations into the hands of "efficient technocrats."[42]

Among miners, the idea of workers' self-management still prevailed, however. The day the government expropriated the petroleum industry, workers belonging to the miners' union seized the ASARCO smelter in Chihuahua. Their actions coincided with on-going work stoppages by ASARCO's Monterrey refinery workers. By the fall of 1938 the walkout had spread to the Phelps Dodge operations, the Cananea mines and the ASARCO complex at Nueva Rosita. As with the oil workers' strike, the primary issue was self-management.[43]

No other foreign-controlled sector generated more government revenues, employment and foreign exchange. Consequently, the miners' strike placed enormous pressure on Cárdenas. As with the oil workers, Cárdenas supported the miners' efforts to secure material benefits but strongly opposed their demands for self-management of the industry. Accordingly, he denounced workers' seizure of private property as "illegal syndicalist measures" and "unpatriotic acts."[44] The turning point came when Phelps-Dodge formally requested of the federal government a lockout of its San Carlos mine. Through its manipulation of Mexican nationalism, the government convinced the miners' leadership to expel some of its members and warn others not to interfere with company operations. To seal the Phelps-Dodge victory, management agreed to give workers a ten percent pay increase. Once again, the Mexican state rejected syndicalism as incompatible with its plans for capitalist development and successfully outmaneuvered militants by securing material benefits for workers.

AMERICAN UNIONS AND MEXICAN NATIONALISM

Helping to legitimize the government's position that PEMEX belonged to the "whole nation" and not to the oil workers, the CTM enlisted support from organized labor in the United States. Because of existing ties between the AFL and the weakened CROM, Confederación de Trabajadores de México representatives initially sought support from William Green, the AFL's president. But Green and the AFL opposed Mexico's expropriation of the oil companies and refused even to meet with a CTM delegation. The CTM then turned to the new Congress of Industrial Organizations (CIO), and its leader, John L. Lewis. Structural changes had occurred within the labor movement in the United States, which complicated the CTM's task.[45]

The CIO had emerged because of the AFL's refusal to respond to a renewed groundswell of militancy by industrial workers in the U.S. during the Great Depression. The CIO pledged complete separation from the pro-business AFL and viewed contact with the Mexican CTM as a way to enhance the organization's prestige. The CTM and CIO had already established *Noticiero Obrero*

C.C. León Jonhaux, French CGT, and John L. Lewis at the 1938 CTM meeting in Mexico City (from Salazar, *La CTM, su historia y su significado,* Mexico City: Ediciones T.C. Modelo, S.C.L., 1956).

Mexicano (Mexican Labor News) and had cooperated during strikes on the U.S. West Coast, Texas and against American-owned firms operating in Mexico. Unlike the AFL, which refused to organize Mexican workers and even supported U.S. government programs to deport them, the CIO had initiated organizing drives among them.[46]

Lewis and the CIO, like the AFL and Gompers, had practical reasons for supporting the Mexican workers and their government. The potential Mexican market represented a huge dumping-ground for American made-goods. With its largest unions representing unskilled workers in the manufacturing sector, Lewis believed that the CIO should support Mexican workers in their struggle for a decent wage, because a greater share of the national wealth for them meant the sale of American goods and jobs for CIO workers. Like the AFL, it too supported the expansion of trade in the Western Hemisphere. Lewis favored industrial unionism in all of Latin America, "as a means of raising wages, living standards, and hence a boost for U.S. trade."[47]

The CIO gave its tacit support for the nationalization of the petroleum industry when it sent Lewis as a delegate to the first meeting of the Confederación Trabajadores de América Latina—Latin American Confederation of Workers (CTAL). Organized by Lombardo and supported by

President Cárdenas, the meeting attempted to rally support for Mexican nationalism, which had come under increasing attack from powerful economic interests within the United States and Great Britain. As a result of the pressure, the United States government had temporarily suspended silver purchases from Mexico, while Great Britain had broken off relations with Mexico completely. In addition, the international oil companies' boycott had produced a replacement-parts shortage for PEMEX.

At the CTAL Mexico City meeting, Lewis challenged the American government to uphold the rhetoric of the "Good Neighbor Policy," which advocated the policy of non-intervention in Latin America. He stressed Mexico's right to self-determination and non-interference by the great powers in its internal affairs. But Lewis stopped short of openly supporting Mexican nationalization. He did officially endorse the goals of the meeting, which were the extension of labor legislation and collective bargaining throughout the hemisphere—ideals that were consistent with his views on trade in the region. Though a formal alliance never materialized, the CIO pledged cooperation with the CTM.[48]

The AFL, which still maintained relations with the weakened CROM, clashed with Lewis over the question of Mexican nationalism. The AFL president, William Green, like his predecessor Gompers, opposed the expropriation of American-owned businesses. The AFL had always advocated the protection of American business in Mexico and Latin America. During the Revolution, the AFL had worked with the CROM and the governments of Obregón and Calles to protect American-owned enterprises. Its position also stemmed from deep ideological convictions that opposed the notion of governmental intervention in the economy. Mexican nationalism conflicted with the AFL's support of private enterprise and its philosophy of "business unionism."[49]

Consistent with its conservative position toward the Mexican oil crisis, the AFL cooperated with elements in American business and the U.S. State Department to devise a strategy that would ultimately lead to rescinding the oil expropriation decree. Robert Haberman, who had worked closely with officials in the American government in the 1920s, collaborated with Luis Morones in an attempt to revitalize the CROM. Haberman and Morones received support from some Mexican industrialists and hoped to challenge the CTM's hegemony within the Mexican labor movement.

Their efforts failed. The CTM and Cárdenas successfully mobilized other Mexican social groups and established a legitimacy based upon their firm commitment to Mexican nationalism. Mexicans supported the oil expropriation decree, which for them represented the culmination of an important goal of the revolution: "Mexico for the Mexicans."[50] The CIO's implicit support of the expropriation decree discredited the AFL and the forces it attempted to mobilize. The CTM, with a firm commitment to a multi-class alliance against the foreigners, reinforced its claim as the legitimate representative of Mexican working people. It successfully postured itself as the defender of the patria and mexicanismo.[51]

THE DEFEAT OF WORKERS' SELF-MANAGEMENT AND THE SHARP RIGHT TURN

Garnering the support of the Mexican nation and elements of organized labor from the United States, the Cárdenas government went on the offensive against oil workers who still hoped to control the industry. Like the foreign oil companies, PEMEX petitioned the Committee of Conciliation and Arbitration to call the long-standing dispute between the union and the company a "conflict of an economic order." It then demanded that the union give up the right to strike. When the board complied with PEMEX's wishes, the union's leadership, represented by Rafael Suárez, threatened a series of strikes. To avert the possibility of work stoppages, the CTM mediated the dispute and arranged an emergency agreement between PEMEX and the union. Despite the agreement, workers carried out several twenty-four-hour *paros* (illegal strikes) in the Poza Rica region. Government reacted and charged that the emergency agreement had been violated by the union.

Outraged, 6,000 members of Locals #4, #5, #6, #7, #8 and #30 voted for a general strike against PEMEX and to leave the CTM.[52] Lombardo and the CTM then attempted to use the issue of Mexican nationalism to discredit the strikers. CTM leaders accused the oil workers of counterrevolutionary activity and of acting as agents of the foreign oil companies. Under the pressure, some elements within the petroleum union joined the chorus of accusations. Local #1 of Ciudad Madero condemned the use of the strike and called the union's national executive committee "traitors to the nation."[53]

The local unions from the Northern Zone backed the government reorganization plan. President Cárdenas, who enjoyed Local #1's support, called on its leadership to take action against the national executive committee and Suárez. The national executive committee retorted that opposition to reorganization was the work of a small group of agitators and claimed that the majority of workers supported the president's *obrerismo*.[54] With the backing of the union's national executive committee, the government went on the offensive, sending federal troops on September 28, 1940, to the Azcapotzalco refinery in Mexico City to break the strike. The government again used nationalistic rhetoric to justify its actions, calling the strike "subversive" and "surely at the service of foreign interests."[55]

While the government refused to allow workers to run the petroleum industry, it did tolerate worker administration and cooperatives in other industries. When the bureaucracy finalized the nationalization of the railroads, union members agreed to drop their demands for a cooperative and settled for worker administration of a state-owned enterprise. In situations where industry resisted labor demands and strikes disrupted operations, the state turned over operations to technical managers and gave workers a voice in administration. Foreign-owned electrical installations and smaller factories frequently became targets of the policy.[56]

The CTM, while opposing worker control of the "strategically important" petroleum industry, supported and helped to legitimize cooperatives in other industries by spreading nationalistic propaganda.[57] Like the CROM of the 1920s, the CTM mixed rhetoric with the concept of workers' control to limit the revolutionary potential of its rank and file. Instead of giving labor real power within the context of production politics, the state assumed the former role of the foreign companies. Accordingly, government became more involved with issues such as wages, working conditions and the right to strike.

The state-CTM alliance also led to the loss of union autonomy and democracy. The breach between leadership and membership widened, especially in the unions of nationalized industries. Many union leaders accepted top administrative positions in nationalized businesses, especially in petroleum where the government created positions to reward cooperative leaders and paid them salaries five times higher than what they had earned previously. The state-CTM affiliation expanded trade-union bureaucracy and tied the working-class movement closer to the government. Lombardo and the CTM justified their policies in the name of Mexican nationalism and the united front against "internal reaction," "imperialism" and "fascism."[58]

The government- and trade-union alliance reached a new level as the 1940 presidential election approached. While many labor and peasant organizations supported the candidacy of Francisco Múgica, a staunch defender of labor's rights and causes within the Cárdenas administration, the out-going president bowed to conservative pressures and chose as his successor, the minister of defense, Manuel Avila Camacho. Despite reservations about Camacho's conservatism and his unwillingness to support labor causes, the CTM solidly backed his candidacy. Progressive forces within the union justified supporting Avila Camacho by stressing the need for continuing the popular front against "imperialism" in the face of impending war in Europe and Asia.

In response to the CTM's support of the Avila Camacho candidacy, several dissident unions within the CTM, including railroad, electricians and petroleum locals, published a manifesto that called for the repudiation of the CTM leadership. Lombardo—the proponent of the popular-front strategy—reacted by declaring the dissident unions "non-existent."[59] Some of the frustrated dissidents joined Luis Morones and the weakened CROM to support the candidacy of Monterrey capitalist Juan Andréu Almazán, who enjoyed the backing of the new conservative Partido Acción Nacional—National Action Party (PAN). Misguided in their thinking, the dissident unionists believed that an Almazán presidency could be manipulated to bring about greater union democracy and autonomy. Instead, the election accelerated the growing labor-state alliance and the bureaucratization of the working-class movement. With the CTM's help, Avila Camacho swept the presidency. Meanwhile, the CTM elected eight senators and twenty-four deputies of their own. The 1940 election capped a twenty-year process in which the state legitimized its goals for national development by bringing popular organizations under its control.

CHAPTER FOUR

ELITE NATIONALISM
AND THE POLITICS OF PRODUCTION

The nationalistic consensus forged during the Cárdenas era remained fragile because it involved the co-existence of a state-building elite in an uneasy relationship with the working-class, in which elements opposed state development and labor policies. That opposition led to the formation of factions within CTM unions as well as new and independent federations that, at first, defended Mexican workers' right to strike and opposed the state's imposition of a professional trade-union bureaucracy.

The conflict between these forces sharpened when the demand generated by World War II increased exports, industrial production and foreign investment. The industrial boom augmented the government's entrepreneurial role and led to the creation of a new class of industrialists that joined older elite groups and state bureaucrats in opposing the development of an independent working-class movement. Control over the trade unions became a central feature of state economic and development policy, as government sought to cut and freeze wages, restrict the right to strike and increase productivity in the workplace. Many workers and union leaders resisted these policies by waging militant strikes and proposing popular alternatives to the labor bureaucracy.

As wartime economic growth produced a rampant inflation that significantly lowered working-class living standards, worker resistance against government labor policy intensified. Between 1939 and 1946, the manufacturing workers' real wage dropped fifty percent because prices for basic necessities increased by 300 percent.[1] Workers responded with a series of spontaneous strikes, most of which the government declared "illegal," and the CTM bureaucracy tried to prevent with "no-strike" pledges. The strike wave reached its peak in 1943 and 1944 and involved traditional militant unions as well as workers in smaller industries who suffered acutely from deteriorating living standards. The trade union became the contested terrain of the labor bureaucracy and elements of the rank and file in a fight over wages, working conditions, union autonomy and the right to strike.

To formalize control over the unions and their leaders, the government and its allies in the CTM received support from organized labor in the United States. This development accelerated after World War II when the American government tried to extend its economic interests in Latin America and while the Mexican government reached out to make accommodations with U.S. financial interests. As the United States emerged from the Second World War as the world's dominant economic power, it initiated a global campaign to undermine militant, leftist-leaning unions. Mexican government leaders demonstrated their support for this policy by maneuvering the ouster of the Marxist Vicente Lombardo Toledano from the CTM and installing conservative leaders. At the same time, U.S. and Mexican government officials, along with their trade-union allies, created the Organización Regional Intra-Americana de Trabajadores (ORIT) to compete against Lombardo's Confederación Trabajadores de América Latina (CTAL) and to steer the Mexican and Latin American labor movement in a more conservative direction.

Despite the maneuvering, Mexican workers continued to strike and call for workers' self-management in state-run industries and demand the further "Mexicanization" of the economy. The state reacted by passing new labor laws that restricted the right to strike and expanded the power of the conciliation and arbitration boards. The government also established "the law of social dissolution," which stipulated long jail sentences for anyone attempting to "dissolve" society through strikes in industries of "great social importance."

Rather than questioning the new laws and the obvious limitations they placed on the workers' right to strike, CTM leaders became willing policemen and got perquisites in exchange for ensuring labor discipline. After years of battling dissident unionists, especially in the large industrial unions where worker militancy had been strident, the state imposed charro leadership, which cooperated with government officials in the enforcement of shop-floor discipline and no-strike clauses. As the Mexican state took a sharp right turn and increasingly accommodated both foreign and domestic capital, charro leadership exercised a key role in lining up organized labor in support of national development policy.

WORKERS RESIST STATE DEVELOPMENT POLICY

Rank-and-file resistance to the government and their trade union allies began in 1940, when petroleum, railroad workers and state employees joined forces in opposing an attempt to destroy the railroad unions' seniority system.[2] When the three unions threatened a strike, the government sent Lombardo to address a meeting of angry workers. He hoped to convince them not to strike and accept the proposed dissolution of the seniority system. Instead, workers hissed and heckled Lombardo as he attempted to speak. In the face of such fierce opposition, the government backed down.[3]

A few days later, Local #15 of the railway union passed a motion demanding the resignation of Lombardo and considering the union's possible withdrawal from the CTM. Rank-and-file railroaders pointed to the example of Rafael Saavedra and the 280 unions of 15,000 workers in the Federal District that he recently led out of the CTM. The unions withdrew from the CTM because they opposed government affiliation and wanted union democracy and autonomy.[4]

Although the railroad union temporarily remained in the CTM, militant leadership and members of other unions increasingly raised the issues of union autonomy and workers' self-management. In October 1940 at Monterrey, employees at the British-owned electric power and light company went on strike and demanded that the government expropriate the industry. During the conflict, an anarchist organization, the Lucretia Toriz Feminine League joined the strikers in calling for the expropriation of the "English-Imperialist" water and sewer systems and placing them under workers' self-management.[5] Miners at American-owned ASARCO facilities paralyzed facilities in Rosita and Piedras Negras, Coahuila, and demanded expropriation and control of the enterprise. The government reacted to both strikes by negotiating wage increases; but it refused to consider the demands for worker control.[6]

Strikes and labor discontent were increasingly troublesome for the Mexican economy, which had grown at unprecedented levels during the Second World War. The state's plan for development entailed cooperation from workers in the name of the "national interest." As a solution, labor bureaucrats supported new legislation that strengthened the power of the conciliation and arbitration boards. The government's actions coincided with the February 1941 expiration of Lombardo's three-year term as general secretary of the CTM. Despite being replaced by the moderate Fidel Velázquez, Lombardo remained a CTM member and exercised considerable influence within the organization and still directed his personally created CTAL. He continued to work with the government and industrialists to enforce the new work discipline, even as the rank and file strengthened its resolve to fight.

On September 23, 1941, 1,000 members of the war materials workers' union marched to the president's house and demanded the dismissal of General Luis Camberos, head of the war production board. The demonstrators protested Camberos' conduct in handling disputes since taking over the board. They claimed that Camberos had violated their right to strike and that the arbitration and conciliation boards had sided with the employers in every dispute. When the workers approached the president's house shouting for action, the military ordered the crowd to disperse. After the demonstration leaders agreed to disband, soldiers fired at the backs of the marchers, killing nineteen and wounding thirty. Although the CTM rank and file protested, the organization's top leaders failed to influence the government to bring the killers to justice.[7]

Although the bloody incident and the increasing partiality of the arbitration and conciliation boards toward employers had reduced the number of "official" strikes between 1941 and 1943, "illegal" strikes continued, and conflict within the CTM reached violent levels. While Lombardo and the official leadership called for a bi-national worker-industrialist alliance against the "fascistic imperialism" of Germany and Japan and condemned "illegal" strikes, militant rank and filers defended their right to strike and advocated union autonomy. On April 24, 1941, Lombardo loyalists shot several "autonomists" after debate on the right-to-strike issue had taken place at a Mexico City union meeting.[8]

In early 1942 the government sent a contingent of federal troops to Dinamita, Durango. There 1,000 workers "illegally" struck the dynamite division of the American-owned Dupont Chemical company and demanded expropriation and workers' self-management of the enterprise. The government ignored the demands, sent the army in to protect company property and backed management's decision to fire strikers who refused to return to their jobs.[9] Infuriated with the CTM's decision to support the government's position in the strike, Alfredo Navarette, a leader of textile, building trades, hotel and restaurant unions in the Federal District, founded the Confederación Proletario Nacional (CPN). Initiated in March 1942, Navarette called the CPN an alternative to the "dictatorial" methods of Lombardo, Fidel Velázquez and Jesús Yuren.[10]

Two months later CTM leaders reacted by requesting that union members refrain from striking for the duration of the war and rely on the conciliation and arbitration boards to settle disputes. In June, Lombardo convinced CROM and CGT leaders to join the CTM in signing a workers' solidarity pact, which included a no-strike pledge for the duration of the war and collaboration with the government's plan for national economic development. Solidarity pact signatories also joined the Ministry of Labor's Workers' Advisory Council, which sought to centralize all existing labor organizations and place them under government tutelage. The council attempted to prevent strikes and promote solidarity between labor, industry and government.

Despite a Supreme Court decision that declared work stoppages "violations of the work discipline," strikes continued, largely due to rising inflation. Between 1941 and 1943 prices in the Federal District rose sixty percent while wages increased only twenty percent.[11] Especially hard hit were workers in the Federal District belonging to the newly formed CPN. While the CPN's leaders had fallen in line and supported the solidarity pact, over sixty percent of all strikes occurring in July 1942 involved CPN rank-and-file workers.[12] The government successfully quelled some labor unrest with modest wage increases, but inflation continued to eat away at working-class living standards. Wages for railroad workers went up only forty-eight percent; miners, thirty; and oil workers, only twenty percent.[13] For the remainder of the decade, workers in these industries struck for higher wages, and government expropriation of foreign-owned enterprises and demanded self-management.

Rank-and-file unrest was widespread in the Mexican mining industry, despite the implementation of no-strike pledges and sporadic wage increases. The outbreak of the Second World War led to the Suárez-Tellez Agreement, which committed the United States to buy at least $1 million worth of Mexican metals at high fixed prices.[14] The agreement also included provisions that obliged the U.S. government to aid Mexico in the purchase of vitally necessary machinery, manufactured goods and raw materials. In return, Mexican officials and labor leaders promised the United States to keep workers' demands "reasonable," based upon the understanding that labor troubles would be controlled to assure precious metal deliveries.[15]

At the same time, the mining companies and the American government wanted Mexican miners to work in the United States to fill labor shortages in the industry. The Mexican government refused, perhaps because it feared a repeat of the revolutionary period, when Mexican miners returning from the United States struck for higher wages and disrupted production.[16] Nonetheless, as production increased and inflation soared, unrest continued. In April 1943 miners carried out an "illegal" strike against the Phelps-Dodge operations at the Moctezuma Copper Company in Nacazori, Sonora. They demanded wage increases, government expropriation of the properties and the placement of operations under workers' self-management. Union leaders

had not sanctioned the strike, and their collaboration with government officials finally forced miners to drop their more militant demands in exchange
for wage increases. While the high prices paid for minerals created foreign
exchange and allowed for wage increases, serving the "national interest"
legitimized the concessions made by the miners on other issues.[17]

Despite efforts by government officials and their trade-union allies to
curb the tide of working-class nationalism, unrest continued. In June 1944 at
ASARCO complexes in Santa Barbara and Avalos, Chihuahua, 80,000 miners
and smelter workers walked off the job. They demanded forty percent
wage increases along with the nationalization of the properties and self-
management of the operations. Like Nacazori the previous year, the strikers
won most wage demands and recouped eighty percent of their wages lost
during the strike in exchange for dropping the demands of nationalization
and self-management.[18] In Monterrey, workers at Pepsi-Cola (Tonelera
Nacional, S.A.) went on strike to protest the company's proposed move away
from the area because of alleged "labor problems."[19] After the conciliation
and arbitration board declared the walkout "illegal," workers at the foreign-
owned telephone company, public utilities and transit system joined the
Tonelera workers in protest.[20] As the number of strikers walking picket lines
in the Monterrey area grew, the government and CTM leaders offered to
negotiate a settlement.[21]

After strikers refused arbitration, Monterrey business and commercial
groups remarked that President Manuel Avila Camacho "was weak" and
unable to "take a stand" against "subversive" elements bent on destroying
order.[22] The Monterrey business establishment called on the president to use
"emergency methods" to stop what had turned into a general strike. As transportation ground to a halt, telephones fell silent and factories dismissed
workers due to a lack of parts, the community's business leaders—long-time,
vehement opponents of organized labor—urged the president to "put people
in their places," and prevent the "beginning of social decline."[23] Finally, the
government intervened and arbitrated the dispute by partially satisfying
some of the workers' demands. Although concessions quelled some labor
unrest, strikes continued throughout the rest of 1944, prompting the government and the CTM leadership to search for a solution.

Meeting with a group of Mexican industrialists in June 1944, Lombardo
proposed binding arbitration of all labor disputes to solve the growing "strike
problem." Lombardo's position immediately received criticism from the rank
and file and local union leaders who charged that he "was killing the right
to strike."[24] Lombardo countered by invoking "class unity" for national

development, claiming that "dissident elements" were trying to destroy "national unity." In almost xenophobic fashion, he added that dissent only served the interests of foreign governments that attempted to disrupt Mexico's plan for national development.[25] As a Marxist, Lombardo adhered to the international communist line of the era, which when applied to Mexico, viewed the industrial and financial elite as progressive forces in an underdeveloped nation dominated by imperialism. Further, Lombardo believed that profits for Mexican industrialists and financiers also meant gains for workers.[26]

THE CTM ENCOUNTERS ORGANIZED RESISTANCE

The CTM's adherence to the idea of a nationalistic alliance between industrialists, financiers and workers produced growing dissension and the formation of organized opposition groups within its ranks. At the CTM's January 1945 annual convention, Iván José Rivera Rojas organized the Bloque Revindicador de la CTM—Revindication Bloc of the CTM, which denounced the CTM's leadership as "government stooges" and "traitors to the working class."[27] In February 1945, the State Federation of Workers in Jalisco left the CTM. Representing 15,000 workers in textile factories, sugar mills, leather tanneries and shoe factories, the federation's leaders attacked the no-strike pledge as an example of the CTM's "dictatorial methods that attempted to destroy union autonomy and place organized labor under government control."[28] In March, Mario Moreno (Cantinflas) and the new motion picture union declined to join the CTM for the same reasons.[29]

Despite desertion and widespread dissatisfaction with its policies, CTM leaders sought closer cooperation with the state and continued the no-strike pledge. Lombardo, the CTAL and the CTM embraced the elite nationalism espoused by the industrial and financial sectors when they agreed to renew the wartime "patriotic alliance for the defense of the nation's independence."[30] Like Morones and the CROM during the 1920s, Lombardo's CTAL and the CTM leadership stressed the "necessity for a complete and lasting agreement between labor, capital, and management," and supported president of the National Chamber of Commerce (CONCAMIN) José R. Colin's statement that "help from foreign capital to aid private enterprise was in the best interests of the nation."[31] In September 1945, the CTM and CONCAMIN formed a "Committee to Prevent Strikes," to ensure labor peace and carry out the government-industry plan for national development.[32]

The CTM's willingness to compromise working-class nationalism and the right to strike at the end of the war did not originate from pressures emanating from the business community or the government. In 1942 the CTM had proposed a pact between industrialists and organized labor in the defense of national interest. To enforce labor discipline and compliance with the pact, the CTM organized "defense committees" in factories to prevent acts of sabotage and insure greater efficiency and productivity from industrial workers. Although employers' organizations had declined to sign a formal labor-industry pact in 1942, the tacit agreement built the foundations for future cooperation between CONCAMIN and the CTM.[33] Lombardo reflected on the labor-capital alliance and the mission of state development policy when he addressed a banquet of business and union leaders. He stated that "The new type of industrialists think like the workers, not just of themselves, but of the entire Mexican fatherland." Unions, he explained, had been transformed from "the old leagues of resistance against capital" to organizations that would collaborate with the new industrialists.[34]

The 1945 Labor-Industry Pact was an attempt to subordinate rank-and-file workers to the elite nationalism propagated by nascent industrialists, government leaders and trade-union officials. Instead of compromising on issues such as job conditions, higher wages and the right to strike, rank-and-file workers continued to advocate the nationalization of foreign-owned industries and defended their autonomy in conflicts with the government that occurred in state-run enterprises. Rank-and-file workers belonging to unions rooted in nationalistic working-class ideology led the fight against the foreign companies and the government. Workers at the Canadian-owned Mexican Street Car company and Swedish-owned Ericcson Telephone company went on strike and demanded the nationalization of the companies and their placement under workers' control.[35] The government seized the political initiative and expropriated the enterprises. At the same time, however, state officials denied workers wage increases and a government loan to begin management of the nationalized enterprises. Instead of exercising self-management, workers became state employees and the government constructed a professional management system to run the new companies. The CTM's support of the government's actions generated worker-employer conflict at other state-run enterprises.[36]

In February 1944 oil workers had initiated a series of sit-down strikes to protest innumerable contract violations by PEMEX. The half-day strikes in the refineries, warehouses and tank farms soon spread to repair shops and offices.[37] When the government intervened a year later, the union and the company still had not reached a settlement. The result was renewed worker protest of the company's non-compliance with collective labor contracts. The traditionally militant unions at Tampico and Poza Rica led the way and carried out a series of daily sit-down strikes protesting low wages and reductions in personnel. Like the conflict with the street car and telephone workers, the CTM supported the government and went even further by denouncing the workers' actions as unpatriotic. The CTM's position reinforced the growing sentiment within some petroleum union locals that real autonomy meant breaking away from leaders whom they called "government-controlled stooges."[38]

Railroad workers also clashed with the CTM over its participation in government efforts to place all existing transportation federations and unions into a single organization. Through centralization, the government hoped to enforce labor discipline more effectively.[39] Work stoppages opposing the government-CTM scheme occurred in Veracruz and the Isthmus of Tehuantepec in what became known as the "July Revolt." When CTM leaders offered to arbitrate to solve the growing strike wave, workers in all railroad unions and federations refused and defended their right to strike.[40] The conflict resulted in a rank-and-file movement to reform the CTM. Late in 1945 factions within the railroad and petroleum workers' unions organized groups called *depuradas* to purify the CTM and to advocate union democracy and autonomy.[41]

As the depuradas intensified their activities, the CTM increasingly came under attack for not observing democratic procedures and for "selling out its membership." Even the Ministry of Labor admitted that "unions were constantly breaking away from the CTM and forming other confederations."[42] In the capital rumors persisted that the railroad workers planned to join the electricians' union in the creation of a federation that would consist of unions working with electricity, including those in manufacturing, communications and streetcar transportation.[43]

In outlying industrial areas the CTM also encountered growing opposition. In January 1946 at Monterrey, CTM dissidents calling themselves *Pro-Congreso* (purified) led walkouts of bus drivers and mechanics at the Lozcano family-owned Círculo Azul. The Pro-Congreso forces joined other workers already on strike at the Cristalería factory, an enterprise of the Cuauhtémoc Brewery Group. The strikers demanded substantial wage increases; CTM General Secretary Fidel Velázquez attempted to mediate the two conflicts. While Velázquez urged the workers to return to their jobs during the negotiations, the strike spread to hotels, restaurants, bars and other businesses.[44]

As the conflict continued, the state governor and the Monterrey press went on the offensive against the strikers. The local papers called the

Pro-Congreso factions "communistic" and urged "loyal Mexican" workers to stop the strike and return to their jobs. Meanwhile, Fidel Velázquez refused to defend the Pro-Congreso forces against such attacks. When the CTM abandoned the strikers, Pro-Congreso leaders faced wholesale firings and arrests. Pro-Congreso newspapers compared Velázquez to an emerging Luis Morones of the CROM and described him as a "leader willing to 'sell out' the rank and file for personal gain."[45]

THE AMERICANS AND THE FALL OF LOMBARDO TOLEDANO

Rising dissension within the CTM's ranks coincided with renewed American interest in the working-class movement throughout Latin America, especially Mexico. The advent of the Cold War and Mexico's increasing economic ties with the United States prompted American government and labor officials to seek greater control over the direction of the Mexican labor movement. The massive expansion of the U.S. economy during World War II reinforced the faith held by American trade unionists in the capitalist system. Friction that had characterized the AFL-CIO relationship of the 1930s withered at the end of World War II as both federations supported U.S. economic expansion abroad and the establishment of anti-communist unionism.[46] At the war's end, union leaders rallied around the idea that continued U.S. economic prosperity was related directly to the expansion of trade abroad.

CIO official Philip Murray expressed this belief when he praised the July 1944 Bretton Woods agreement (which, among other things, established the rules for world trade, created the World Bank and pegged the U.S. Dollar to the gold standard). Declaring that it represented the "best guarantee of an expanded world trade that will afford protection to American businessmen," Murray explained that this meant markets for "American farmers and jobs for American workers."[47] In 1945 Jacob S. Potofsky, chairman of the CIO Latin American Affairs Committee, told the Ways and Means Committee of the U.S. House of Representatives: "As we look at the U.S. economy one thing is clear; our country is set up to produce, in several lines, more goods than we ever have consumed here or are likely to."[48] Although U.S. industrial/labor relations had declined in 1945 and 1946 with the outbreak of numerous strikes, World War II institutionalized cooperation between organized labor and American industrialists, and it carried over into the post-war period and Cold War years, especially in foreign policy.[49]

The nature of U.S. investment in Latin America in the immediate post-war years reinforced the collaboration. Because less than twenty percent went to the development of manufacturers, the investment strategy corresponded with the American trade-union movement's long-term policy toward U.S. business expansion in the region. As long as workers south of the border did not take manufacturing jobs from American workers, unions supported government and corporate policy objectives in the Western Hemisphere. In

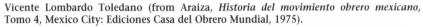

Vicente Lombardo Toledano (from Araiza, *Historia del movimiento obrero mexicano*, Tomo 4, Mexico City: Ediciones Casa del Obrero Mundial, 1975).

1947 Stanley Ruttenberg, director of research and education for the CIO, confirmed this line of thinking, stating that "over 3 million jobs in America were dependent on foreign trade." He added that "maintaining foreign markets for our goods and importing vital materials necessary for our industrial production will play an essential part in keeping our industrial potential."[50]

For the U.S. government and its trade-union allies, an important component of this policy was opposition to economic nationalism in all of its forms, because they believed it invited communist penetration.[51] In Mexico the policy translated into attacks against the Lombardo-led CTAL. The CTAL and Lombardo supported protectionist tariffs and state-directed development of basic industries. Lombardo's strident economic nationalism, combined with his openly declared Marxism, made him a special target of U.S. government officials and union leaders. Too many times Lombardo had spoken of the "dangers of American capital," which he summarized in his resignation speech before the 1941 CTM Congress. He stated: "If we are to continue to be squeezed by the great Yankee monopolies as one squeezes an orange ... the price of the peso will be fixed by the producers, merchants, and bankers of the United States."[52]

During the war U.S. diplomats, through Sidney Hillman, then vice-president of the CIO and for a time member of the War Production Board (WPB), attempted to block links that Lombardo was trying to forge with U.S. labor.[53] As early as 1943 U.S. diplomats and trade union leaders sought to neutralize Lombardo and undercut the CTAL's influence in Latin America. Through the Office of Inter-American Affairs (OIAA) with Nelson Rockefeller as its coordinator, the U.S government initiated a policy of financing the extension of pro-U.S. unions in Latin America. The goal was to cultivate elements within the Latin American labor movement that were sympathetic to U.S. interests in the region. This policy became even more urgent when Lombardo and the CTAL led the Mexican opposition to the U.S. Clayton Plan, unveiled at the February 1945 Chapultepec Conference in Mexico City. The plan promoted lower tariffs for American products and the free and uninhibited investment by foreign capital in the region. Lombardo and the CTAL condemned the plan as a conspiracy to promote uncontrolled investment by American capitalists, which they argued would result in the continued "backwardness" of Mexico and the rest of Latin America.[54]

For Mexican officials, Lombardo's openly declared Marxism was more troublesome. As early as 1940 supporters of Manuel Avila Camacho had considered ousting Lombardo, by force if necessary, and replacing him with the more conservative Fidel Velázquez.[55] But because he supported the government's industrialization program, the Avila Camacho administration and the business community used his leadership skills to promote elite nationalism and enforce wage freezes, no-strike pledges and increased management control at the shop-floor level. Disciplining rank-and-file workers and subordinating them to the state's interests—one of accelerated industrial development—depended upon cooperation from trade-union leadership. Lombardo played an instrumental role in helping government and industry put the enforcement machinery in place and facilitate the emergence of a new class of trade-union bureaucrats, identical to the CROM's of the 1920s. The bureaucratization of the trade-union movement enabled the government to rely upon leaders like Fidel Velázquez increasingly rather than on ideologues such as Lombardo to discipline the rank and file. American government and union leaders joined Miguel Alemán's administration to weaken Lombardo and oust him from the CTM.

As in the past, the American trade-union leadership and government officials relied on Robert Haberman, the one-time collaborator with Luis Morones. Haberman openly criticized Lombardo, the Labor-Industry Pact and claimed that its aims were "protectionist" and against the true "national interests" of Mexico. Lombardo responded to the charges through the CTM, which officially denounced Haberman as an "agent of U.S. Imperialism," and demanded that the Mexican government deport him to the United States.[56] The CTM's harsh indictment of Haberman stemmed from his past involvement in Mexican labor affairs. Dating back to the founding of the CROM, Haberman had worked closely with the Obregón and American governments in breaking anarchosyndicalist-led strikes and deporting foreign-born radical labor leaders. In 1938 Haberman cooperated with the AFL and the CROM in an attempt to rescind the Mexican government's oil expropriation decree. Haberman's long history of collaboration with corrupt labor leaders and his opposition to Mexican nationalism weakened his credibility among the ranks of organized labor. Unlike the 1920s, when Haberman's effectiveness earned him favor with certain labor leaders and government officials, his maneuvering during the 1940s proved futile.

Although Lombardo successfully discredited Haberman and his charges, he faced more serious challenges from within the ranks of the CTM. CTM depuradas attacked him and other leaders as "corrupt," "racketeering" and betraying the working class by continuing the no-strike pledge.[57] Unions also protested his support of the election of Velázquez and Fernando Amilpa to top posts in the CTM. They cited his open collaboration with state industrial policy as the reason for their opposition to the two candidates.[58]

On July 11, 1946, in the midst of a heated election campaign, the powerful and influential petroleum workers' union left the CTM. In a manifesto, the union declared that the CTM's backing of PEMEX management policy had resulted in layoffs and a faster work pace and led to the decision to break away.[59]

As observers watched the CTM's troubles mount, American labor leaders escalated their attacks on Lombardo. The AFL's George Meany criticized the CTAL's structure and Lombardo's methods as "dictatorial" and "undemocratic." He also called for the breakup of the CTAL and the creation of a new hemispheric federation.[60] In the campaign against Lombardo and the CTAL, Mexican government officials and union leaders cooperated with Serafino Romauldi, the AFL's chosen inter-American representative. In 1946 Romauldi made two trips to Mexico, making contacts with pro-U.S. unionists and state functionaries to establish a new hemispheric labor federation to rival the CTAL. Because Lombardo headed the CTAL and it was affiliated with the Soviet-created World Federation of Trade Unions (WFTU), both Romauldi and the U.S. State Department viewed it as a communist-directed organization. George Meany clearly identified Romauldi's mission when he said: "it was up to the AFL to see that the workers of Latin America understand our philosophy," adding that "it is our desire to create a solid front among working people of the hemisphere and to see to it these people do not listen to the mouthings of those who receive their orders from Moscow."[61]

Lombardo responded to the attacks by denouncing the American AFL as an organization that attempted to buy the support of Mexican labor leaders.[62] He also charged that officials from rival Mexican federations, such as the CROM, were fighting over funds that had been provided for the founding of a hemispheric organization to challenge the CTAL.[63] While attacking the Americans, Lombardo represented himself as a defender of Mexican nationalism by accusing the AFL of being an instrument of "Yankee Imperialism" that attempted to "rollback" the gains made by the Mexican revolution.[64]

Despite his defense of Mexican nationalism and the Revolution, Lombardo's problems continued with the rank and file and from leaders of leftist political organizations. Dionosio Encina, general secretary of the Mexican Communist party, accused him of repudiating the tactic of class struggle in the name of espousing national unity. Encina denounced the labor-industry pact and said that the "class struggle is not something to be chosen or rejected at will but an historic fact which exists independently of the plans and desires of men."[65] He added that "the workers' movement in

Mexico had lost its independence as a result of a 'false interpretation' of its historic responsibility as a class by promoting national unity with the bourgeoisie."[66] When asked about the validity of Encina's remarks, Lombardo retorted that "the Communist Party was not the inherent and obligated director of the working-class movement."[67]

Although Lombardo dismissed Encina's comments as "meaningless," because they came from the leader of an organization that had no real leverage within the CTM, his belief in the progressive character of the Mexican bourgeoisie led to continued problems with the CTM's rank and file. CTM depuradas criticized Lombardo's "selling-out" the right to strike and his backing of Fidel Velázquez and Fernando Amilpa in the upcoming elections for the organization's national committee. He replied that "national unity should be defended at all costs," and that the workers should back Amilpa and Velázquez to ensure it. The depuradas alleged that Lombardo's calls for unity were just more pleas and demagogic poses for the purpose of fortifying the power of dishonest leaders headed by Velázquez. Instead, the depuradas backed Velázquez's opponent, Luis Gómez Z., the leftist leader of the powerful railroad workers' union.[68]

Similar attacks against Lombardo occurred at the CPN's January 1947 "Seventh Ordinary Council," when speakers lashed out at Lombardo, Velázquez, Amilpa, Valentín Campa and Gómez Z., calling them "traitors" to the working-class and blaming them for the current crisis in the labor movement. The meeting also produced calls for a labor movement independent of the state and denunciations of federal intervention in labor-management conflicts.[69] Another source of opposition to the official slate (Amilpa and Velázquez) came from members of the Monterrey CTM Pro-Congreso. They expressed their dissatisfaction with Velázquez's behavior during the Cristalería strike. During the 1946 strike, the government expropriated the brewing enterprise, but soon afterward rescinded ownership and awarded CTM bureaucrats a contract favorable to the company's terms. The Pro-Congreso backed the Gómez Z. slate.[70]

Finally, in late 1947, the opposition to Lombardo and the dissension among the rank and file crystallized with the founding of a rival labor federation, the Confederación Unica de Trabajadores (CUT). The CUT, led by defeated insurgent CTM general secretary candidate Gómez Z., and electrical workers' union president Adolfo Escalante, pledged abstention from electoral politics and repudiated governmental tutelage. The CUT accused the CTM of corruption and declared in its manifesto that, "it is necessary for the working class and its labor organizations to refuse subsidies or gifts from either the government or the capitalist class."[71] The 2,700 delegates, which represented about 350,000 workers, also condemned the "imperialist" actions of the AFL and promised to remain affiliated with the CTAL.[72]

The CPN, led by long-time labor activist Enrique Rangel, also supported the CTAL against AFL attacks. The CPN claimed a membership of 115,000

Fernando Amilpa (from Araiza, *Historia del movimiento obrero mexicano*, Tomo 4, Mexico City: Ediciones Casa del Obrero Mundial, 1975).

with strength in Puebla, the Federal District, Veracruz, Sonora, the State of Mexico and Nuevo León. Rangel, a former anarchosyndicalist, detested communism and called it an authoritarian system. The CPN and Rangel advocated a democratic form of socialism instead, while denouncing Lombardo as a tool of the Soviet Union, and calling the AFL an instrument of "Yankee Imperialism."[73]

Although the CPN's numbers were exaggerated, Rangel's position on Lombardo, the CTM and the AFL probably represented the sentiments of rank-and-file Mexican union members and elements within the government. The CTM leadership was reluctant, however, to harmonize relations with the AFL and move against Lombardo. President Miguel Alemán, frustrated with the CTM's leadership, tried to work through the CTM depuradas. During an August 1947 trip to the United States, Alemán encouraged CTM dissidents who accompanied him on the visit to meet with AFL President William Green and discuss the possibility of creating a hemispheric alternative to the Lombardo-controlled CTAL.[74] Because rank-and-file opposition had been building against Lombardo and defections from the CTM occurred almost daily, the government's task of removing Lombardo became more urgent. The opposition had grown stronger in recent weeks since Lombardo had declared his intentions to form a "Popular Party" to rival the new, government-controlled Partido Revolucionario Institucional (PRI). Alemán's flirtations with the CTM dissidents pressured the resignation of Fidel Velázquez as secretary of the CTAL. It coincided with the AFL's more active role in other Latin American countries, such as Chile, Cuba and Costa Rica, where it participated in creating conservative labor federations to rival leftist labor unions.[75]

On January 5, 1948, the Thirty-third National Council of the CTM met and ratified the ouster of Lombardo. Fernando Amilpa chaired the sessions. He justified Lombardo's removal by blaming him for the recent desertions from and rebellions in the CTM. Amilpa also accused Lombardo of attempting to steer the Mexican labor movement in the direction of Stalin and the Soviet Union. He declared "Communist maneuvering" a failure and urged the passage of resolutions that forbade CTM members from belonging to Lombardo's Popular Party. Members were also forbidden to participate in "incidental" committees protesting against such things as the high cost of living in Mexico and the American Clayton Plan.

Amilpa called organized actions against the Clayton Plan as "nothing more than demonstrations led by demagogues and divisionists."[76] Delegates at the meeting also resolved to suspend relations with the CTAL and the WFTU as long as Lombardo served as president and vice-president of those organizations.[77] Three years later, Velázquez and the CTM aided Serafino Romauldi and the AFL in creating ORIT to undercut the CTAL's influence in Mexico and the rest of Latin America.

INTRANSIGENT MILITANTS
AND THE EMERGENCE OF THE CHARRO SOLUTION

Days before Lombardo's expulsion, rank-and-file workers and union leaders in the railroad, mining and petroleum workers' unions met to discuss strategy against the CTM leadership and their American allies. The respective leaders Daniel García, José López Malo and Jesús Chinas signed a pact of friendship and mutual aid to combat the stratagems and attacks of "Yankee Imperialism." They declared that "now more than ever, it was intervening in the domestic affairs of Latin America countries." The leaders described the pact as a common defense of "class interests," and a new beginning to refute the CTM's leadership of Amilpa and Velázquez.[78] The secretary general of the petroleum workers' union, Eulalio Gutiérrez, pledged to fight the foreign monopolies and the "Yankee Imperialists" by uniting with the rest of the world's workers. He added that the large industrial unions would continue to support the CTAL and the WFTU and vehemently oppose the AFL and its efforts to construct a "pro-imperialist" regional federation.[79]

The alliance of the major industrial unions against the CTM posed a significant challenge to the government and its allies. The state and its trade-union supporters reacted to the potential threat with a two-pronged policy. First it sought to curtail the right to strike; second it initiated an offensive to impose government-approved leaders as union heads. Although rank and filers and some union officials prevented the government from limiting the workers' right to strike, they failed to stop the imposition of government-sanctioned leaders.

In February 1948, the Mexican Supreme Court postulated what later became known as the "Corona Thesis," which stated that Mexican workers had no right to strike during the length of the work contract. The initiative failed because all major labor federations, save the CTM, staged demonstrations and rallies in front of the Supreme Court building. Detachments of workers from the CUT, mine, rail, electricians and petroleum workers' unions swelled the number of demonstrators to over 100,000. Speaking in front of the huge throng, Gutiérrez compared the "Corona Thesis" to the recently passed Taft-Hartley Act in the United States, which among other things restricted the right of workers in some industries to strike. Because of the workers' impressive show of unity, the government backed down and the thesis never became law.[80]

The unity exhibited by the industrial unions in opposition to the Corona Thesis reinforced the government's determination to impose a top-down leadership upon a rank and file that continued to resist wage freezes and to defend the right to strike. The immediate post-war period brought on economic readjustment that caused inflation and unemployment. The government attempted to control the rampant inflation with wage freezes, a strategy that major industrial unions opposed. The state's problems compounded when the miners, petroleum and railroad workers discussed the idea of creating an alternative labor federation. The absence of these powerful unions from the CTM's ranks meant that the government's goal— a compliant labor force—faced a formidable task without the participation of the trade-union leadership of the industrial unions.

Within the context of the Cold War, the removal of Communists and leftists from key union posts provided a convenient vehicle to subordinate "independent" union leaders and rank-and-file members simultaneously. The successful establishment of a new labor bureaucracy that complied with the state's economic development policy meant that union bosses of all political leaning who opposed the government's intrusion into labor's affairs were labeled "communist," "corrupt" or "unpatriotic."

The purge of autonomy-minded labor leaders began with the railroad workers' union (STFRM). The organization had exercised a leadership role in the newly created Confederación Unica, which opposed the CTM-promoted worker-industrialist alliance. Under the leadership of Luis Gómez Z. and Valentín Campa, the railroad workers' union had withdrawn from the CTM in early 1947. The organization and its leaders spearheaded the fight against the deteriorating living and working conditions facing Mexican workers. Because Campa and Gómez Z. were Communists and many activists in the railroad workers' union were leftists, both the union and the leadership were vulnerable to attacks from government officials and conservative leaders of rival unions. After railroad workers led petroleum workers and teachers in a demonstration against rising prices and a peso devaluation in August 1948, the government maneuvered to depose the Communist leaders.

To remove Gómez Z. and Valentín Campa, bureaucrats used the services of Jesús Díaz de León, the newly elected general secretary of the railroad workers' union and a friend of Carlos Serrano, President Miguel Alemán's closest advisor. After taking office, Díaz de León, also known as *El Charro* because of his passion for dressing in the traditional charro style with silver-buckled trousers and a wide-brimmed sombrero, accused Gómez Z. of embezzling several hundred thousand pesos. Before the union executive board could conduct an independent investigation, Díaz de León carried the matter to the district attorney of the Federal District to decide the issue. Upon learning of Díaz de León's actions, the union executive board claimed that politicians had collaborated and conspired with him to "involve the state in the internal life of the union." They also called the government's actions "aggression against the Mexican working class."[81]

Fearing that rank and file and leaders from other unions would join the railroaders' battle to defend their autonomy, the government sent 100 policemen disguised as workers to assist Díaz de León in taking over union headquarters. As Díaz de León and the police successfully occupied headquarters, federal soldiers seized all other railroad locals in Mexico City. The government then accused Valentín Campa of sabotage and corroborated its charges by torturing two workers into saying that Valentín Campa had ordered them to steal a locomotive from a shop and have it collide with another train in Guadalajara. One worker died during interrogation, while police extracted a public confession of sabotage from the other. The state prosecuted, convicted and sentenced Valentín Campa to eight years in prison.

Díaz de León greatly influenced production politics in state-run industries. With the autonomists removed from leadership, Díaz de León accepted a conciliation and arbitration decision to allow the state company to close shops, terminate routes, change job titles and work rules, lay off workers and leave vacancies unfilled. The defeat of the railroad activists paved the way for similar attacks against other industrial unions. The workers in the state-owned petroleum industry became the next target.

The move to impose the charro system on the petroleum workers actually began at their January 1947 convention. There Lombardo and Fidel Velázquez supported Antonio Hernández Abrego's candidacy for the post of general secretary. Hernández Abrego had opposed a recent wave of strikes by the union and supported the government's plan for post-war economic development. Unwilling to give up the right to strike and have their wages frozen, rank and file factions fought Hernández Abrego after he won the election with the help of Velázquez and Lombardo. The rank and filers also opposed Hernández Abrego's actions in bringing the union back into the CTM. Their resistance to the CTM's dictatorial methods and blind compliance with the government's plan for post-war readjustment resulted in the removal of Abrego Hernández from his post and the election of Eulalio

Gutiérrez. Immediately afterward, the rank and file voted to leave the CTM and join the Confederación Unica along with the miners and railroaders.

By March 1949, however, the successful imposition of charrismo in the railroad workers' union had weakened the Confederación Unica and made the petroleum workers' union open to government manipulation. Contract

Fidel Velázquez (from Araiza, *Historia del movimiento obrero mexicano*, Tomo 4, Mexico City: Ediciones Casa del Obrero Mundial, 1975).

negotiations stalled. When the government finally settled the dispute, several locals rejected the new contract. Internal conflict escalated and the government used the situation to impose new leadership. At the petroleum workers' Sixth Convention in December 1949, the government monitored proceedings closely. State officials and police packed the meeting and prevented rank and filers from entering. The absence of workers allowed a bogus election of Gustavo Roldán Vargas, a bureaucrat formerly accused of misusing union funds. Internal dissension, police agents and anti-democratic tactics carried out by the government had resulted in the imposition of charrismo in the nation's most important industry.

By the end of 1949 the charro movement had spread to other unions. Lombardo, now an outsider, tried to stop its momentum. He and several other unions had joined together in June 1949 to form the General Union of Workers and Peasants of Mexico (UGOCM). The group wanted to reverse the growing loss of autonomy and anti-democratic trends running rampant within the trade unions. After supporting government wage freezes, no-strike pledges by unions, and using the power of the CTM's bureaucracy to stifle rank-and-file participation in union policy, Lombardo had lost much credibility with the nation's workers. His attempts to reverse the tide of charrismo failed, and the government went on the offensive against the last remaining major industrial union, the miners.

The Miners' and Metallurgical Workers' Union (SNTMMSRM) had been particularly outspoken in its opposition to the government's salary freeze. Communists like Adan Nieto led rank-and-file resistance against government post-war readjustment policy. The government wanted to oust Nieto and other leftists and convince companies like ASARCO, which by 1950 controlled about sixty-five percent of all mining firms operating in Mexico, that it could maintain labor peace and guarantee low wages. In May 1950 the state moved to impose charro leadership on the miners' union at the Sixth Convention.

Secretary of Labor Manuel Ramírez Vázquez tried the same tactics that he had used against the railroad workers and petroleum workers—packing the meeting with illegitimate delegates and using police and thugs to exclude the duly elected representatives. With Ramírez Vázquez's delegates in the majority, the convention elected Jesús Carrasco general secretary. In so doing, the charro-controlled convention expelled *Lombardista* supporter and Fundidora Monterrey steel mill employee, Antonio García Moreno, General Workers' Confederation official Agustín Guzmán and Adan Nieto. Fearing the rank and file, Carrasco then moved to suspend the rights of the more militant locals: #14 in Nueva Rosita; its subsection in Cloete; #28 in Palau; and #97 and #123 of La Consolidada, S.A.[82]

Imposing charrismo on the entire membership of the miners' union presented problems, however. The union represented workers in different private and state-owned mining companies and metal-working plants throughout Mexico. Within locals there existed distinct occupational specializations, varying contracts, wage and benefit levels and working conditions. These conditions produced a tradition of strident intra-union rivalries and separatist movements. Accordingly, the excluded delegations protested Carrasco's actions and held a rival convention, which elected García Moreno as general secretary of the new National Miners' Union. The new union advocated autonomy, opposition to wage freezes, freedom of political affiliation for its members and solidarity pacts with other industrial unions. The government reacted to the insurgency by notifying employers that Carrasco's union had exclusive bargaining rights. It then used police to break up dissident meetings and cooperated with employers in firing workers who resisted Carrasco's authority.[83]

Despite widespread intimidation and repression, the rank and file continued to fight. The peak of the resistance began on June 12, 1950, during a strike against ASARCO's Nueva Rosita facility. ASARCO had been a symbol of foreign economic domination since the days of the Revolution, and workers had struck its mines and smelters on countless occasions. They frequently had called for ASARCO's expropriation. In northern Mexico ASARCO controlled powerful subsidiaries, such as Carboníferas Sabinas and Mexican Zinc. Managers and executives ran the company towns and bribed public officials, including the police and military.[84]

The rebel national miners' union, which represented 5,800 members of Local #14, demanded wage increases, better safety in the mine, more holidays, construction of roads between the mines and local towns, recognition of occupational diseases, housing and a farm to grow food for the miners' families. ASARCO refused to meet the demands and the committee of conciliation and arbitration declared the strike "illegal." Rather than face a confrontation, however, the government urged that ASARCO and the rebel union sign a contract. ASARCO agreed, primarily because the recent outbreak of the Korean War had boosted the price of various metals sixty percent. Although ASARCO wanted production to continue at Nueva Rosita, nonetheless, it was unwilling to abide by the new agreement. After three months of laboring under such conditions and exhausting all legal recourse through the committee of conciliation and arbitration, miners at Nueva Rosita went on strike.

Their defiance prompted the government to seize the initiative. Fearful that the Nueva Rosita strike might trigger other sympathy walkouts, the government confiscated the union's funds. It also shut off gas and electricity, closed the miners' local consumer cooperative and enlisted the support of the local chamber of commerce, which prohibited local merchants from selling food to the strikers. The government then declared martial law and ordered the army into the area to protect scabs running the operations. Within the repressive atmosphere, red-baiting of local union leaders escalated. The secretary of labor accused the strike leaders of being Communist agitators, and the local clergy attacked the strikers from the pulpit.[85]

The propaganda campaign took its toll. By the end of December, 3,600 of the 5,800 union workers had returned to their jobs despite breaking of an effigy piñata of Jesús Carrasco by miners' children on Christmas day. As they broke the piñata, the miners' children shouted: "Long live the right to strike! Death to Jesús Carrasco! Death to the scabs!"[86] When the desperate miners and their families marched to Mexico City in January 1951 to redress their grievances, police beat them and made arrests. With the government's complicity, ASARCO blacklisted hundreds of miners and helped to entrench Carrasco in power. The charrismo system had penetrated the three major and most militant industrial unions in Mexico.

CHAPTER FIVE

THE AMERICANS AND CHARRO ENTRENCHMENT

The state's efforts to enlist the support of organized labor for a national development policy of industrialization reached a climax during the early years of the Cold War. The Mexican development project converged with U.S. business and government desires for new markets and outlets for capital investment. Because the industrialization program required continued capital flow from the U.S. to reinvest profits and establish joint ventures with American companies, leaders from both countries realized that profits and returns depended on social stability, which to a great extent rested upon the ability of the Mexican trade-union bureaucracy to manage rank-and-file discontent.[1] As U.S. investment poured into Mexico, government leaders embraced and employed the anti-communist politics of the Cold War to consolidate charro rule and rid the trade unions of independent elements that opposed state development policy.

American union leaders cooperated with U.S. government officials in opposing economic nationalism in all of its forms, and in the process shaped the development and direction of the Mexican labor movement. Working through ORIT and the U.S. embassy, American trade-unionists provided cooperating Mexican labor leaders with logistical and financial support in their battle against forces within the movement that resisted charrismo.[2] The AFL's activities in Mexico were part of a larger effort by U.S. officials to bolster centrist, pro-capitalist unions at a global level.[3]

The American policy focused particularly on gathering information on the Mexican labor movement by inviting labor leaders to the U.S. Through these contacts, U.S. officials designed a strategy to provide crucial technical and financial assistance to Mexican labor leaders who increasingly embraced the anti-communism of the Cold War. U.S. State Department personnel relied heavily on AFL leader George Meany as a point man for selling their policy objectives to Mexican labor leaders. Meany and other U.S. trade union leaders played instrumental roles in escalating anti-communist rhetoric by alleging that Mexican unions had been infiltrated by communists and agents of Russia. Meany explained that the AFL goal in Latin America was "to create friendship and support for the U.S. in opposition to the Communists who sought the same support and friendship of Russia."[4]

The communists and agents Meany had referred to were elements within the Mexican labor movement that opposed placing economic growth before the rights of workers and improvement in their living standards. Although the Mexican economy grew and foreign investment increased, inflation continued to eat away at wages. New labor federations and factions within unions emerged to defend the workers' right to strike and earn a decent living. Although these new labor groups generally supported Mexico's drive to industrialize, they welcomed foreign investment only if it contributed to the authentic progress of Mexico. Upholding working-class nationalism and the gains made by workers during the Revolution, these labor groups were the first line of defense against state attempts to impose development policy through charro leadership. The struggle between autonomists and charro forces reached a climax during the teachers' rebellion and the railroad workers' strike of 1958-1959, both of which the government successfully suppressed.

THE AMERICANS AND THE CTM'S STRUGGLE FOR HEGEMONY

The government-CTM campaign to manage rank-and-file discontent and tie organized labor to state development policy evolved into a two-track strategy. First, the CTM attempted to "raid" smaller independent unions that opposed the state's industrialization program. The second strategy entailed the removal of "autonomists" and "independents" from key leadership positions at both local and national levels in the major industrial unions. Both of these strategies involved the direct participation of ORIT, U.S. trade unions and the American government. The internationalization of the conflict strengthened the hand of the state and their trade-union allies as they forced the opposition to engage in ideological debate rather then welding unity around the fight for higher wages and union autonomy. Armed with American dollars and anti-communist ideology, the CTM attempted to absorb and to transform smaller unions that resisted charrismo and state development policy.

In an effort to defend smaller unions against CTM encroachment, the Confederación Unica and remnants of older federations merged to form the Confederación Revolucionaria de Obreros y Campesinos (CROC).

Representing around 100,000 workers, the CROC suffered from personality conflicts and ideological differences.[5] Leaders subordinated the fight for wage increases to quarrelling over international affiliation. While railroad union leader Luis Gómez Z. promoted affiliation with the leftist CTAL and opposed Enrique Rangel, a former anarchosyndicalist, who argued for joining ORIT, other CROC leaders opted for an alliance with the Agrupación de Trabajadores Latino Americanos Sindicalistas (ATLAS). ATLAS attempted to unite all Latin American workers' organizations under the aegis of the Argentine government and its president, Juan Domingo Perón, who successfully had placed the labor movement in that country under tight state control.[6] While Rangel rejected affiliation with ATLAS because it was a government-controlled federation, Gómez Z. argued that joining ORIT was no different, because it would also lead to state control of the Mexican labor movement. At the same time, however, Gómez Z. defended Perón's economic nationalism by comparing it with Mexico's situation. He added that the U.S. opposed ATLAS and the CTAL because both represented a challenge to American economic hegemony in Latin America.[7]

While the CROC remained non-affiliated to an international labor federation, the ideological bickering weakened its resolve to combat the CTM's raiding of smaller unions. In early 1954 the CROC further discredited itself when the CTM threatened a general strike during the government's devaluation of the peso. Instead of joining the CTM in opposing the devaluation plan, the CROC attempted to curry government favor. The strategy backfired as the CTM signed a "pact of friendship" and "bloc of unity" with the CROM, the CGT and the charro union leadership of the miners, railroad, electrical and Federation of State Workers (FSTSE). While negotiating meager wage hikes for their members, the participants received official labor status from the ruling PRI in exchange for pledging to fight communist and subversive activities within their respective locals.[8] The financial assistance provided by ORIT facilitated the unity and played an even more important role in the CTM's campaign to absorb smaller unions.[9] The help provided by ORIT was particularly timely because the Mexican government had curtailed subsidies to the CTM and all "friendly" labor organizations. Fidel Velázquez personally requested assistance from the CIO's Latin American representative, Ernst Schwarz, who assured him that ORIT's resources would be available for CTM operations in the absence of Mexican government funding.[10]

The financial pledge was an integral part of ORIT's strategy in aiding the CTM in the removal of communists and independents from Mexico's industrial unions. A key component of ORIT funding involved the printing and distribution of literature and propaganda critical of radical unionism. Initially, the CTM-ORIT propaganda offensive targeted the traditionally militant miners' union, in which communists and independents held a number of high posts. The campaign began after a 1953 Mexico visit by Paul Reed, the United Mine Workers' international representative. With ORIT money and the support of Serafino Romualdi, the AFL's point man on Latin American labor relations, Reed hoped to convince the miners' national leadership to join the CTM and take measures to rid their local unions of communists. Although Reed's lack of spoken Spanish and knowledge about Mexico's labor movement contributed to his failure to convince the miners to join the CTM, he did manage to negotiate an agreement between the American government's United States Information Service (USIS) and the miners' union.[11]

Through the agreement, the USIS distributed films and forty projectors for use in miners' locals throughout Mexico. The content of the films represented the best in Cold War propaganda as they pointed out the dangers of communism, extolled the virtues of business unionism and emphasized labor-government cooperation. The USIS also printed and distributed free pamphlets to union locals throughout Mexico and donated fifty books to a new labor library in San Luis Potosí.[12] As miners' locals were flooded with USIS propaganda, Reed proposed the formation of a Latin American miners' federation that would function under ORIT authority. The long-range strategy to tie the miners' union to ORIT also included financing the campaigns of charro and anti-communist candidates in local union elections.[13]

The USIS and ORIT dollars elected a substantial number of anti-communist union officials, some of whom captured posts at the national level. As a means to consolidate charro power, ORIT funded a speaking tour of the elected officials to other union locals to convince the membership of the necessity of removing the communist threat from the miners' union. With the cooperation of the mining companies, the charros succeeded in obtaining the dismissal of about twenty-four active Communist Party members as well as independents and communist sympathizers.[14]

Although effective, the charro tactics failed to eliminate all independents and communists in many mining locals, especially in Coahuila and Chihuahua. In those states, leaders allied with Lombardo Toledano and the CTAL to counter ORIT dollars by offering the national union $1,500 in disaster relief for the families victimized by a disaster at the Dolores Mine in Michoacán during April 1954. They also invited the miners' union on a paid trip to the leftist-leaning World Federation of Trade Unions (WFTU)

Congress in Vienna, Austria. Attempting to counter growing anti-communist sentiment, Lombardo stressed that the invitation entailed no ideological commitment.[15]

With more funds at their disposal, ORIT overcame Lombardo's shrewd maneuvering. Through the use of the Mexico City newspaper, *Noticiario Obrero Interamericano*, ORIT denounced Lombardo and all anti-charro elements within the miners' union as communist agents in the service of the Soviet Union. Complementing the propaganda offensive, Paul Reed enticed the miners' leadership with American dollars to pay for additional staff and services. With ORIT dollars, mining locals enhanced their prestige and visibility on a national level. Commanding more resources, ORIT and Reed convinced the miners' national leadership to reject Lombardo's invitation. In effect, Reed and ORIT had bought the miners' union leadership and helped to entrench the charro administration of Filiberto Rabalcava.[16]

The CTM and ORIT also worked to influence the leadership of the federal workers' union. Once again, financial resources were a central feature of ORIT strategy. Federal workers' union leaders affiliated with the American Cultural Institute in the United States Embassy. Through the institute, they received instruction in English and collaborated in the development of a new course in industrial relations at the National University of Mexico.[17] The American embassy also awarded promising union leaders USIS Leader Grants to travel to Washington and receive further training.

The Leader Grants were an outgrowth of the Mutual Security Act, which empowered President Harry Truman's "Point Four" programs initiated in 1949 and designed to fight communism in developing countries through U.S. economic expansion. Sections 516 and 528 of the Mutual Security Act called on the United States to encourage the development of "free labor" union movements. In practice this involved identifying pro-U.S., anti-communist trade-unionists to send to the United States for training. The grants were part of a broader strategy to assist in the struggle against communist and independent unionists, a category that included nationalists, socialists and intransigent rank and file. As part of the program, public employees' union Presidents Abelardo de la Torre and Florencia Maya received extensive labor relations training through the study of labor statistics, collective bargaining, safety inspection and wage and cost-of-living indexes.[18] Besides providing training the USIS grants allowed Mexican trade-union leaders to establish cordial and working relationships with U.S. public employee unions like the postal workers.[19] Other grant recipients followed and stayed in the United States for six months, in which, after three weeks of intensive English, they studied labor economics, statistics and American history. Grantees spent their final weeks observing operations of unions and visiting work sites.[20]

When labor leaders returned from training, ORIT financed travel and lectures for them throughout Mexico. With ORIT and USIS dollars, Mexican labor leaders published dozens of books, articles and pamphlets that extolled the virtues of AFL-style unionism and partnership between government, industry and organized labor. One result of the propaganda was the founding of an association of labor leader grant recipients, called the Círculo Samuel Gompers.[21] Instrumental in starting the group was former anarchist and trade-union leader Rosendo Salazar, who with USIS and ORIT money, published a biography of Samuel Gompers. The USIS distributed the Gompers biography to union locals throughout Mexico free of charge.[22]

The ORIT financing also helped Círculo Samuel Gompers members publish newspapers for smaller unions in remote areas of Mexico. This contributed to the CTM's efforts to incorporate these unions into its ranks, all of which had been struggling financially. Key to the CTM's success was the ORIT and U.S. industrial unions' financing of the construction of a new office building and headquarters. Besides providing ample space for the CTM national directorate and all of its affiliates, the structure also housed ORIT's executive operations. The building provided a symbol of strength for the CTM and served to legitimize its policies. It also facilitated the CTM's absorption of smaller unions that struggled to provide logistical and staff support for their membership. ORIT funding enabled these organizations to affirm their existence; in the process they strengthened the CTM's position within the Mexican labor movement against the forces that opposed charrismo.[23]

In the immediate years ahead, government officials and charro leaders put their extensive training into practice when they settled close to 40,000 labor disputes, most of which provided for minuscule wage increases.[24] To enforce the new contracts, the CTM and charro union leaders formed the Bloque de Unidad Obrera—Workers' Unity Bloc (BUO), whose sole purpose was to legitimize agreements drawn up by industry, charro-controlled unions and the government. Although these maneuvers limited the expression of workers' demands, they were not able to repress rank-and-file militancy and convert unions into passive instruments of the state.

RANK-AND-FILE REBELLION AND THE CHARRO COUNTERATTACK

The overwhelming financial backing of American labor unions to charro leaders failed to quell discontent. Rank and file continued to protest wage freezes, no-strike pledges and attempts to discipline them in the workplace. As workers' incomes stagnated and the distribution of wealth skewed upward, rank-and-file union members joined insurgent movements within the established trade unions and federations in opposition to charro leaders. Although some insurgent leaders were communists, socialists and ideologues, the majority merely sought the democratization and autonomy of their unions as a means to achieve higher wages and better working conditions. They viewed these goals as tantamount to defending the rights guaranteed to workers in the 1917 Constitution.

An insurgent movement among communication workers began on February 6, 1958, when 7,000 telegraph workers walked off the job in protest of the secretary of communications and public works violation of contract work rules. The secretary had transferred what he called thirty-seven communist agitators to posts outside Mexico City. Strikers called for a fifty percent pay increase and defied government and charro demands for a return to work by cutting off the Federal District's internal telephone services. The strike gained momentum when nearly 500 international telephone operators struck, severing communications with dozens of countries. On February 15, 1960, Radio Chapultepec employees and hundreds of telegraph workers who operated direct lines in banks and aviation companies began walking picket lines. As postal workers threatened to join their ranks, charros desperately sought a solution to the conflict.[25]

In conjunction with the charro leadership of the Federation of State Workers' union, the secretary of communications revoked the transfer order and petitioned the government for a modest wage increase, infuriating the charro leadership. Instead of negotiating, the charros denounced the secretary's concession to communist agitators and insisted that no negotiations take place until the strikers returned to work. The strikers responded by sharply criticizing the union leadership for not representing genuine worker sentiment. The government, trying to avoid making martyrs of the strikers during an election year, timidly watched as charro leaders attempted to defuse the situation during a February 16, 1958, Mexico City meeting.[26]

The meeting witnessed strikers shouting down Federation of State Workers' union General Secretary Abelardo de la Torre as he attempted to speak and to offer them a meager seven percent wage increase. Strike leaders stood on chairs and denounced the union's leadership as traitors. The speakers repudiated the leadership's authority and declared that only they should represent the membership in negotiations with the government. As the walkout progressed, strikers clandestinely received financial support from other unions. The expression of solidarity ultimately led to the formation of a new union—Alianza. Immediately the press and the charro leadership orchestrated a propaganda campaign to discredit the Alianza by calling it unpatriotic and communistic. The Cold War rhetoric eventually produced cracks in the Alianza's leadership and pressure mounted for a negotiated settlement. The strikers finally accepted the original offer of a seven percent wage increase under the name of the Alianza, not the charro-led union.[27]

The communications workers' rebellion gave railroad and petroleum workers new faith. Stymied by charro manipulation of parliamentary procedures, railroad rank and filers followed former union heads Valentín Campa and Luis Gómez Z. in an attempted forceful takeover of six local union headquarters. The insurgents targeted a group of charro leaders called "October 14," which was led by Fidel Velázquez's cousin, Ricardo Velázquez Vázquez. After barricading themselves inside the local union halls for several hours, police and federal soldiers used tear gas and nightsticks to dislodge them. The authorities' actions ensured the continuation of charro leadership.[28]

In the petroleum workers' union, charro leaders conspired with the secretary of labor to hold a secret-ballot referendum that would nullify previous elections where independents and communists had won a majority of the national union posts. With government complicity, the charro slate of candidates stuffed ballot boxes and lost ballots, as well as other frauds, to win the election.[29] The results demoralized the independent forces and led to more labor-management agreements that limited union autonomy and held down wages. Working-class living standards continued to deteriorate.

While the real wages of federal employees had fallen fifty percent between 1938 and 1952, teachers' salaries suffered a worse fate. Urban primary school teachers, especially the 15,582 of Mexico City, experienced acute inflationary pressures.[30] In 1956, after suffering attacks from charros and failing to win wage increases, members of the National Education Workers' Union (SNTE) decided to organize an independent faction much like the CTM depuradas of the 1940s. Under the leadership of Othón Salazar, a former member of a communist youth organization, teachers formed the Comité de Lucha y Democratización.

Based in the Federal District, the Comité de Lucha attempted to regain control of its local unions from the charro leaders. When the national union refused to conduct elections and called for the dissolution of the rank-and-file committee, the insurgents held their own convention. With over 15,000 Mexico City teachers in attendance, they elected Othón Salazar as general secretary. The committee asserted that the national union leadership had betrayed the Mexican Revolution, and accordingly, had changed its name in late 1957 to the Teachers' Revolutionary Movement (MRM). The Revolutionary Movement hoped to attract nationalistic elements within the PRI by backing Adolfo López Mateos, the ruling party's official candidate for the presidency in 1958. The Revolutionary Movement leaders based their strategy on advice given to them by Lombardo Toledano, head of the People's Party (PP), and Dionisio Encino, general secretary of the Communist party. Lombardo and Encino suggested that the rank and file work through the established political system and not challenge the charros directly.[31]

While supporting López Mateos, the Revolutionary Movement called for a forty percent wage increase and retirement after forty years' service. It attempted to present the demands during an April 12, 1958, demonstration in Mexico City where police greeted them with tear gas, clubs and pistols. The repression prompted the Revolutionary Movement's leadership to call for a strike of Mexico City kindergartens and primary schools. Teachers responded and shut down the schools for several weeks, generating a propaganda offensive by the national teachers' union charros and Unity Bloc leader Jesús Yuren, a Leader Grant recipient and Círculo Samuel Gompers member, accusing Salazar and the Revolutionary Movement of being part of a "plan of an international character," bent on destroying national worker unity, and creating a climate of anarchy.[32] Despite the attacks, the strike continued and received support from parents, students and other unions, such as the electricians and railroad workers. The unity expressed by rank and filers prohibited the charros from recruiting strike-breakers, and thus forced the government to grant a substantial enough pay increase to end the strike.

The charro bureaucracy still refused to recognize Salazar and others, however, as the legitimate heads of the Mexico City locals. On September 6, 1958, the Revolutionary Movement organized a demonstration at the Monument of the Revolution and called for the recognition of the union's democratically elected officials. Police attacked the demonstrators and arrested 208 persons, including Salazar, whom authorities charged with conspiring to "dissolve" the state. The seriousness of the charges reflected the Mexican and U.S. government's concern over the growth of the anti-charro movement. U.S. officials working in Mexico expressed concern about the growing discontent among Mexico's lower classes and the communist influence within trade unions. They specifically identified Othón Salazar and railroad worker Demetrio Vallejo as communist agitators and as threats to Mexico's stability.[33]

Although the concern about a communist threat was probably exaggerated, the rank-and-file challenge to the charro system was genuine. Telegraph workers already had left the communications workers' union and had joined teachers in their efforts to form a committee that advocated labor union democracy and autonomy. A month prior to Salazar's arrest, petroleum workers belonging to Locals #34 and #35 staged a hunger strike in the PEMEX building to pressure the secretary of labor to recognize anti-charro leaders Carlos Castillo and Ignacio Hernández Alcala as presidents of their respective unions. As with the teachers, police used tear gas and clubs to remove the workers from the PEMEX facility.

The repression strengthened the resolve of the anti-charro forces, and, as a consequence, the government began negotiations and promised to release all of the arrested teachers, except strike leaders, provided that the work stoppages ended immediately. In another tactical move, the labor department exerted pressure on the national teachers' union leadership to hold new elections. The Revolutionary Movement insurgents easily won the fairly held elections. On December 4, 1958, three days after López Mateos became president, the government released Salazar and other union officials and recognized the anti-charro officials in the petroleum workers' union. The rank-and-file victories encouraged workers in other unions to demand democratization as the path to better working conditions and a decent wage.

THE GREAT REBELLION OF 1959

Despite almost a decade of widespread repression against rebellious elements in the railroad workers' union—which included a reign of terror by paramilitary groups—rank-and-file members organized local committees to agitate for immediate wage increases. On May 2, 1958, they gathered their forces at the union's national headquarters to pressure the charro leadership.[34] The dissidents were part of a group called *pro-aumento salarios* (for salary increases). Historically railroad workers had resisted government tutelage and fought tenaciously against wage discrimination. During the Porfiriato they had struggled against the American management's practices of discrimination against Mexican nationals. They had resisted joining the CROM and demanded self-management during the Cárdenas era. Railroad workers now called for an immediate monthly pay increase of 350 pesos at the government-controlled Mexican National Railway. Their leaders, Demetrio Vallejo and Roberto Gómez Godínez from Local #13 in Matías Romero, Oaxaca, came under attack from charro Samuel Ortega Hernández, the railroad union's general secretary. Ortega Hernández denounced them as "communist agitators" and demanded that the commission they headed cease its activities. While Vallejo dismissed Ortega's comments and continued to challenge his authority, the Mexican Communist Party (PCM) central committee sided with the charro bureaucrats and called for a wage increase of only 250 pesos a month.[35]

When the director of the Mexican National Railway asked for sixty days to study the situation, rumors spread that the state-run enterprise was only prepared to offer the railroad workers sixty pesos per month, 140 less than the charro local executive boards had asked for. In Matías Romero, Vallejo reported to Local #13 members the events from Mexico City, despite the local general secretary's attempts to stop the meeting. Local #13 members responded by electing a new executive committee and voted to support the 350-pesos-a-month demand. Although not officially recognized, the local executive board convened a special meeting on June 11, 1958, to discuss the wage issue. The membership gave the company ten days to meet their demands or face a series of work slowdowns. Known as the "Plan of the Southeast," the demand for 350 pesos became the cry of rank and filers in Southern Mexico after Vallejo and Local #13 members had organized dissidents in other locals.[36]

In an attempt to defuse the situation, Ortega Hernández agreed to meet with a group of representatives from six Southern Mexico locals on June 25, 1958. A day later, when the general secretary refused to support the proposed wage increase, workers went on strike. After two consecutive days of two-hour, system-wide shutdowns, the company asked to negotiate with Vallejo's commission instead of the national union leadership. On the strike's third day, oil workers, teachers and students joined the railroaders in street demonstrations. The show of solidarity forced the government to compromise. Despite Vallejo's reservations, railroad workers accepted an increase of 215 pesos, a raise three times greater than originally proposed by the company and more than the union executive committee had demanded.[37]

Spurred on by their victory, the commission forces rallied on July 12, 1958, at the General Union Convention and elected Demetrio Vallejo as their new general secretary. The overthrow of the charros stunned the secretary of labor and the national company. They reacted by refusing to recognize the new leadership. The unionists immediately gave both the company and the secretary of labor an ultimatum: either accept the election results or face another series of work stoppages. Government attempts to negotiate the impending walkouts failed when the secretario de gobernación insisted that the charro leaders return to power. As the shutdown commenced, strikers received support from electrical workers' union leader Agustín Sánchez Delint and representatives of the teachers' union.[38]

An alarmed government ordered the army and the police to seize the railroad workers' union halls. Authorities arrested over 100 strikers and used tear gas to break up daily street demonstrations, which included participants from several other unions. The government combined the use of repression with offers of bonus pay and salary increases. State officials hoped to convince enough strikers to abandon the picket lines and begin operating some of the trains. In Monterrey and San Luis Potosí, where the company tried to run the trains, the strikers' wives physically blocked operations.[39] When efforts to run the trains failed, the government announced that strikers would no longer receive pay. Other unions, such as the telegraph workers, responded by holding one-hour sympathy strikes. When authorities countered by arresting a strike leader, the walkout spread until the army occupied telegraph offices with battalions of infantry and communications personnel. Even as telegraph workers slowly drifted back to their jobs, the show of solidarity forced the government to compromise.[40]

On August 5, the Ministry of Labor announced that an agreement had been reached. It called for an end to the strike and a government promise to allow new elections within fifteen days. In addition, the government withdrew all troops from railroad stations and union halls, released all prisoners with no reprisals, and awarded strikers back pay. Without charro interference, the Vallejo slate of candidates won a landslide victory.[41]

As the 120,000-member railroad workers' union fell to anti-charro forces, the emboldened rank and file began carrying out acts of revenge against supervisory personnel and workers who had remained loyal to the company. In Monterrey, Vallejo supporters seized divisional headquarters and severely beat the superintendent. They also physically abused several of his assistants and union members who had refused to strike. The rank and file's actions left the Monterrey division of the Mexican National Railway without management personnel for more than a week. As attacks against supervisors and charros escalated, the government ordered the 7th Military District to police the railway and provide protection for employees.[42]

After settling scores with old union bureaucrats and management personnel, the new union executive committee drew up an economic analysis of the Mexican National Railway that called for the complete restructuring of the state-owned enterprise. Presented by Demetrio Vallejo to President López Mateos, it called the railroad a "tool of foreign interests" and demanded that the company raise rates and terminate the subsidies given to American-owned mining and metal companies. The report concluded that the proposed changes would make the railroad more profitable and, thereby, enable the business to provide higher wages and better working conditions for employees. The union's critique of the company reflected the enduring

On strike! A railroad worker addresses a Mexico City crowd in 1959 (from Alonso, *El movimiento ferrocarilero en México, 1958-1959*, Mexico City: Ediciones Era, 1972).

working-class nationalism, which traditionally had opposed subordinating labor's interests to the demands of U.S. corporations. The nationalistic overtones in the executive committee's report directly challenged the government's economic plan of continued industrialization through foreign investment.

Soldiers and strikers, 1959 (from Alonso, *El movimiento ferrocarilero en México, 1958-1959,* Mexico City: Ediciones Era, 1972).

When the government refused to consider the proposed company reorganization, union leadership rallied its members around the plan in the upcoming contract negotiations with the Mexican National Railway. The plan served as a springboard to develop a strategy to secure higher wages and improved working conditions on smaller lines, which routinely violated contractual terms with their employees. The union set a target date of February 25, 1959, for a general railroad strike if company officials refused to meet the demands for a 16.66 percent raise over the previous 215 pesos, medical attention and medicine for workers' families and new workers' housing or daily rent subsidies paid for by the company.[43] The CTM reacted by initiating a propaganda campaign against the union's leadership, denouncing it as communistic and unpatriotic. The Unity Bloc joined the campaign by accusing the union of "planning acts of sabotage that would lead to the communist leadership's goals of changing the public order."[44]

In spite of the labor bureaucracy's attempts to discredit their demands, Vallejo initiated the strike as planned on February 25, 1959. Immediately, the Ministry of Labor declared the strike illegal. While the union sought injunctions to continue the strike, the government placed police and soldiers in most train terminals. Meanwhile, Vallejo worked through the union's council to try to reach an agreement with President López Mateos. Finally, the government and the union came to terms. The agreement granted workers a 16.66 percent pay increase and promised to rectify previous violations of the contract. The union's willingness to negotiate and remove the red-and-black strike flags stemmed in part from Vallejo's eagerness to respond to the orchestrated propaganda campaign against the strikers. Vallejo insisted throughout the conflict that rather than trying to disrupt and destroy the existing social order as critics claimed, the union intended to work through the system and exercise the workers' constitutional right to strike.[45]

Despite the legality of the union leadership's actions, the entrenched labor bureaucracy continued the verbal assault. Fidel Velázquez charged Vallejo and his followers with "wanting to create a climate of agitation for the benefit of their communist theories."[46] Railroaders working on private lines, however, chose to listen to Vallejo and the union. The recently negotiated victory and Vallejo's defense of Article 123 prompted employees of the Ferrocarril Mexicano to demand wage hikes as well. Workers employed by the Ferrocarriles Unidos de Yucatán and the Ferrocarril del Pacífico followed suit and set late March strike deadlines. Militancy spread to the telegraph workers as they carried out a series of two-hour strikes and pressed for an election to oust their charro leaders. Both the railroad and telegraph companies refused to negotiate for higher wages because they claimed running contracts did not expire until July 1960.[47]

While workers on the private lines remained militant, Vallejo and the union leadership intervened and set March 25 as a uniform deadline for the walkout. Despite the fact that the strike deadline appeared to increase the bargaining leverage of the private line workers, the companies refused to meet the union's demand for a thirty-five peso daily wage increase. Even as the government prepared army units to intervene, the strike involving 14,000 workers began on schedule. Immediately, the government declared the strike "non-existent" and ordered troops to occupy the rail yards.

The strike affected the Mexican public because it shut down rail traffic at the peak of Holy Week, a traditional time for travel. The strike's effectiveness increased when workers on other lines conducted thirty-minute sympathy strikes. The railroaders received further support when longshoremen in Veracruz walked off their jobs and joined other workers in street demonstrations. Vallejo countered government and charro claims that the strike was "unpatriotic" by consistently stating that the railroad workers were only exercising their constitutional right. He used legal channels to contest the state's ruling and even pledged to determine the sentiment of the rank and file by conducting an election that would decide whether to resume work if the government's position did not change.[48]

The strike held together when Vallejo and the union attained a seventy-two-hour injunction from the court that challenged the government's "non-existent" ruling. The court's action froze the strike's legal status and delayed the possible mass dismissal of employees. Mexican National Railroad workers seized the opportunity by staging one-hour sympathy strikes in Torreón, Durango, Aguascalientes and Tampico. The sympathy strikers even threatened to expand the time of the shutdowns from one to two hours. The government reacted by threatening to initiate mass firings. Union leaders in four Federal District locals responded to the threats by promising a system-wide walkout if the dismissals took place.[49]

On March 28, the government and the private rail companies began mass firings. Strikers on the Mexicano lines also faced dismissal, despite the protection they received from the injunction against the government. Simultaneously, the government began recruiting replacements and rejected Vallejo's offer to renew negotiations. On the Nogales-Guadalajara and Mexico City-Veracruz lines, troops occupied the trains and protected replacement workers and supervisors. While some lines operated at a limited capacity, the workers on the National Railways continued to halt most of the nation's rail traffic. Soon, however, the repression began to take its toll. While the army protected an increasing number of replacement workers, sympathy strikes by Veracruz longshoremen and other unions failed to materialize.[50]

Meanwhile, police made sweeping arrests throughout the country; in Mexico City they jailed the principal leaders, including Vallejo. Initially, the arrests involved about 450 strikers. Authorities charged them with inciting disorder and sedition. Subsequent apprehensions resulted in the jailing of over 1,500 strikers. In Guadalajara alone, authorities incarcerated several hundred strikers. With the militants in jail, the government moved to create a new charro leadership. The morning after Vallejo's arrest, the charros selected a group of workers to convene a meeting and designate a four-man national representative committee as a provisional directorate of the union. The relatively unknown directorate repudiated Vallejo and his tactics and issued a statement that urged the union members to return to their jobs as "good" Mexicans.[51]

The majority of railroad workers ignored the call. Railway operations continued to run only at twenty percent capacity nationwide. Conflict also erupted between pro-Vallejo forces and charro supporters. On April 1 in Monterrey, Vallejo supporters attempted to meet inside the railway union building that police and pro-government unionists had occupied. A pitched battle followed and finally a crowd of about 3,000 strikers moved to the electrical workers' union headquarters where an overwhelming majority voted to reject the government-sponsored bosses. They also vowed to continue the strike until the railroad administration recognized Vallejo's authority and complied with the previous agreement. Finally, as a condition for their return to work, they demanded the release of all jailed union members.[52]

The strikers' bold actions—sabotage and mass street demonstrations—temporarily stopped the government's back-to-work movement. During one protest in Mexico City, police arrested forty Vallejo supporters as they attempted to block the entrance to railroad shops and prevent replacements from working. In Torreón and Durango, strikers destroyed bridges and burned freight cars. The government reacted to the escalating militancy by threatening to cancel the seniority rights of strikers who did not report back to work by April 2.[53]

The ultimatum was effective: key railroad employees such as engineers and mechanics returned to their jobs. By April 3, an estimated sixty percent of Mexico City's National Railway workers, as well as those on other lines had returned to work. As the strike ended, the government-sponsored charros announced that they would conduct negotiations with all companies for the reinstatement of fired workers and the restoration of seniority rights. A delegation of pro-government Tampico union members even solicited support from the American consulate for financial aid to reconstruct its local under anti-communist, anti-Vallejo leadership.[54] Even sympathetic elements in other unions joined the anti-Vallejo chorus. Sánchez Delint, leftist leader of the electrical workers' union, condemned the Vallejo-led strike as illegal. He added that his union wholeheartedly supported the government and repudiated tactics that would be "detrimental to the economic needs of the government."[55]

As former allies deserted Vallejo and his followers, repression against the strike movement escalated. During the first two weeks of April the government made mass arrests of union leaders and jailed them incommunicado. In the Nogales Division authorities arrested fifteen key union leaders along with sixty strikers accused of disrupting rail communications in the local terminal. The CTM placed full-page bulletins in the nation's major newspapers that denounced the strike as communist inspired and supported the actions taken by the government. The Mexican press went as far as blaming the Soviets for the strike and called for the immediate expulsion of its diplomatic delegation. The only exception to the press onslaught against the strikers was an editorial in *El Noreste*, which defended the railroad workers' constitutional right to strike.[56]

As the press escalated its attacks against Vallejo, the government formally indicted him on charges of "social dissolution." The charges included acts of sabotage, subverting national institutions, committing provocative acts to disturb the public peace, paralyzing the nation's communications system, endangering the economy by impeding the movement of merchandise and creating shortages of supplies, coercing and interfering with public policy and making threats against constituted authority.

Vallejo answered the charges by insisting that he strictly adhered to the provisions of the Federal Labor Code throughout the negotiations and the strike. He also claimed that he tried to prevent illegal walkouts but was unable to because the strikes represented the "will of the rank and file." Vallejo complained that the government's actions were unjust and that they were only carried out to prevent the existence of trade unions independent of the state.[57] The charges against Vallejo did indeed indicate that the government intended to sweep the union of militants and independents. Authorities declared only two minor union officials of the sixty-five arrested eligible for release on bail. In Vallejo's case, the charge of attempting "social dissolution" made him ineligible.

Despite the charges brought against Vallejo, which resulted in his fifteen-year incarceration, the state's efforts to restore the charro system in the railroad workers' union encountered problems. Even after the government selectively cut the number of regular employees by 5,000 to eliminate "undesirable" elements, the charro leadership failed to consolidate its authority and rebel factions loyal to Vallejo continued to emerge.[58] Pro-Vallejo sentiment remained strong among union members in Oaxaca, Tapachula, and in Tonala, Chiapas, as well as in Guadalajara and Monterrey, where workers continued to call for the "Defense of the Collective Agreement." In Monterrey on June 21, 1959, 500 Vallejo supporters seized Local #19's hall and held an assembly to denounce the national union leadership and the Monterrey charros. The government reacted immediately, ordering troops to seize the building and remove the rebels. As radical workers in Saltillo, Torreón and Nuevo Laredo followed the example of Monterrey union members, the army occupied union headquarters and rail installations. The rebel workers responded by holding solidarity demonstrations to celebrate the first anniversary of the Vallejo-led June 25, 1958, strike.[59]

Finally, the government used widespread layoffs and more arrests in an attempt to reinforce the charro leaders. Meanwhile, the new charro leaders, Alfredo A. Fabela and Francisco Calderón, accused Vallejo and his administration of robbing the union's treasury of ten million pesos. They claimed that Vallejo had disbursed the majority of money to dissident factions in other unions. In order to tie the union closer to the state and consolidate the government's authority over its activities, Fabela and Calderón secured a thirty million peso loan from the national treasury.[60] Repression, company retrenchment and the actions of the new charro leaders assured state power in a union that had long advocated autonomy and resisted government meddling in its internal affairs. More importantly, the failure of the railroad workers' challenge to the charro system facilitated governmental ability to impose charro control in other unions and tighten its grip over organized labor.

The 1959 railroad strike represented organized labor's greatest challenge to state authority since the 1916 Casa general strike. Like Vallejo's fifteen-year prison sentence, the severity of that challenge explains the harsh punishment given to the strikers' leadership. But it also demonstrated that charro effectiveness in containing labor unrest would have to become more flexible and responsive to the rank and file. As a result, both the CTM and the government pursued more conciliatory policies toward labor demands after the 1959 conflict. Nonetheless, government control of the movement through political links and violence against intransigent, militant and independent trade-union activists remained the cornerstone of state policy.

Crucial to the development of this strategy during the 1950s was the U.S. labor movement's participation in consolidating the Mexican charro system. American labor officials exercised their traditional role, which dated to the revolutionary period, as liaisons for American corporations and the United States government. During the era of the Cold War, when the U.S. labor movement fell in line with the American government's anti-communist foreign policy, the help that American unionists gave the Mexican government and the CTM bureaucrats was crucial. Using ORIT resources and dollars, the CTM and the Mexican government eradicated militant and independent forces in organizations that opposed state policy. As economic ties between the U.S. and Mexico increased and industrialization accelerated, a disciplined labor movement void of militant and independent elements became essential. Mexico's role in the post-war international division of labor—that of providing raw materials and inexpensive labor markets for more economically advanced countries like the United States—depended upon the entrenchment of the charro system.

Although the 1950s witnessed the advancement and entrenchment of the charro system, unionized workers still demanded a decent wage, better working conditions and the right to strike. As the Mexican economy grew, peaceful industrial relations depended upon the state's open manipulation of trade-union officials and the use of brute force against intransigent rank and file. Legitimizing charrismo required organized labor's total ideological allegiance to a state that increasingly favored capital, both foreign and domestic. As capital enhanced its position against labor in the decades that followed, the contradictions that surfaced between the working-class and the state during the 1950s emerged once again.

CHAPTER SIX

LEGACY:
CHARRISMO AND THE CRISIS OF MEXICAN POLITICAL ECONOMY

Crushing the 1958-1959 working-class insurgency accelerated the Mexican business and industrialists' growing political influence versus organized labor. By 1990 the relationship between the business elite and the state has ushered in a model of economic development that embraces the expansion of export manufacturing. Influenced by external factors as well as the growing power of the private sector, the Mexican state has rapidly established a neo-liberal development strategy that cuts social spending, welcomes foreign investment with little restriction and carries out a labor policy that is based upon greater union subservience to the regime's policies. The capstone of this policy is the North American Free Trade Agreement (NAFTA), which among other things, has transformed the long relationship between organized labor in the United States and Mexico.

During the last three decades the appointments of businessmen as state officials and the government's consultation with business leaders on issues like economic development and labor relations has become commonplace. Mexican business leaders have acquired veto power over policies, and the core of the state bureaucracy has filled itself with technicians and experts, whose discourse has moved the state toward an orthodox pro-business policy. As state officials accumulated wealth through business activities and businessmen entered the state bureaucracy in larger numbers, the business-government alliance has been consolidated and institutionalized. This process is clearly reflected in the sphere of labor relations, where both business and government have cooperated to entrench the charro system and stifle the autonomy and independence of organized labor. Facilitating this trend was the increasing centralization of labor organization, reflected by the creation of the Congreso del Trabajo—Workers' Congress (CT) in 1966, an umbrella organization which incorporated most major unions and labor federations.

As the Mexican economy grew and the business elite increased its share of national income and political power, a greater number of Mexicans saw their standard of living deteriorate and the political system closed to them. The conditions helped to produce the tumultuous year of 1968 when students, workers and intellectuals challenged the regime's legitimacy. Despite the protest's defeat, the broad-based popular uprising forced the government to make policy adjustments.

During the administration of Luis Echeverría (1970-1976) the state fostered the belief that economic growth and income distribution were compatible. It emphasized the "social wage" and increased outlays for education, housing, distribution of food, health care and sanitation. Business associations expressed fears that the policies would lead to a renewed popular movement, much like the 1930s, and believed that its emergence would seriously limit their powers and hard-won influence in the state bureaucracy. Echeverría and his successor, José López Portillo (1976-1982), never sought the genuine participation of the masses in the elite-dominated party structure but implemented the "social wage" from the top down. Nonetheless, the most conservative businessmen (the Monterrey group) philosophically resisted the state's concept of "shared growth." In 1971 the business elite issued a seven-point program for the government to adopt.

The program's key components called for the privatization of parastate industries and an increase in direct foreign investment. The bold proclamation reflected the private sector's organizational transformation that had slowly welded the old and new industrial firms and banks into interlocked "national economic groups." It quickly translated into political power, and the Echeverría government passed laws that recognized the legitimacy of holding companies, creating new opportunities for foreign investment. The model of economic growth, accompanied by long-standing management practices of holding down wages, ultimately resulted in a sharp reduction in the income received by the bottom forty percent of the population.[1] The new set of conditions represented a decline in the relative autonomy of the state and reflected the private sector's growing capacity to shape policy.

But the implementation of the social wage and the idea of shared growth raised working-class expectations. Union members demanded organizational autonomy, democracy and an end to charro rule. By 1976 the labor insurgency represented a political threat to the regime because it complemented other challenges from the middle class, students and intellectuals to the government's legitimacy. For their part, workers in a number of unions—including the important and expanding automobile industry—elected more militant leaders.

Auto workers, electricians, metal, telephone and university employees joined forces to protest charro rule. Like the 1958-1959 insurgency, the movement began with demands for higher wages and attacked the charro system as the barrier to that goal. In contrast to 1958-1959, however, the insurgency of the 1970s encompassed more sectors of the labor movement and endured longer. It presented the possibility of coordinated actions and solidarity with students and participation in newly formed leftist political parties.

The most serious challenges to the charro system came from the Tendencia Democrática—Democratic Tendency (DT) and the Frente Auténtico del Trabajo—Authentic Labor Front (FAT). The Frente Auténtico, founded in the early 1960s by Nicolás Medina, a worker in a shoe factory in León, Guanajuato, initially engaged in the political expression found in the Christian Democratic parties and labor unions throughout Latin America. Like its Latin American counterparts, the Frente Auténtico espoused the reconciliation of social classes and other liberal ideals that were popular among sectors of the Roman Catholic Church. As the Frente Auténtico attempted to direct the rank-and-file rebellion it became more radical, and, as a consequence, expanded the organization's influence among workers in dynamic industrial sectors such as automobiles, electronics, mining and metallurgy. It registered success because it substituted the philosophy of class peace with calls for organizational autonomy, democracy and the right to strike as the means for workers to better themselves materially.

The government thwarted the Frente Auténtico's challenge by supporting the formation and activities of a new "independent" labor movement, the Independent Worker Unity (UOI). In effect, Workers' Unity was really a new labor bureaucracy to substitute for the CTM in the automobile, chemical, textile and transportation industries, where the government had failed to dislodge the Frente Auténtico.[2] Like its government-backed predecessors, Workers' Unity never had difficulty attaining legal recognition for its local unions or contracts, while the Frente Auténtico did. As in the past, the government and its trade-union allies had blunted a wave of working-class protest with a combination of responses. With Workers' Unity cooperation, the state relied on legal powers to deny unions recognition, declare the legality of strikes and build a new labor bureaucracy to act as an alternative to radical unionism. And, as in the past, the state exercised coercion when flexible responses failed.

While the government effectively neutralized the Frente Auténtico, it had more difficulty defeating the challenge posed by the Democratic Tendency. Led by Rafael Galván, the Democratic Tendency was an outgrowth of rank-and-file caucuses within the electrical workers' union. Throughout the early 1970s the Democratic Tendency advocated working-class nationalism and articulated its ideas through *Solidaridad*, an old anarchosyndicalist newspaper acquired by the union during the 1950s. Using *Solidaridad*, it advocated the further "Mexicanization" of the economy and an end to charro rule.[3]

Galván asserted that revolutionary nationalism could survive only if the mass movements of labor and the peasantry remained central to the direction of the state's economic development. He condemned the state's "sterilizing bureaucracy," and blamed the degeneration of the Mexican Revolution on the United States government, which he claimed "attempted to control the Mexican economic and political system." Galván added that Mexican capitalists and government bureaucrats had joined financial interests from the United States to reverse the progress of the Mexican Revolution. Charros, Galván argued, served as instruments of foreign capitalists and constituted the most treacherous and disloyal group of traitors in Mexican society. He advocated a workers' alliance to overthrow the system and the rebirth of the democratic revolutionary state.[4]

Through its revolutionary nationalist program, embodied in the "Declaration of Guadalajara," the Democratic Tendency garnered broad-based support among workers, students, and intellectuals. The document called for a union democracy movement and a comprehensive program to fight for the nationalistic goals of the Mexican Revolution. When the Democratic Tendency rallied hundreds of thousands of Mexican workers, students and peasants into the streets, the Echeverría government used military force and vigilantes hired by the charro-dominated CTM to crush the protest. The state's combination of force and co-optation had once again defeated working-class nationalism. By 1976, the regime successfully had wiped out organized labor's renewed challenge to its authority.[5]

The insurgency's defeat coincided with a new capitalist offensive. Business associations that formerly had allied themselves with statist economic development joined the Consejo Coordinador Empresarial (CCE)— Business Advisory Board. It grouped together the Monterrey industrialists, large commercial capital and the new industrial elite. The board immediately created the Center for Economic Studies (CEESP), which became a major source of economic analysis that reflected the University of Chicago and

Professor Milton Friedman's free-market philosophy. In 1976 the economic studies center launched a propaganda campaign in the nation's daily newspapers. It occurred while the International Monetary Fund (IMF) and Mexico negotiated a three-year debt repayment program. One of the program's components was a 100 percent devaluation of the peso, which reinforced the economic studies center's propaganda that blamed Mexico's failing economic health on Echeverría's model of "shared growth." Simultaneously, the IMF and the Mexican government agreed upon a stabilization program that called for cutting the state's deficit, freezing wages, easing government price controls and the promotion of exports to pay the deficit.

Jose López Portillo delayed full implementation of the agreement. Temporarily, high world oil prices had saved Mexico. López Portillo's announcement of the government's intention to exploit recently discovered petroleum reserves gave the government considerable counter bargaining power with the IMF. The new regime declared that Mexico's problem was now the "management of abundance." Although the oil boom generated revenue, payment on Mexico's long-term debt had left the country's international capital flow either close to zero or negative.[6] While the government continued to borrow abroad, it gave the private sector expanded subsidies, tax exemptions and tariff benefits. Most profits made by the state seemed to end up in the private sector as capital transfers and benefits to the business elite grew from 3.6 percent of GNP in 1970 to 13.4 percent of GNP in 1981.[7] While the private sector reaped profits and invested their capital abroad, the minimum wage fell by ten percent during the six years of the oil boom; real wages declined steadily from 1976 onward.[8] Between 1977 and 1981, labor's share of national income fell by nine percent.[9]

Bankrupt, the Mexican government negotiated a "structural adjustment" plan with the International Monetary Fund to limit the economic activities of the state. Almost immediately after Miguel de la Madrid Hurtado became president in 1983, his administration made major changes in Articles 25, 26 and 28 of the Mexican Constitution. The most important changes were in Article 28, which resulted in limiting the state's industrial activity to petroleum, petrochemicals, nuclear energy, electricity and satellite communications, all defined as strategic areas of the economy. Authorities enforced laws prohibiting strikes in industries of "national interest." Invoking Article 923 of the 1980 Labor Reform Law, the state denied the mostly female membership of the Coordinadora Democrática Nacional de Telefonistas union registration in compliance with IMF directives to hold down costs in government-run industries.[10]

In addition to the IMF, the World Bank had been deeply involved in formulating "structural adjustment," and by 1986 Mexico had become the largest single recipient of World Bank funding. At the heart of the World Bank's program lay the idea that parastate firms should be privatized because they contributed to the state's deficit. A serious move toward privatization—a long-standing demand of the most powerful elements among the business elite—had begun.

Privatization also marked the beginning of an informal political pact between the private sector and state technocrats. Many of the new technocrats had been trained in the free-market school of economics at major U.S. universities, which were tied ideologically to multilateral agencies like the IMF and the World Bank. This development facilitated the growing link between the strategy of privatization and production for the export market. This process accelerated as the economic situation deteriorated and the nation's capitalists rallied behind the Partido de Acción Nacional—National Action Party (PAN) program to force a shift toward the right in PRI policies. By 1985 the state had reversed a 1982 bank nationalization decree and fundamentally had changed its approach to long-term problems facing the economy.

A year later Mexico joined the General Agreement on Tariffs and Trade (GATT). In so doing, the state abandoned its long-time argument that agreements of international organizations should never supersede national sovereignty. The decision to join GATT reflected a significant shift in Mexico's long-term economic development policy. By joining GATT, the regime accelerated its program of "comparative advantage" low-wage manufacturing, which was accompanied by a renewal of loans from foreign banks and the relaxation of laws mandating fifty-one percent Mexican participation in direct foreign investment. Structural change and low-wage export production were seen as the paths to a fully modernized Mexican economy by the businessmen and state technocrats, who hoped to convert the nation into an intermediate industrial power by the late 1990s.

The de la Madrid administration's structural adjustment was really an outgrowth of an already existing manufacturing export program started in the 1960s. The Mexican Border Industrialization Program (BIP), begun in 1965, allows foreign owners a majority ownership of plants on a strip of land 12.5 miles wide along the length of the U.S.-Mexico border. There Mexican workers are employed in electronic assembly, automobile parts manufacturing, clothing and other industrially produced items. All finished products are re-exported to the United States.

Called the *maquiladora*, it provides for the duty-free importation of components and a value-added tax on finished products. The maquiladora industry is a striking diversity of technology, unionization and working conditions. It is dominated by large foreign-owned corporations, such as RCA, Zenith, Ford and General Motors. In recent years, the Mexican government has permitted the establishment of maquiladoras in the interior of Mexico as well. In December 1990 the Mexican government reported the existence of 1,909 maquila plants, 1,464 of which were located on the border, and 445 in other parts of the country. According to the same government report, maquiladoras employed 371,780 workers of whom 145,297 were men, while 226,483 were women. In 1990, counting technicians and administrative and management employees, the plants employed a total of 459,837 persons.[11]

Although CTM unions exist in various maquiladoras along the border and in the Mexican interior, many maquiladora workers have refused to join, calling the unions "useless and ineffectual." Maquiladora workers have charged the CTM with cronyism, injustice and corruption.[12] At least in Nuevo Laredo, the home of over 100 maquiladoras, conditions in the industry reflect the workers' concerns. There the unions perform many of the normal U.S. corporate personnel management functions, such as recruiting, training, discipline and the hiring and firing of workers.[13] Because of the "official" unions' practices, an antagonistic relationship has developed between maquiladora workers and labor representatives in Nuevo Laredo. An April 1989 wildcat strike by workers at the Ford Motor Company's plant illustrated that tension and revealed many problems of the existing nature and future of foreign-owned export manufacturing operations in Mexico.

On April 24, 1989, 1,500 workers at the Ford Motor Company's Nuevo Laredo LAMOSA manufacturing facility occupied the plant and set up picket lines. They demanded a reduction of the work week from forty-eight to forty hours. The CTM, which "officially" represented the workers, refused to back them. Instead, CTM bureaucrats supported management's call for the strikers to return to their jobs. The strikers refused and for two days they threw rocks and blocked the entrances of plant gates. Although the short-lived strike failed to win anything for workers, the incident illuminated larger issues, such as Mexico's membership in GATT and the onset of NAFTA agreement and their significance for the maquiladora industries and the state's export manufacturing strategy.[14]

The LAMOSA plant, unlike electronic and other auto parts maquiladoras, engages in heavy manufacturing, that of the production of stabilizer and torsion bars for the American automobile industry. Until recent negotiations between the United States and Mexico over the movement to more open markets, U.S. law prohibited heavy manufacturing in foreign-based plants controlled by American corporations. This factor, along with the employment at LAMOSA of young men under the age of sixteen (which is against Mexican law), demonstrates how Mexico's GATT membership has accelerated the removal of technical barriers to trade and regulations that govern or specify the way certain goods are produced.[15] In many cases, Mexico's GATT membership supersedes national laws that govern working conditions and child labor. Indeed, Article XX of the GATT treaty bans slavery but says nothing about child labor, sweatshop conditions or minimum safety standards. And, although NAFTA contains side agreements to protect workers' rights, no real mechanism for their enforcement exists.

Although the Mexican business elite and the state argue that foreign investment will bring capital-intensive production methods, the Ford Motor Company's LAMOSA "heavy manufacturing" maquiladora tells another story. Most of the machinery the workers use in the plant is of 1960s and 1970s vintage. According to management personnel at the plant, the weekly $35 U.S. average earned by workers enables Ford to make labor-intensive manufacturing profitable. Skilled workers required for various functions at the plant are trained on-site and receive no increase in pay for the work they perform. If conditions at LAMOSA are any indication, Mexico's move toward privatization and its open invitation to foreign investment for export manufacturing primarily is based upon the availability of a disciplined and low-wage workforce.

The maquila industry is strikingly Porfirian. State technocrat policies of the late twentieth century resemble those of Porfirio Díaz's *científicos* of a century ago. In pursuit of modernization, policy makers have employed effective deunionization and favorable concessions to foreign capital at the expense of Mexican workers. Despite sporadic worker protest, foreign investors, especially from the U.S. and Asia, continue to establish maquila operations. In the last ten years, employment in the maquiladoras has doubled. According to the Mexican Institute of Statistics (INEGI), as of May 1996 nearly 2,700 maquiladoras employed 890,412 persons, more than any other industry in Mexico.[16]

The growth of the maquiladora industry coincides with the Mexican workers' falling wages. In 1975 United States workers had a salary 4.4 times greater than Mexican laborers. By 1985 wages in the U.S. were 10.4 times more than those in Mexico; and this occurred while American workers' real wages were falling by twenty percent. Since 1982, real wages for Mexicans have deteriorated by sixty percent, and a CTM study adds that since 1987 the minimum wage has lost almost sixty-five percent of its purchasing power.[17]

As U.S. and other foreign manufacturers rush to Mexico for lower wages, the tripartite alliance between American capital, American labor unions and the "official" Mexican labor movement crumbles. The tripartite consensus that evolved among American trade unions, corporate representatives and U.S. officials on how best to confront the revolutionary nationalism spawned by the Mexican Revolution has been transformed.[18] Since the days of the Revolution, the American labor movement supported U.S. economic expansion in tandem with reform unionism. The tripartite consensus solidified during the era of the Cold War when U.S. business and labor leaders accepted the need for collective bargaining and a gradual rise in the standard of living. Increased productivity and more management control meant shorter work weeks, safer factories and higher wages.

But increasing competition from Europe and Japan soon led to the spread of American industrial production to countries where low wages, less regulation and deunionization prevail. Until recently, the U.S. labor bureaucracy has responded to the events with the protectionist slogan, "Buy American!" The transfer of American jobs to places like South Korea, China, Taiwan and Mexico weakened the U.S. labor movement politically. Although the labor movement has rebounded, its failure to stop NAFTA's initiation symbolizes an emerging political consensus in the U.S. that stresses the necessity for American workers to compete with low-wage countries in an increasingly globalized economy within the framework of a new international division of labor. Recently, however, small cracks have begun to appear in this loosely bound political consensus.

While the new international division of labor has meant lower wages and weaker unions for American workers, it has translated into even lower pay and effective deunionization for some Mexican laborers. Recent attacks on the once powerful petroleum workers' union by the Mexican government coincided with the World Bank's insistence that Mexico's national oil industry no longer be considered strategic and off limits to foreign investment. The rush to NAFTA has paralleled the rapid privatization of parastate companies, which in most cases, like the airline and fishing industries, has resulted in deunionization. From 1994 to 1997, the Mexican government's national companies entered into 300 mergers or partnerships with foreign companies and issued 186 permits for the exploitation of the goods and services of the nation.[19]

The new arrangement with foreign capital has threatened the power base of the charro labor bureaucracy. The restructuring of the Mexican economy has resulted in a significant decline in union membership. From 1988 to 1996, the oil, railway, mining and metal unions collectively witnessed a forty percent reduction in membership. The result has been that national industrial unions represent less than ten percent of the country's labor force of forty million persons. Overall, less than fifteen percent of the entire economically active population are now union members.[20] During the *sexenio* of the Carlos Salinas de Gortari and the Ernesto Zedillo administrations, the old-guard charro labor bureaucracy gradually has been shunted aside as neither the state nor management views it as essential to the realities of globalization. With the absence of any threat to mobilize its members, the labor bureaucracy has little or no voice in defining the economy as a whole.

As the effects of globalization continue to grip Mexico, and GATT and NAFTA regulations increasingly supersede Mexican national laws, Mexican workers face an environment of effective deunionization, necessary to attract foreign investment in the new international division of labor. With a charro bureaucracy in deep ideological and political crisis and the worker's share in the national wealth declining, elements of organized labor have begun to take independent action.

Reacting to the economic, social and political crises, which have included the indigenous uprising in Chiapas and the collapse of the peso, sectors of the labor bureaucracy have distanced themselves from the CT, CTM and the ruling PRI. The most serious challenge to the charro system was the emergence of the Foro Sindicalismo ante la Nación. Founded in February 1995 and initially consisting of twenty-five major unions, most of which belonged to the CT, the Foro represented moderate resistance to the more odious aspects of the Mexican government's economic policies. The Foro opposed IMF-inspired economic adjustment policies as well as the privatization of the social security system, which provides workers' pensions, health care and disability payments. Despite its failure to stop the privatization of social security and the government's neo-liberal policies, the Foro became an important vehicle for rank-and-file discussion of organized labor's direction and position within Mexican society.

The Foro's most prominent leader was Francisco Hernández Juárez, head of the telephone workers' union. While repeatedly calling for the creation of a new federation of labor to rival the CTM and the CT, many rank-and-file participants in the Foro criticized Hernández Juárez for his support of the privatization of the Mexican Telephone Company (TELMEX) and a new unionism based upon worker productivity and cooperation with management. In the spirit of this new unionism, Hernández Juárez was instrumental in creating the Federation of Unions of Goods and Services (FESEBES). Many within organized labor argued that Hernández Juárez sought to lead a new federation, which would have become the new link between labor and the state in establishing a new system of worker exploitation.[21]

Much of the rank-and-file criticism of Foro leadership came from members of the Coordinadora Intersindical Primero de Mayo, formed in March 1995 to organize an independent May Day demonstration. In contrast to the Foro, the Intersindical seeks to weld efforts to reform unions to movements struggling for a democratic transformation of Mexican society. Accordingly, Intersindical cobbles together various leftist perspectives, which include communist and anarchosyndicalist groupings as well as elements of the Partido Revolucionario de la Democrática (PRD). Rather than attempting to modify the state's neo-liberal project, Intersindical receives its inspiration from the January 1994 Zapatista uprising in Chiapas, and, therefore, looks to construct an alternative project that would place Mexican workers and campesinos at the center of any economic development model.

At its first national congress held September 3-5, 1997, Intersindical delegates voted to reject participation in the new Foro-dominated National Union of Workers (UNT), subsequently founded in November. The Intersindical delegates predicted that the UNT would follow the bureaucratic and conservative practices of the CTM and the CT. Fernando García Guzmán, a spokesman for Intersindical, said that "since conditions are not ripe for the creation of a new workers' central, any new alternative to the CTM and CT would only represent a continuation of the old-style unionism."[22] Herón Rosales, former president of the National Council of Workers (CNT), stated in the press that, "Hernández Juárez wants to become the next Fidel Velázquez," who after fifty years of presiding over Mexico's labor bureaucracy, passed away a month before the Intersindical congress.[23]

The 253 delegates attending the congress adopted a radical program. Representing the workers' union of the National Autonomous University (STUNAM), the Independent Union of Workers of the Metropolitan Autonomous University (SITUAM), the Fishing Industry Workers' Union (STP) and a myriad of left-wing groupings, they called for the repudiation of Mexico's foreign debt, stopping the government's neo-liberal economic policy and an end to the militarization of Mexico.[24]

Despite the biting criticism from Intersindical, the leadership of the Foro founded the UNT independent of the ruling PRI and is dedicated to internal union democracy. Claiming to represent 1.5 million workers in 200 organizations, the UNT leadership denounces state-party control of trade unions and labor federations. In principle, the UNT supports the notion of complete freedom for workers to affiliate with any political party that best represents their interest.[25] While delegates elected PRI members Hernández Juárez and Antonio Rosado García, head of the National Union of Social Security (SNTSS), as two of the UNT's presidents, a third president, Agustín Rodríguez Fuentes, head of the workers' union at the National Autonomous University, sympathizes with the PRD. He is joined by two vice presidents, Benedicto Martínez of the Frente Auténtico and Alejandra Barrales Magdaleno, former president of the flight attendants' union and new head of the FESEBES.

Especially important is the election of Martínez, who, as a member of the National Coordinating Committee of the Frente Auténtico and general secretary of the Union of Metal, Steel, Iron and Allied Industry Workers (STIMAHCS), played a major role in moving the UNT to a more radical position. As a particpant in Foro discussions, he earned a reputation for his persistent advocacy of untainted independent unionism. His influence is reflected in the UNT program, which calls for a reversal of state neo-liberal policy. The UNT program raises the demand that the Mexican state guarantee workers' health, social welfare and pension programs as well as a living wage. Central to the program, however, is the call for a new relationship between the state, political parties and the unions to guarantee the independence of the labor movement. The UNT seeks to resolve this set of issues by writing a new Federal Labor Law, which federation leaders hope would end the control of labor unions by the PRI and, at the same time, spawn labor relations correspondent to the new global economy.[26]

The push to amend the Federal Labor Law does not emanate exclusively from trade-union reformers. The Mexican business elite and multinational employers are also advocates of changes in the law that would permit more flexible work arrangements, better productivity and more quality control. Ricardo Martínez Rojas, head of the CCE articulates a position which has become known as "the new labor culture." Martínez Rojas and his supporters advocate modifying existing labor codes to permit the use of casual and part-time workers, pay by the hour rather than by the day or week, and the elimination of automatic seniority increments in pay.[26]

On August 13, 1997, the business elite and the charro labor bureaucracy renegotiated a labor-management-government pact, known as the Alliance for Growth (APEC). While APEC focuses on such issues as productivity, cooperation and union acquiescence to new forms of labor organization in the workplace, CTM and CT signatories of the pact oppose changes to the existing Federal Labor Law. Through representation on the boards of conciliation and arbitration and benefitting from its PRI status as the "official" labor movement, charro leaders of the CTM and the CT have used the law to maintain their power. Since the boards can deny independent unions legal status and refuse them rights to bargain with employers, charro leaders effectively have eliminated independent and democratic opposition movements. Essentially, both the CT and the CTM view changes in the existing Federal Labor Law as an assault on their privileges and protected status.

But the old-guard charro bureaucracy has increasingly become politically isolated. Dissident political parties, which include the PRD and the PAN, the UNT, the Frente Auténtico and major employer associations such as the CCE, all advocate radical reform of the Federal Labor Law. Fostering this process is Mexico's increasing integration into the U.S. market and world economy. U.S. corporations now account for almost seventy percent of all direct foreign investment in Mexico.[27] Major foreign companies have constructed many modern manufacturing facilities that utilize the most advanced technology and new forms of work organization. For multinational employers, the Mexican business elite, the Mexican worker and emerging reformist labor organizations, the entrenched charro bureaucracy and the legal system are archaic institutions irrelevant to the realities of globalization.

Globalization has been illuminated in the maquila industry, where battle lines have been drawn to reflect the crisis within Mexican political economy and the tensions that flow out of the contradictions between the state, foreign employers and the resurging labor movement. In Tijuana 200 factory workers employed by the Korean-owned Han Young plant, a Hyundai subsidiary, fought and believed they had won the right to form an independent union. The Han Young workers, who make tractor-trailer parts, voted to affiliate with the Frente Auténtico's Metal, Steel, Iron and Allied Workers' Union, founded by UNT Vice-President Benedicto Martínez. Ostensibly, the workers previously had been represented by the Confederación Revolucionaria de Obreros y Campesinos (CROC), a CT affiliate. The CROC's position within the Han Young plant, that of official representative of the workers, is illustrative of how the Federal Labor Law allows charro unions to provide "protection contracts" to employers.

Protection contracts are designed to protect employers from genuine unionization. The contracts create ghost unions, which arrange for a union to exist in name only in exchange for kickback payments to labor bureaucrats. These organizations are officially recognized by the boards of conciliation and arbitration, consequently preventing a competing union from gaining legal status. This type of racketeering is prevalent in Mexico City, the largest industrial area in the country, and exists on a smaller scale in the maquila industry as in the example of the Ford- LAMOSA facility in Nuevo Laredo. Having a protection contract in place, Han Young management refused to recognize the results of the election, which lacked a secret ballot and subsequently left independent union supporters open to retaliation. International publicity and pressure, especially from the AFL-CIO and labor solidarity groups in the U.S., finally forced Han Young management to recognize the workers' union. But the agreement contained a provision requiring the state to recognize officially the union's right to exist. In traditional fashion, the state of Baja California, which enforces the Federal Labor Law at the local level, refused to sign the agreement.[28]

The issues surrounding the events at Han Young have been magnified, in part due to the transformation taking place within labor in the United States. Both U.S. rank-and-file activists and official union leadership pointed to the Han Young case as proof that NAFTA failed to protect American workers from being undercut by Mexican workers, who are poorly paid and unprotected by a corrupt labor system.[29] The new AFL-CIO leadership has been supportive of the creation of alternatives to the charro labor system. Reinvigorated by the UPS strike and committed to a scale of organizing activity not seen since the 1930s, labor leaders are in agreement with the statement that "NAFTA has brought us to the realization of the importance of international solidarity."[30] Labor representatives from the U.S. attending the Frente Auténtico's eleventh annual convention in November 1997 supported the federation's pledge for a globalization from below to be carried out by an international alliance of labor unions, social movements and political opposition parties.[31]

Stanley A. Gacek, assistant director of the international affairs department of the AFL-CIO, spoke at the convention, telling delegates that "we must globalize our methods, whether they be work stoppages, boycotts, political mobilizations or campaigns against multinational corporations."[32] Dick Martin, speaking on behalf of the Canadian Labor Congress and as new president of ORIT, addressed the convention by calling the struggle over NAFTA the "biggest battle between capital and labor."[33] The AFL-CIO's recent transformation has resulted in renewed political clout. The U.S. Congress' rejection of President Clinton's fast-track NAFTA proposal for the remainder of the Western Hemisphere is a reflection of the AFL-CIO's ability to mobilize public support and marshal resources to influence U.S. politics.

Partly due to AFL-CIO efforts, the Han Young dispute has drawn the attention of dozens of U.S. lawmakers, who claim that Han Young demonstrates NAFTA's failure to protect workers on both sides of the border.[34]

Much like the globalization that transpired nearly 100 years ago, late twentieth-century capitalism is unsettling social relations in many parts of the world. In Mexico, as during the Porfiriato, the forces of global capitalism are transforming labor, the political system and other crucial sectors of society. The situation has generated political fragmentation, popular uprisings, increasing violence, militarization and a volatile economy. Within this context organized labor seeks to redefine itself.

Although events are unfolding at a rapid pace, it is certain that workers and their organizations will occupy important space in the national dialog surrounding the resolution of Mexico's current crisis. In the new global economy, labor's success in influencing the outcome of that dialog depends largely upon its ability to answer Ricardo Flores Magón's call of nearly a century ago to internationalize working-class organizations. And, although current circumstances certainly point to that possibility, it must be noted that the UNT, the largest new federation to challenge the old labor system, is an amalgam of conservatives, moderate reformers and radicals. Only time will reveal if organized labor can redefine itself independently and thereby contribute to the resolution of the crisis that now grips Mexican society.

ACRONYMS USED IN THIS VOLUME

AFL: American Federation of Labor

APEC: Alianza Para Crecemiento Económico (Alliance for Growth)

ATLAS: Agrupación de Trabajadores Latino Americanos Sindicalistas (Latin American Workers' Group)

ASARCO: American Smelting and Refining Company

BUO: Bloque Unidad Obrera (Workers Unity Bloc)

Casa: Casa del Obrera Mundial (House of the World Worker)

CGOCM: Confederación General de Obreros y Campesinos de México (General Confederation of Workers and Peasants of Mexico)

CGT: Confederación General de Trabajadores (General Confederation of Workers)

CIO: Congress of Industrial Organizations

CNDP: Comité Nacional de Defensa Proletaria (National Committee of Proletarian Defense)

CNT: Cámara Nacional del Trabajo (National Chamber of Labor) and Consejo Nacional de Trabajadores (National Council of Workers)

CONCAMIN: Confederación de Cámaras de Industria (Confederation of Chambers of Industries)

CROC: Confederación Revolucionaria de Obreros y Campesinos (Revolutionay Confederation of Workers and Peasants)

CROM: Confederación Regional Obrera Mexicana (Regional Confederation of Mexican Workers)

CSF: Confederación de Sociedades Ferrocarrileras (Confederation of Railroad Societies)

CT: Congreso del Trabajo (Congress of Labor)

CTAL: Confederación de Trabajadores de América Latina (Confederation of Latin American Workers)

CTM: Confederación de Trabajadores de México (Confederation of Mexican Workers)

CUT: Confederación Unica de Trabajadores (Sole Confederation of Mexican Workers)

FAT: Frente Auténtico del Trabajo (Authentic Labor Front)

FESEBES: Federación de Sindicatos de Bienes y Servicios (Federation of Unions of Goods and Services)

FCPM: Federación Comunista del Proletariado Mexicano (Communist Federation of the Mexican Proletariat)

FSODF: Federación de Sindicatos Obreros del Distrito Federal (Federation of Workers' Unions of the Federal District)

FSTDF: Federación de Sindicatos de los Trabajadores del Distrito Federal (Federation of Federal District Workers)

FSTSE: Federación de Sindicatos de Trabajadores al Servicio del Estado (Federation of Unions of Workers at the Service of the State)

GATT: General Agreement on Tariffs and Trade

IAM: International Association of Machinists

IWW: Industrial Workers of the World

MRM: Movimiento Revolucionario del Magisterio (Teachers' Revolutionary Movement)

MTW: Marine Transport Workers' Union

ORIT: Organización Regional Intra-Americana de Trabajadores (Inter-American Regional Organization of Workers)

PAFL: Pan American Federation of Labor

PAN: Partido Acción Nacional (National Action Party)

PEMEX: Petróleos Mexicanos (Mexican Petroleum Company)

PL: Partido Laborista (Labor Party)

PLM: Partido Liberal Mexicano (Mexican Liberal Party)

PNR: Partido Nacional Revolucionario (National Revolutionary Party, f. 1929—today the PRI)

PRD: Partido de la Revolucionario Democrática (Revolutionary Democratic Party)

PRI: Partido Revolucionario Institucional (Institutional Revolutionary Party)

SITUAM: Sindicato Independiente de los Trabajadores de la Universidad Autónoma Metropolitana (Independent Union of the Workers of the Metropolitan Autonomous University)

SME: Sindicato Mexicano de Electricstas (Electrical Workers' Union)

SNTE: Sindicato Nacional de Trabajadores de la Educación (National Union of Education Workers [Teachers' union])

SNTSS Sindicato Nacional de Trabajadores de Seguro Social (National Union of Social Security Workers)

SNTMMSRM: Sindicato Nacional de Trabajadores Mineros, Metalurgicos y Similares de la República Mexicana (Miners' and Metallurgical Workers' Union)

STIMAHCS: Sindicato de Trabajadores de la Industria Metalúrgica, Acero, Hierro y Compañias Similares (Union of Metal, Steel, Iron and Allied Industry Workers)

STFRM: Sindicato de Trabajadores Ferrocarrileros de la República Mexicana (Railroad Workers' Union)

STP: Sindicato de Trabajadores de la Industria de la Pesca (Fishing Industry Workers' Union)

STPRM: Sindicato de Trabajadores Petroleros de la República Mexicana (Petroleum Workers' Union)

STRM: Sindicato de Teléfonistas de la República Mexicana (Telephone Workers' Union of Mexico)

STUNAM: Sindicato de Trabajadores de la Universidad Nacional Autónoma de México (Workers' Union of the National Autonomous University of Mexico)

TD: Tendencia Democrática (Democratic Tendency)

UGOCM: Union General de Obreros y Campesinos de México (General Union of Workers and Peasants of Mexico)

UOI: Unidad Obrera Independiente (Independent Workers' Unity)

UNT: Union Nacional de Trabajadores (National Workers' Union)

WFTU: World Federation of Trade Unions

NOTES

INTRODUCTION: GLOBALISM AND REVOLUTION REVISITED

1. For the complete text of Ricardo Flores Magón's "Manifesto to the Workers of the World," see Colin M. MacLachlan, *Anarchism and the Mexican Revolution: The Political Trials of Ricardo Flores Magón in the United States* (Berkeley: University of California Press, 1991), 121.

2. *Ibid.*

3. A controversy among scholars of the Revolution over the importance of working-class participation and the role of nationalist ideology in the Revolution has emerged in recent years. While Ramón Eduardo Ruiz in *The Great Rebellion: Mexico, 1905-1924* (New York: Norton Books, 1980) and John Mason Hart in *Revolutionary Mexico: The Coming and the Process of the Mexican Revolution* (Berkeley: University of California Press, 1987) emphasize the importance of workers and their organizations to the growth of Mexican nationalism and the outbreak of the Revolution, Alan Knight in *The Mexican Revolution* 2 vols. (Cambridge: Cambridge University Press, 1986) and Jonathan Brown in *Oil and Revolution in Mexico* (Berkeley: University of California Press, 1993) maintain that nationalism was not a significant ideological force in the struggle against Díaz and that working-class organization exercised a peripheral role in the process and outcome of the 1910 Revolution.

4. For a discussion of Madero's political philosophy and its impact upon his decision making as president see Colin M. MacLachlan and William H. Beezley, *El Gran Pueblo: A History of Greater Mexico* (Englewood Cliffs, New Jersey: Prentice Hall Publishers, 1994), 185-87.

5. Donald Hodges, *Mexican Anarchism After the Revolution* (Austin: University of Texas Press, 1995), 149-56.

6. Antonio Gramsci, *Selections from the Prison Notebooks* (New York: International Publishers, 1971), 323.

7. *Ibid.*, 333.

8. For a recent study of the AFL and its activities in Mexico during the Revolution and an examination of AFL philosophy, see Gregg Andrews, *Shoulder to Shoulder? The American Federation of Labor, the Mexican Revolution, and the United States, 1910-1924* (Berkeley: University of California Press, 1991).

9. *Ibid.*, 199.

10. *Ibid.*

11. James Weinstein, *The Decline of Socialism in America, 1912-1925* (New York: Monthly Review Press, 1967), 30.

12. MacLachlan, *Anarchism*, 53.

13. Thomas F. O'Brien, *The Revolutionary Mission: American Enterprise in Latin America, 1900-1945* (Cambridge: Cambridge University Press, 1996), 303.

14. Barry Carr, *Marxism and Communism in Twentieth-Century Mexico* (Lincoln: University of Nebraska Press, 1992), 142-86.

15. Andrews, *Shoulder to Shoulder?*, 199-200.

ONE: A REVOLUTION FRAGMENTS

1. *El Imparcial*, 19 August 1906, 5 July 1906.

2. As explained in John M. Hart, *Anarchism and the Mexican Working Class, 1860-1931* (Austin: University of Texas Press, 1978), 12-18, the syndicalism espoused by Mexican industrial workers was rooted in the nation's precapitalist *agrarista* movements, which specifically demanded local autonomy from centralized government. Hart attributes the success of the *agraristas* to their ability to raise demands that were compatible with the values, traditions and aspirations of the sedentary-indigenous people, which incorporated egalitarianism, a distrust of government officials, absentee landlords and a suspicion of politics. The hypothesis that syndicalism incorporated all movements calling themselves anarchosyndicalist, revolutionary syndicalist, etc., is powerfully advanced in Robert Holton, *British Syndicalism, 1900-1914* (London: Pluto Press, 1976), 19-23.

3. Hart, *Revolutionary Mexico*, 61-62. For a more complete explanation of Porfirian labor policy see David Walker, "Porfirian Labor Politics: Working Class Organizations in Mexico City and Porfirio Diaz, 1876-1902," *The Americas* 37 (January 1981): 257-89.

4. Ruiz, *The Great Rebellion*, 63.

5. While MacLachlan and Beezley in *El Gran Pueblo* emphasize the rigidity of the political system as the principal cause of elite alienation, Hart stresses in *Revolutionary Mexico* the overwhelming North American economic presence in northern Mexico as the important component in understanding the roots of elite dissatisfaction.

6. For the PLM's activities in Puebla see David LaFrance, *The Mexican Revolution in Puebla, 1908-1913: The Maderista Movement and the Failure of Liberal Reform* (Wilmington: Scholarly Resources, 1989).

7. Rodolfo Acuña, *Occupied America: A History of Chicanos*, 3rd. ed. (New York: Harper & Row Publishers, 1988), 98. Also see Phil Mellinger, "The Men Have Become Organizers: Labor Conflict and Unionization in the Mexican Mining Communities of Arizona, 1900-1915," *Western Historical Quarterly* 3 (August 1992): 323-48.

8. For a discussion of the Western Federation of Miners see Melvyn Dubofsky, *We Shall Be All: A History of the IWW* (Chicago: Quadrangle Books, 1969), 36.

9. Herbert O. Buyer, "The Cananea Incident," *New Mexico Historical Review* 13 (October 1938): 387-415.

10. *Miners Magazine* (Denver), 21 February 1907; also see Juan Luis Sariego, "Anarquismo e historia social minera en el norte de Mexico, 1906-1918," *Historias* 8-9 (enero-junio 1985): 118-19.

11. Hart, *Revolutionary Mexico*, 72.

12. MacLachlan and Beezley, *El Gran Pueblo*, 186.

13. As cited in Hart, *Revolutionary Mexico*, 237.

14. *Ibid.*

15. For works that explore early railroad organization in Mexico and the influence of the AFL Brotherhood unions and the Knights of Labor on Mexican workers along the border and inside Mexico, see Richard Ulric Miller, "American Railroad Unions and the National Railways of Mexico: An Exercise in Nineteenth-Century Proletarian Manifest Destiny," *Labor History* 15 (Spring 1974): 239-60; Lorena Parlee, "The Impact of United States Railroad Unions on Organized Labor and Government Policy in Mexico (1880-1911)," *Hispanic American Historical Review* 64 (August 1984):

443-75; and Emilio Zamora, *El movimiento obrero en el sur de Texas, 1900-1920* (México, D.F.: SEP, 1986).

16. For Casa recruitment during 1913 see Hart, *Anarchism and the Mexican Working Class*, 124, 125, and for the *Tribuna Roja's* organizing in Tampico, 157.

17. Luis Araiza, *Historia del movimiento obrero mexicano*, vol. 3 (Mexico City: Edicíones Casa del Mundial, 1966), 138-58. For Villareal's efforts in recruiting urban workers to the Constitutionalist cause, see: Jacinto Huitrón, *Orígenes e historia del movimiento obrero en México* (Mexico City: Editores Mexicanos Unidos, 1975), 134-35.

18. Hart, *Revolutionary Mexico*, 278. Hart identifies Obregón as a member of what he calls the socially mobile *pequeña burguesía*. Obregón had business experience and varied family connections that tied him to the Sonoran oligarchy (his mother's name was Salido, and Hart refers to him as Obregón Salido throughout his book). He developed a very close relationship with W.R. Grace and Company as a chickpea farmer and personally witnessed some of Sonora's pre-1910 labor unrest.

19. Hart, *Anarchism and the Mexican Working Class*, 132-33.

20. Marjorie Ruth Clark, *Organized Labor in Mexico* (Chapel Hill: University of North Carolina Press, 1934), 30-31.

21. *Ibid.*, 32.

22. As cited in MacLachlan, *Anarchism and the Mexican Revolution*, 54.

23. *El Rebelde* (Los Angeles), 1 March 1915; also see *El Rebelde*, 15 March 1915.

24. Hart, *Revolutionary Mexico*, 307-08. Hart provides strong evidence that arms left at the port of Veracruz and later used by the Constitutionalist forces provided those forces with the margin of victory. While others—like Alan Knight in his two-volume study of the revolution, *The Mexican Revolution* (Cambridge: Cambridge University Press, 1986)—have downplayed the participation and importance of Mexican workers during the struggle, Hart's evidence also suggests that the military role of the Mexican working-class was central to the outcome of the 1910 Revolution.

25. Hart, *Anarchism and the Mexican Working Class*, 136-39; also see: John M. Hart, "The Urban Working Class and the Mexican Revolution: The Case of the Casa del Obrero Mundial," *Hispanic American Historical Review* (February 1978), 18-19. For *Ariete's* circulation in the United States see issues of *El Rebelde* (Los Angeles) from 1915 to 1917.

26. Hart, "The Urban Working Class," 140-41.

27. *Ibid.*

28. *Ibid.*, 152.

29. *Ibid.*, 154-55.

30. S. Leif Adelson, "The Cultural Roots of the Oil Workers' Unions in Tampico, 1910-1925," in Jonathan C. Brown and Alan Knight, eds., *The Mexican Petroleum Industry in the Twentieth Century* (Austin: University of Texas, 1992), 44.

31. For the IWW's role in organizing Chilean workers see Peter DeShazo, *Urban Workers and Labor Unions in Chile, 1902-1927* (Madison: University of Wisconsin Press, 1983). Information on the MTW's international meeting of union seamen can be found in Adolfo García, "The Workers Look to Montevideo," *Industrial Pioneer* (Chicago), January 1925, 7.

32. For Madero's overture to the WFM and the UMWA see MacLachlan, *Anarchism and the Mexican Revolution*, 53; for the IWW locals in Torreón see, "producción y trabajo," in *Luz* (Mexico City), 1 September 1917.

33. The Casa's activities in Tampico are discussed in S. Leif Adelson, "Cultural Roots," 34. The MTW and IWW's arrival in the area and its cooperation with the

Casa are highlighted in *Solidarity* (Cleveland), 3 February 1917. Information on IWW and Casa activity in Tampico can also be found in NARAW, State Department Records (hereafter cited as SD Records), Record Group 59 (hereafter cited as RG 59), 812.504/134; see confidential letter from Department of Treasury agent, Wilbur Carr, to the Secretary of State, 27 August 1917.

34. S. Leif Adelson, "Cultural Roots," 37-41.

35. George Rudé, *The Crowd in History, 1730-1848* (New York: Wiley & Sons, 1964), 234.

36. S. Leif Adelson, "Cultural Roots," 42.

37. *Ibid.*

38. *Ibid.*

39. *Ibid.*

40. *Ibid.*

41. *Ibid.*, 43.

42. Robert E. Quirk, *The Mexican Revolution and the Catholic Church, 1910-1929* (Bloomington: University of Indiana Press, 1973), 18.

43. *Ibid.*

44. Donald C. Hodges, *The Intellectual Foundations of the Nicaraguan Revolution* (Austin: University of Texas Press, 1986), 29-72. Hodges studies the origins of the Nicaraguan revolution and examines Augusto César Sandino's experience as a worker for the Huasteca Petroleum Company during the 1920s. Hodges points out the weakness of the Catholic Church and the strength of Freemasonry, and Mexican Spiritualism in the Tampico area. He correctly identifies Mexican Spiritualism, begun by Father Elías, a recalcitrant Roman Catholic priest, in 1861 as a countercultural movement against Roman Catholicism during the period when Mexico suffered foreign invasion, civil war and the socially disrupting effects of nascent industrialization.

45. Harry Braverman, *Labor and Monopoly Capital: The Degradation of Work in the Twentieth Century* (New York: Monthly Review Press, 1974). Braverman's analysis elevated the idea that the continuing degradation of work under capitalism would inexorably homogenize the conditions that working people confront on the job. He argued that capitalist dynamics continually transform the labor process, increasingly subjugating workers to their employers and fragmenting their jobs. This thesis is also powerfully advanced in David M. Gordon, Richard Edwards and Michael Reich, *Segmented Work, Divided Workers: The Historical Transformation of Labor in the United States* (Cambridge: Cambridge University Press, 1982).

46. Norman Caulfield, "Wobblies and Mexican Workers in Mining and Petroleum, 1905-1924," *International Review of Social History* 46 (1995): 56-57.

47. NARAW, SD Records, RG 59, 812.504/46, letter from American Consul Claude I. Dawson to the Secretary of State, 6 April 1916.

48. *Ibid.*

49. *Ibid.*

50. *El Rebelde* (Los Angeles), 3 February 1917; also see *Solidarity* (Cleveland), 10 February 1917.

51. NARAW, SD Records, RG 59, 812.504/81, telegram from Dawson to the Secretary of State, April 23, 1917.

52. *Ibid.*

53. *Ibid.*

54. *Ibid.*, 812.504/82; 812.504/85, telegrams from Dawson to the Secretary of State, 24 and 26 April 1917.

55. *Ibid.*, 812.504/86, telegram from American Ambassador to the Secretary of State and Consul Dawson, 27 April 1917.

56. *Ibid.*, 812.504/87, telegram from Dawson to the Secretary of State, 30 April 1917.

57. *Ibid.*, 812.504/91, telegram from the USS *Tacoma* to the Secretary of Navy, 2 May 1917.

58. *Ibid.*, 812.504/95, letter from Consul Dawson to the Secretary of State, 2 May 1917.

59. *Ibid.*, 812.504/107A, telegram from Secretary of State Robert Lansing to American Consul Dawson. Information was received by Lansing from the Department of Navy, 18 June 1917 (812.504/114), telegram from Dawson to Secretary of State Lansing, 16 July 1917; for the strike's progression and activities see *El Rebelde* (Los Angeles), 11 August 1917.

60. *Ibid.*, 812.504/116, letter from Pierce Oil Corporation Vice-President Eben Richards to Assistant Secretary of State Frank L. Polk, 24 July 1917. Reply was given to Pierce Oil from the State Department on 27 July 1917. For MTW Local #100's activities during the 1917 strike see *El Rebelde* (Los Angeles), 11 August 1917.

61. *Ibid.*, 812.504/117, telegram from Dawson to the Secretary of State, 24 July 1917.

62. *Ibid.*, 812.504/117, telegram to Mexican Petroleum Company, New York, N.Y., from George Paddleford, local manager in Tampico, 26 July 1917.

63. *Ibid.*, 812.504/124, Special Situation Report from Captain Richardson, Commander of Mexican Patrol, to the Department of Navy, 25 July 1917.

64. *Ibid.*

65. *Ibid.*, 812.504/124, telegram sent to Naval Operations Office, Washington, D.C., 30 July 1917, from the USS *Annapolis*. Also see 812.504/124, letter sent from Pierce Oil Corporation, Vice-President Eben Richards to the Acting Secretary of State, Frank L. Polk, 2 August 1917. For the arrest of IWW members see *El Rebelde* (Los Angeles), 11 August 1917.

66. NARAW, SD Records, RG 59, 812.504/151, letter from American Consul Claude Dawson to the Secretary of State, 21 November 1917; also see 812.504/154, telegram from USS *Annapolis* to the Department of Navy, Washington, D.C., 11 February 1918.

67. *El Rebelde* (Los Angeles), 25 August 1917.

68. Rosendo Salazar and José G. Escobedo, *Las pugnas de la gleba* (Mexico, D.F.: Editorial Avante, 1923), 192; also see Rosendo Salazar in *La Casadel Obrero Mundial* (Mexico, D.F.: Costa-Amic, 1962), 229.

69. Salazar and Escobedo, *Las pugnas de la gleba*, 244.

70. Hart, *Revolutionary Mexico*, 332.

71. Clark, *Organized Labor*, 50.

TWO: FOREIGN INTERESTS, ELITES AND ORGANIZED LABOR IN TRANSITION

1. Rodolfo Acuña, *Occupied America: A History of Chicanos* (New York: Harper & Row, 1988), 166.

2. "The Strike at Ajo," *Miners' Magazine* (Denver), January-February 1917; also see Philip S. Foner, *Labor and World War I, 1914-1918*, vol. 7 in the *History of the Labor Movement in the United States* (New York: International Publishers, 1973), 265-66.

3. Foner, *Labor and World War I*, 265-66.

4. *Ibid.*

5. *Ibid.*, 267.

6. *Ibid.*, 269.

7. *Ibid.*

8. *Ibid.*, 267.

9. *Ibid.*, 273.

10. *Ibid.*, 275. See also *The Journal of Arizona History,* 18 (Summer 1997), passim.

11. NARAW, MID, RG 165, 10110-12, letter from M.H. McLearn, manager of the Phelps-Dodge Corporation, Morenci, Arizona, 17 May 1917, to Agent R.L. Barnes, Fort Sam Houston, San Antonio, Texas. In the letter McLearn stated that he was working closely with Department of Justice Agent Harris.

12. NARAW, MID, RG 165, 10110-85, page five (5) of a report prepared by Justice Department Agent S. Guzmán on "IWW activities in the Globe-Miami District," 25 September 1917.

13. *Ibid.*, excerpts of Rodríguez and Blanco's speeches are found in S. Guzmán's report on "IWW activities in the Globe-Miami District," under the subtitle, "Prominent Members and Officials of the IWW Movement."

14. *Ibid.*

15. *Ibid.*, 10110-13, Report from S. Guzmán on "IWW activities at Globe-Miami," 14 March 1918.

16. N. Gordon Levin, Jr., *Woodrow Wilson and World Politics: America's Response to War and Revolution* (London: Oxford University Press, 1968), 193.

17. *Ibid.*, 10110-85, report from S. Guzmán on "IWW activities in the Globe-Miami District," 25 September 1917.

18. *Ibid.*

19. *Ibid.*, 10110-12, report from Agent John W. Ganzhorn on "IWW Activities at Globe and Vicinity," 24 February 1918.

20. *Ibid.*, 100110-3, report from S. Guzmán concerning the arrests of IWW agitators, Azuara, Martínez and Negreira, 22 March 1918. For a sample of Martínez's contributions to *El Rebelde*, see "Latigazos a los mártires de la A.S.F. of L. de Morenci, Arizona, Local #2," in *El Rebelde* (Los Angeles), 26 December 1915.

21. *Ibid.*, 10110-12, report from Agent S. Guzmán on "IWW activities in Globe-Miami," 6 March 1918.

22. Foner, *Labor and World War I*, 279.

23. *Ibid.*, 280.

24. *Ibid.*

25. *Ibid.*

26. Andrews, *Shoulder To Shoulder?*, 1-12. This work is a major reinterpretation of the AFL's role in the Mexican Revolution. In the introduction, where Andrews presents a sweeping review of the literature on the subject, he posits that Gompers and the AFL promoted reform unionism in Mexico to stabilize the revolution, improve living standards and thereby provide a market for manufactured goods produced by American workers. For other accounts on the role of the AFL in Mexico see Harvey A. Levenstein, *Labor Organizations in the United States and Mexico: A History of Their Relations* (Westport: Greenwood Publishing Company, 1971); Sinclair Snow, *The Pan-American Federation of Labor* (Durham: Duke University Press, 1964), and Jack Scott, *Yankee Unions, Go Home! How the AFL Helped the U.S. Build and Empire in Latin America* (Vancouver: New Star Books, 1978).

27. Hart, *Anarchism and the Mexican Working Class*, 158.

28. *Ibid.*

29. As cited in Andrews, *Shoulder to Shoulder?*, 85. Andrews points out that the secret aim of the AFL leaders was to use Mexican labor's influence with Carranza to convince him to support the Allied war effort in Europe, but Iglesias, Lord and Murray did not mention the war during their Mexican visit.

30. *Ibid.*

31. *Ibid.*, 85-86.

32. *Ibid.*, 90.

33. *Ibid.*, 91.

34. Paco Ignacio Taibo, *Los Bolshevikis: historia narrativa de los orígenes del comunismo en México, 1919-1925* (Mexico: Editorial Joaquín, 1986), 19-20.

35. *Ibid.*, 21.

36. *Ibid.*, 21-22.

37. Hart, *Anarchism and the Mexican Working Class*, 159.

38. Archivo General de la Nación, México, D.F., hereafter cited as (AGN) Ramo de Presidentes, Obregón-Calles, numero de expediente 601-M-2, hereafter cited as no. exp. A series of letters written to the president of the republic from the undersecretary of the Department of Hacienda, Manuel Padres, and the undersecretary of Foreign Relations, Aarón Sáenz, dated from 4 August 1920 to 21 July 1921, reveal that Morones received payments between 1,000 to 2,007.78 pesos to attend PAFL meetings in the United States from July 1919 to July 1921.

39. Andrews, *Shoulder to Shoulder?*, 95-96.

40. *La Nueva Solidaridad* (Chicago), 14 October 1919; also see the text of Borrán's statement in U.S. Congress and Senate, *Investigation of Mexican Affairs, 1919-1920*, 2826-28.

41. Ignacio Taibo, *Los Bolshevikis*, 57-60.

42. AGN, Departamento de Trabajo (DT), Caja 213, no. exp. 33, Gómez Hare and E. Artasanchy to Srio. de Industria, Comercio y Trabajo, 27 de febrero 1920.

43. *Ibid.*

44. *Ibid.*, 60-61.

45. Linn A.E. Gale, "The War Against Gomperism in Mexico," *One Big Union Monthly* (Chicago), November 1919.

46. Andrews, *Shoulder to Shoulder?*, 96-98.

47. José Refugio Rodríguez, "Mexican IWW Permanently Organized," *One Big Union Monthly* (Chicago), August 1920; also see "The Mexican IWW," *One Big Union Monthly* (Chicago), December 1920.

48. "The Mexican IWW," *One Big Union Monthly* (Chicago), November 1919.

49. NARAW, SD Records, RG 59, 812.504/152, letter to R.C. Tanis, Division of Mexican Affairs, U.S. State Department, from William Yeandle, Jr., of the United States Smelting, Refining and Mining Co., 5 December 1917.

50. NARAW, MID Records, RG 165, 10058-0-9, letter from C.D. Garrison, Army Intelligence Officer, Douglas, Arizona, to A.C. of S. for M. 8th Corps Area, Fort Sam Houston, San Antonio, Texas, 15 November 1920. For a chronology of the IWW's activities in Cananea, Sonora, Chihuahua and Arizona see *El Rebelde* (Los Angeles), 15 March 1915; letter from Tomás Martínez, "Compañeros de la Unión Obrera de Cananea, ¡Alerta! in *El Rebelde* (Los Angeles), 28 August 1915; also see *Luz* (Mexico City), 1 May 1919, letter from IWW members Benito Pavón, Edmundo Ibarra and Pablo Ollo to Jacinto Huitrón, editor.

51. NARAW, MID Records, RG 165, 10058-0-9, letter from Garrison to M.I. 8th Corps Area, Fort Sam Houston, San Antonio, Texas, 15 November 1920.

52. *Ibid.*

53. Marvin D. Bernstein, *The Mexican Mining Industry, 1890-1950* (Albany: State University of New York, 1964), 127.

54. NARAW, MID Records, RG 165, 10058-0-9, letter from C.D. Garrison to Headquarters, Fort Sam Houston, San Antonio, Texas, 15 November 1920.

55. NARAW, SD Records, RG 59, 812.504/260, letter from American Consular Agent J.M. Gibbs in Cananea to the Secretary of State and to the American Consul, Francis J. Dyer at Nogales, Sonora, 6 October 1920. Agent Gibbs states in the letter that he received the information from Cananea Company officials George Young and T. Evans.

56. NARAW, MID Records, RG 165, 10058-0-9, letter from C.D. Garrison, Intelligence Officer, Douglas, Arizona, to Headquarters, Fort Sam Houston, San Antonio, Texas, 15 November 1920.

57. NARAW, SD Records, RG 59, 812.504/262, letter from Consul Blocker at Piedras Negras, Coahuila, to the Secretary of State, 3 November 1920.

58. *Ibid.*

59. *Ibid.*, 812.504/278: telegram from Consul William Blocker at Eagle Pass, Texas, to the Secretary of State, 22 November 1920; letter from Consul Blocker at Piedras Negras to the Secretary of State, 11 December 1920.

60. NARAW, SD Records, RG 59, 812.504/222, telegram from Consul Dawson at Tampico to the Secretary of State, 9 July 1920. For the IWW's role in the strike and their cooperation with *El Grupo Hermanos Rojo*, see *Solidarity* (Chicago), 10 January 1920.

61. Julio Valdivieso Castillo, *Historia del movimiento sindicato petrolero en Minatitlán, Veracruz* (Mexico, D.F.: Imprenta Mexicana, 1963), 24-25; also see Francisco Colmenares, *Petrolero y lucha de clases en Mexico, 1864-1982* (Mexico, D.F.: Ediciones El Caballito, S.A., 1982), 43-44.

62. NARAW, SD Records, RG 59, 812.504/222, telegram from Consul Dawson at Tampico to the Secretary of State, 9 July 1920.

63. Andrews, *Shoulder to Shoulder?*, 100-02.

64. M. Paley, "The Pan-American Federation of Labor," *Solidarity* (Chicago), 19 February 1921.

65. *Ibid.*

66. *Ibid.*, 26 February 1921.

67. *Ibid.*

68. *Ibid.*, 19 February 1921.

69. Ignacio Taibo, *Los Bolshevikis*, 113-16.

70. Paco Ignacio Taibo, II, "El breve matrimonio rojo: comunistas y anarchosyndicalistas en la CGT en 1921," *Historias* 8-9 (octubre-diciembre): 50.

71. *Ibid.*, 113-16, 137, 141.

72. *Ibid.*, 118-19.

73. Ignacio Taibo, "El breve matrimonio rojo," 50-51.

74. G. Baena Paz, "La confederación general de trabajadores 1921-1931," *Revista Mexicana de Ciencias Políticas y Sociales* 83 (enero-marzo 1976): 113-86; also see Arnaldo Córdova, "En una época de crisis 1928-1934" in vol. 9 of *La clase obrera en la historia de México*, Pablo González Casanova, ed. (Mexico, D.F.: Siglo Veintiuno Editores, 1980); and *Solidaridad* (Veracruz), 10 de julio 1921.

75. *El Demócrata*, 30 May 1921.

76. Ignacio Taibo, "El breve matrimonio rojo," 52; Robert J. Alexander, *Communism in Latin America* (New Brunswick: New Jersey University Press, 1957), 320.

77. *Solidaridad* (Chicago), 30 December 1921.

78. *Ibid.*, 18 June 1921.

79. S. Leif Adelson, "Coyuntura y conciencia: factores convergentes en la fundación de los sindicatos petroleros de Tampico durante la década de 1920," *El trabajo y los trabajadores en la historia de México/Labor and Laborers through Mexican History* (Tucson: El Colegio de México and the University of Arizona Press, 1979), 640.

80. "Un congreso obrero que resultó político," *Solidaridad* (Veracruz), no. 1, 10 July 1921; *El Demócrata*, 2, 3, and 15 July 1921.

81. Hart, *Anarchism and the Mexican Working Class*, 161.

82. Andrews, *Shoulder to Shoulder?*, 107-23. In his chapter on Mexican Reconstruction, Andrews demonstrates that despite the Harding administration's anti-labor stance in the U.S., he and other members of his administration were willing to work with Gompers and the AFL to smooth over relations with the Obregón government. The efforts culminated with the signing of the Bucareli Accords in August 1923, which gave the Mexican government formal diplomatic recognition from the United States.

83. *Ibid.*, 116-17.

84. *Ibid.*, 109-10.

85. Clark, *Organized Labor*, 101; Hart, *Anarchism and the Mexican Working Class*, 164-65.

86. Clark, *Organized Labor*, 193-97. Based on solid primary research, Clark discusses conditions in the textile industry and explains the battle between CGT and CROM unions as well as the tactic of lockout by employers.

87. Clark, *Organized Labor*, 180.

88. In late 1922, Haberman discussed the plan to destroy the CGT with Louis DeNette, an agent from the United States Justice Department's Bureau of Investigation. Calling himself the author of a "well-guarded secret in Mexican Governmental circles," Haberman appears to have correctly forecasted what occurred during the streetcar strike in Mexico City during January and February 1923 and also in the textile industry during the summer of that year. See Andrews, *Shoulder to Shoulder?*, 158. Haberman, in an interview with J. Edgar Hoover on 2 August 1921, discussed the deportations and confirmed that they had received full approval from the CROM and the AFL. During the interview Haberman offered himself as an informant on labor activity in Mexico, NARAW, SD Records, RG 165, 10058-D-91.

89. Andrews, *Shoulder to Shoulder?*, 122.

90. *Ibid.*, 124.

91. NARAW, SD Records, RG 59, John Wood to the Secretary of State, 21 December 1923, 23 February 1924, 812/26647, 812/27026.

92. *Ibid.*

93. *Ibid.*, 812.504/520, letter from American Vice-Consul at Chihuahua Thomas McEnelly to the Secretary of State, 8 November 1923. McEnelly worked closely with J. Norris Hobart, ASARCO's welfare representative, who complained of constant IWW agitation at company facilities in Chihuahua.

94. *Solidaridad* (Chicago), 5 April 1924.

95. *Ibid.*, 2 June 1923.

96. *Ibid.*

97. *El Diario* (Chihuahua, Mexico), 2 May 1923.

98. NARAW, SD Records, RG 59, 812.504/565, letter from American Consul Thomas McEnelly to the Secretary of State, 24 May 1924. Also see *Solidarity* (Chicago), 21 May 1924, and *Solidaridad* (Chicago), 12 July 1924.

99. *Ibid.*

100. NARAW, SD Records, RG 59, 812.504/567, letter from American Consul McEnelly to the Secretary of State, 27 May 1924. Also see *Solidaridad* (Chicago), 31 May 1924.

101. *Solidaridad* (Chicago), 26 July 1924.

102. The willingness of American-owned mining companies to pay higher wages and work with reformist AFL-style unions is documented before and after the 1924 Santa Eulalia strike. Andrews, in *Shoulder to Shoulder?*, 85-86, points out that in 1918, employers in the mining industry were agreeable to pay higher wages if Mexican labor would change its philosophical orientation and comply to company work rules. Clark in *Organized Labor*, 118, cites Rafael García's *La situación de la industria minera* (1928), which states that mining management would pay higher wages if they could increase the efficiency of the workers.

103. NARAW, SD Records, RG 59, 812.504/533, letter to Secretary of State Charles Evans Hughes from Guy Stevens, the director of the Association of Producers of Petroleum in Mexico, New York, N.Y., 19 February 1924. For another report on the 1924 Tampico strike see "Tampico: A Class War Skirmish," *Industrial Pioneer* (Chicago), January 1925.

104. See *Solidarity* (Chicago), 28 May 1924 and 4 June 1924 for the support given to the El Aguila strikers by other Tampico unions.

105. As cited in Andrews, *Shoulder to Shoulder?*, 134.

106. *Ibid.*, 133.

107. As cited in Severo Iglesias, *Sindicalismo y socialismo en México* (Mexico, D.F.: Grijalbo Press, 1970), 98.

108. Cited in Rosendo Salazar, *Historia de las luchas proletarios de México* (Mexico City: Avante, 1938), 200.

THREE: WORKING-CLASS NATIONALISM AND THE POLITICS OF PRODUCTION

1. Clark, *Organized Labor*, 112-13.

2. Colmenares, *Petrolero y lucha*, 65-70; Barry Carr, *El Movimiento obrero y la política en México, 1910-1929* (Mexico City: Ediciones Era, 1981), 171.

3. *Ibid.*, 114-15.

4. *Ibid.*, 117; also see Carr, *Movimiento obrero*, 172-73.

5. Typical of organizations that searched for new alternatives to the CROM were the textile and Federation of State Employees in Orizaba, Veracruz, a CROM stronghold. The issues of their newspaper, *Pro-Paria*, from October 1928 to December 1929, consistently criticize Morones and the CROM's leadership failures to fight for workers' rights embodied in the 1917 Constitution.

6. James D. Cockroft, *Mexico: Class Formation, Capital Accumulation and the State* (New York: Monthly Review Press, 1983), 122.

7. Miguel Angel Calderón, *El impacto de la crisis de 1929 en México* (Mexico, D.F.: SepSetentas, 1982), 82-96.

8. Alex Saragoza, *The Monterrey Elite and the Mexican State, 1880-1940* (Austin: University of Texas Press, 1988), 156.

9. *Ibid.*, 134.

10. *Ibid.*, 143.

11. *Ibid.*, 159.

12. *Ibid.*, 164.

13. Francie R. Chassen de López, *Lombardo Toledano y el movimiento obrero mexicano, 1917-1940* (Mexico: Extemporaneous, 1977), 91-92. This work is the most comprehensive treatment of Lombardo's political career as a Mexican trade unionist, Marxist and politician.

14. Chassen de López, *Lombardo Toledano*, 158.

15. Córdova, *En una epoca de crisis, 1928-1934* vol. 9 of *La clase obrera en la historia de México* (Mexico: Siglo Veintuno Editores, 1980), 64, 65, 69-75.

16. Cockroft, *Mexico*, 126-27.

17. Arturo Anguiano, *El estado y la política obrera del cardenismo*, 3rd ed. (Mexico, D.F.: Ediciones Era, 1978), 55-57.

18. Saragoza, *The Monterrey Elite*, 174; also see Anguiano, *El estado y la política obrera*, 70-72.

19. Saragoza, *The Monterrey Elite*, 178.

20. *Ibid.*

21. *Ibid.*, 179.

22. *Ibid.*, 180.

23. For analysis of the February 1936 lockout by Monterrey businessmen see Saragoza, *The Monterrey Elite*, and Rosendo Salazar, *La CTM, su historia y su significado* (Mexico: Ediciones T.C. Modelo, S.C.L., 1956), 181-83; for an elaboration on Cárdenas' Fourteen Points see Joe Ashby, *Organized Labor and the Mexican Revolution under Lázaro Cárdenas* (Chapel Hill: University of North Carolina Press, 1967), 27.

24. Ashby, *Organized Labor*, 43.

25. "La huelga de los ferrocarriles sofocada. Protesta de la CTM," *Futuro* 4 (junio 1936): 7. Also see Sergio L. Yañez Reyes, *Génesis de la burocracia sindical cetemista* (Mexico: Ediciones El Caballito, 1984), 109.

26. *Ibid.*

27. "Significado de la reciente huelga eléctrica," *Futuro* 34 (diciembre 1938): 42. Also see Yañez Reyes, *Génesis*, 119.

28. "El porqué de la huelga eléctrica" (transcription from public interview given by Lombardo Toledano), in *Confederación de Trabajadores de México, (CTM), 1936-1941* (Mexico: Talleres Tipográficas Modelo, S.A., 1942), 109; Also see Samuel León González and Ignacio Marván, *En el cardenismo, 1934-1940*, vol. 10 of *La clase obrera en la historia de Méxicoa* (Mexico: Siglo Veintiuno Editores, 1985), 227.

29. For oil worker unionization in the early 1930s see José Rivera Castro, "Periodización del sindicalismo petrolero," in Javier Aguilar, ed., *Petroleros*, vol. 1 of *Los sindicatos nacionales en el México contemporáneo* (Mexico: G.V. Editores, 1986), 22-28.

30. Cited in Andrews, *Shoulder to Shoulder?*, 113.

31. For a discussion of oil unions in Poza Rica, see Alberto J. Olvera, "The Rise and Fall of Union Democracy in Poza Rica, 1932-1940," in Jonathan C. Brown and Alan Knight, eds., *The Mexican Petroleum Industry in the Twentieth Century* (Austin: University of Texas Press, 1992), 71.

32. *Ibid.*, 64.

33. *Ibid.*

34. *Ibid.*, 75.

35. Two major works treat the subject of the worker administration controversy. Joe Ashby writes an account supportive of Cárdenas in *Organized Labor*, 256-71; and Fabio Barbosa Cano takes the side of labor in his essay "El movimiento petrolero en 1938-40" in Aguilar, *Petroleros*, 59-111.

36. Harvey Levenstein, "Leninists Undone By Leninism: Communism and Unionism in the United States and Mexico, 1935-1939," *Labor History* 2 (Spring 1981): 255.

37. Olvera, "The Rise and Fall of Union Democracy."

38. *Ibid.*

39. *Ibid.*

40. *Ibid.*

41. *Ibid.*, 78.

42. Cited in Ashby, *Organized Labor*, 33.

43. O'Brien, *The Revolutionary Mission*, 303-04.

44. *Ibid.*, 306.

45. For an excellent overview of the CIO's role in Mexico during the oil expropriation, see Henry W. Berger, "Crisis Diplomacy, 1930-1939," in Willam Appleman Williams, ed., *From Colony to Empire: Essays in the History of American Foreign Relations* (New York: John Wiley & Sons, 1972), 294-336.

46. *Mexican Labor News*, 1 July 1936. For active cooperation between the CTM and the CIO during strikes on both sides of the border, and the CIO's efforts to organize Mexicans in the U.S. see *CIO News*, 2 July 1938.

47. For the AFL's view on trade see the *American Federationist* 39 (April 1932): 379. The Lewis quote is taken from the *CIO News*, September 1938.

48. *Mexican Labor News*, 30 September 1936, 2.

49. For the AFL's ideology during the 1930s when it encountered bitter conflict with the CIO on a number of questions, see Irving Bernstein, *The Turbulent Years: A History of the American Worker, 1933-1941* (Boston: Houghton & Mifflin, 1971), 682-767.

50. This thesis is powerfully advanced in Ashby, *Organized Labor*.

51. For the CTM's advocacy of a multi-class alliance against foreigners and the fascist threat, see Vicente Lombardo Toledano, "La CTM ante la amenaza fascista," *Futuro* (marzo 1938), 9-14. For the CTM's defense of the oil expropriation and the development of a multi-class alliance to defend it, see Vicente Lombardo Toledano, "Nuestra democracia y el petróleo," *Futuro* (abril 1939), 12-14.

52. Aguilar, *Los sindicatos*, 72-73.

53. *Ibid.*

54. See Ruth Adler, "Worker Participation in the Administration of the Petroleum Industry, 1938-1940," in Brown and Knight, *The Mexican Petroleum Industry*, 140-144.

55. Aguilar, *Los sindicatos*, 72-73.

56. Cockroft, *Mexico*, 132.

57. Vicente Lombardo Toledano, "El cooperativismo y los trabajadores," *Futuro* (enero 1938).

58. Nora Hamilton, *The Limits of State Autonomy* (Princeton, New Jersey: Princeton University Press, 1982), 235-36.

59. Jorge Basurto, *Cárdenas y el poder sindical* (Mexico: Ediciones Era, 1975), 162-63.

FOUR: ELITE NATIONALISM AND THE POLITICS OF PRODUCTION

1. Cited in Cockroft, *Mexico*, 154.

2. NARAW, SD Records, RG 59, 812.504/1960, George Shaw to the Secretary of State, 19 March 1940.

3. *Excélsior*, 2 February 1940.

4. *Ibid.*, 22 April 1940.

5. *El Norte* (Monterrey), 19 October 1940.

6. NARAW SD Records RG 59, 812.5045/2027, G.R. Wilson, American Consul at Piedras Negras, to the Secretary of State, 10 October 1940.

7. *El Popular*, 24 September 1941.

8. NARAW, SD Records, RG 59, 812.5043/48, U.S. Embassy to the Secretary of State, 16 June 1941.

9. *Ibid.*, 812.5045/985, letter from J. Edgar Hoover to Adolph A. Berle, Jr., 18 February 1942.

10. *Ibid.*, 812.504/2115, Harold Finley, First Secretary of the U.S. Embassy, to the Secretary of State, 14 September 1942.

11. *Ibid.*, 812.5045/1037, U.S. Embassy to the Secretary of State, 5 April 1944.

12. *Ibid.*, 812.504/2115, Harold Finley, First Secretary of the U.S. Embassy, to the Secretary of State, 14 September 1942.

13. *Ibid.*, 812.504/4-445 for Ailshie's interpretive report to the Secretary of State; Annual Reports from the *Ministry of Labor* and the *Banco de Mexico*, August 1944.

14. Bernstein, *Mexican Mining*, 226.

15. *Ibid.*, 226-28.

16. *Ibid.*

17. For the Phelps-Dodge walkout see *1906* (Cananea), 25 March 1943, weekly newspaper published by the mining union at Cananea, Sonora; for the outcome of the strike see NARAW, SD Records, RG 59, 812.5045/1021; American Consul at Agua Prieta to the Secretary of State, in *Monthly Report*, April 1943.

18. NARAW, SD Records, RG 59, 812.5045/6-1544, Messersmith to the Secretary of State, *Monthly Report*, April 1944.

19. *Ibid.*, 812.5045/1017; Henry S. Waterman, American Consul at Monterrey, to the Secretary of State, 20 March 1944.

20. *Ibid.*, 812.5045/1017, Waterman to the Secretary of State, 1 April 1944.

21. *El Porvenir* (Monterrey), 1 April 1944.

22. *Ibid.*

23. *Ibid.*

24. *Excélsior* (Mexico City), 14 June 1944.

25. *El Popular* (Mexico City), 17 June 1944.

26. See Chassen de López, *Lombardo Toledano*; and Robert Millon, *Mexican Marxist: Vicente Lombardo Toledano* (Chapel Hill: University of North Carolina Press, 1966) for an examination of Lombardo's politics, philosophy and career as a trade-union leader.

27. NARAW, SD Records, RG 59, 812.5041/1-1845, Henry F. Holland to the Secretary of State, 16 January 1945.

28. *Ibid.*, 812.504/2-1545, Ailshie's interpretive comment on Mexican labor to the Secretary of State, 15 February 1945.

29. *Ibid.*, 812.504/4-445, Ailshie's interpretive reports on Mexican labor, February and March 1945.

30. *Ibid.*, 812.504/2-1545; Ailshie's interpretive comment on Mexican labor to the Secretary of State, 15 February 1945.

31. *El Popular* (Mexico City), 24 March 1945.

32. *Excélsior* (Mexico City), 21 September 1945.

33. For an excellent analysis of the collaborationist policies of the CTM during this period see Jorge Basurto, *Del avilacamachismo al alemanismo* (1940-1952), vol. 11 of *La clase obrera en la historia de México* (Mexico: Siglo Veintiuno, 1984), 72-76; and Virginia López Villegas-Manjarrez, *La CTM vs. otras organizaciones obreras* (Mexico: Ediciones El Caballito, 1983).

34. As cited in Stephen R. Niblo, *War, Diplomacy, and Development: The United States and Mexico, 1938-1954* (Wilmington, Delaware: Scholarly Resources, 1995), 199.

35. NARAW, SD Records, RG 59, 812.504/2-1545, interpretive comment on Mexican labor by Ailshie, 15 February 1945.

36. *Ibid.*, 812.504/4-445, interpretive comment on Mexican labor by Ailshie for February and March, 1945; 812.504/5-345, interpretive comment on Mexican labor by Ailshie, April 1945.

37. NARAW, SD Records, RG 59, 812.5045, letter from William A. Conkright, Senior Economic Analyst at the U.S. Embassy in Mexico City, to the Secretary of State, 3 March 1944.

38. *Excélsior* (Mexico City), 6 December 1945.

39. NARAW, SD Records, RG 59, 812.504/12-1145, Ailshie's monthly report on Mexican labor, June 1945.

40. *Excélsior* (Mexico City), 15 July 1945.

41. *Ibid.*, 6 December 1945.

42. NAWRAW 812.5043/10-3145, Manifesto issued by the Federation of Jalisco Workers, and Ailshie's report to the Secretary of the State, 30 September 1945.

43. *Ibid.*

44. *Ibid.*, 812.5045/7-146, Politico Labor Report, "Círculo Azul Strike," by Henry S. Waterman, American Consul General at Monterrey, 1 July 1946.

45. *Ibid.*

46. On the differences between the AFL and the CIO with regard to Mexico in the 1930s see Levenstein, *Labor Organizations*, ch. 10.

47. *CIO News*, 12 March 1945.

48. *Ibid.*

49. For an extensive treatment of the cooperation forged between organized labor and American industrialists during World War II see Robert Zieger, *The CIO, 1935-1955* (Chapel Hill: University of North Carolina Press, 1995).

50. As cited in Scott, *Yankee Unions*, 195.

51. *Ibid.*, 210.

52. NARAW, SD Records, RG 59, 812.504/2273, Ailshie, "Memorandum of Conversation with Mr. Lombardo Toledano by a member of the Staff of the Embassy," 17 April 1944.

53. Niblo, *War, Diplomacy, and Development*, 10-11.

54. Scott, *Yankee Unions*, 208-09.

55. NARAW, SD Records, Central Files, 800/850.4, Information on Lombardo's proposed ouster by Camacho supporters was given to American Consul George P. Shaw by FBI agent Gus Jones on 11 January 1940. Jones received his information from an informant, Francisco de la Garza of San Antonio, Texas, a close friend and confidant of President Camacho.

56. *El Popular* (Mexico City), 31 July 1945; also see *CTAL News* (Mexico City), August 1945.

57. *Excélsior* (Mexico City), 12 February 1946.

58. *Ibid.*, 19 February 1946.

59. *Ultimas Noticias*, 31 July 1946.

60. NARAW, SD Records, RG 59, 812.504/6-2146, Ailshie to the Secretary of State, 21 June 1946.

61. George Meany, "Pan-American Day Address," cited in Serafino Romauldi, *Presidents and Peons: Recollections of a Labor Ambassador* (New York: Funk & Wagnalls, 1967), 47.

62. *CTAL NEWS*, 24 June 1946.

63. *El Popular* (Mexico City), 1 August 1946.

64. *Ibid.*, 22 August 1946.

65. *La Voz de México* (Mexico City), 3 November 1946.

66. *Ibid.*

67. *El Popular* (Mexico City), 23 November 1946.

68. For the rank and file's opposition to the Lombardo-backed slate of candidates for the 1947 CTM elections see *El Popular* (Mexico City), 8 and 9 January 1947.

69. *El Popular* (Mexico City), 10 January 1947.

70. NARAW, SD Records, RG 59, 812.5045/1-1647, Dwight Dickinson to the Secretary of State, 13 February 1947.

71. Statutes of the *Confederación Unica de Trabajadores*, as cited in *La Prensa* (Mexico City), 20 March 1947.

72. *El Universal* (Mexico City), 23 March 1947.

73. NARAW, SD Records, RG 59, 812.5043/4-1847, letter from Juan de Zengotita to the Secretary of State, 27 March 1947.

74. *Ibid.*, 812.5043/8-1547, letter from S. Walter Washington to the Secretary of State, 15 August 1947.

75. *Ibid.*, also see 812.5043/11-647, Washington to the Secretary of State, 15 August 1947.

76. *El Nacional* (Mexico City), 10 January 1948.

77. *Ibid.*

78. *El Popular* (Mexico City), 6 January 1948.

79. The Solidarity Pact's Manifesto as cited in *El Popular* (Mexico City), 13 January 1948.

80. NARAW, SD Records, RG 59, 812.5045/2-1648, Dwight Dickinson to the Secretary of State, 17 February 1948.

81. Mario Gill, *Los Ferrocarrileros* (Mexico: Editorial Extemporaneos, 1971), 148-49.

82. Basurto, *Del avilacamachismo*, 246.

83. Federico Besserer, Victoria Novelo, and Juan Luis Sariego, *El sindicalismo minero en México: 1900-1952* (Mexico: Ediciones Era, 1983), 51-53.

84. Armando Rodríguez Suárez, "¡Nueva Rosita! Drama y Ejemplo de Hombres Dignos," in Mario Gill, ed., *La huelga de Nueva Rosita* (Mexico: MAPRI, 1959), 67, 113.

85, Rodríguez Suárez, "¡Nueva Rosita!" 22.

86. *Ibid.*

FIVE: THE AMERICANS AND CHARRO ENTRENCHMENT

1. For discussion on the growing relationship between the Mexican state, industrialists and American capitalists see Cockroft, *Mexico*, 178. *Latin American Weekly Report*, 16 November 1979, reported that between 1945 and 1979 Latin America received roughly twenty percent of all U.S. investment in the Third World and added that the highest return on investments came from Mexico, which averaged nineteen percent.

2. Norman Caulfield, "Mexican State Development Policy and Labor Internationalism, 1945-1958," *International Review of Social History* 42 (1997): 45-66.

3. Cited in Hobart A. Spalding, Jr., "Unions Look South," in *NACLA Report on the Americas* 22 (May/June 1988): 15.

4. NARAW, SD Records, 820.06/3-2353, memorandum of J.T. Fishburn, State Department labor advisor, to John Moors Cabot, 23 March 1953.

5. NARAW, SD Records, RG 59, 812.062/5-952, R. Smith Simpson to the Secretary of State, 9 May 1952.

6. *Ibid.*, 812.06/9-1153, Stephansky to the Secretary of State, 11 September 1953.

7. *Ibid.*

8. *Ibid.*

9. *Ibid.*, Stephansky to the Secretary of State, 17 March 1954.

10. *Ibid.*

11. *Ibid.*

12. *Ibid.*

13. *Ibid.*

14. *Ibid.*

15. *Ibid.*, 812.06/10-1454, Stephansky's Semi-Annual Labor Report to the Secretary of the State, 14 October 1954.

16. *Ibid.*

17. *Ibid.*, 812.06/3-1754, Stephansky to the Secretary of State, 17 March 1954.

18. *Ibid.*, 812.06/11-2652, Report from Windsor Stroup, American Labor Officer in the U.S. Embassy in Mexico, to the Secretary of State, 26 November 1957.

19. *Ibid.*

20. Caulfield, "Mexican State Development Policy," 61.

21. NARAW, SD Records, RG 59, 812.06/11-2657, Stroup to the Secretary of State, 26 November 1957.

22. *Ibid.*, Ironically Salazar had opposed Gompers and the AFL's activities during the early 1920s when he was an important intellectual leader of the anarchosyndicalist CGT. As early as 1926, however, he began working with Morones and the CROM. The title of his Gompers biography is *Samuel Gompers: presencia de un líder* (Servicio Informativo y Cultural de los Estados Unidos [USIS], 1957).

23. *Ibid.*, 812.06/6-657, Stephansky to the Secretary of State, 6 June 1957.

24. *Ibid.*, 812.06/3-2057, Stephansky's 1956 Annual Labor Report, 20 March 1957.

25. NARAW, SD Records, RG 59, 812.0621/3-1258, A. Kramer, labor attaché of the American Embassy, to the Secretary of State, 12 March 1958.

26. *Ibid.*, A. Kramer, labor attaché of the American Embassy, reported that Mexican government officials were concerned that forceful intervention in the strike might produce martyrs for the strikers, something the ruling party did not want during an election year.

27. *Ibid.*

28. *Ibid.*

29. *Ibid.*, 812.06/3-1754, Stephansky to the Secretary of State, 17 March 1954.

30. Aurora Loyo Brambila, *El movimiento magisterial de 1958 en México*, 2nd ed. (Mexico: Ediciones Era, 1980), 29.

31. Gerardo Peláez, *Historia del sindicato nacional de trabajadores del la educación* (Mexico: Ediciones de Cultura Popular, 1984), 91.

32. Loyo Brambila, *El movimiento*, 46-49.

33. NARAW, SD Records, Central Files, 712/8-2985, 712.00/8-2958, telegram from the U.S. Embassy in Mexico City to the Department of State, 29 August 1958.

34. José Luis Reyna and Raúl Trejo Delarbe, *De Adolfo Rúiz Cortines a Adolfo López Mateos, 1957-1964*, vol. 12 of *La clase obrera en la historia de México*, Pablo González Casanova, ed. (Mexico: Siglo Veintiuno Editores, 1981), 79-81.

35. Demetrio Vallejo, *Las luchas ferrocarrileras que conmovieron a México*, 4th ed. (Mexico: Editorial Hombre Nuevo, 1975), 5-6. Also see Arnoldo Martínez Verdugo, ed., *Historia del comunismo en México* (Mexico: Grijalbo, 1985), 248-49.

36. Vallejo, *Las luchas*, 18.

37. *Ibid.*, 20.

38. *Ibid.*, 26, 27.

39. *Ibid.*

40. Antonio Alonso, *El movimiento ferrocarrilero en México: 1958-59*, 3rd ed. (Mexico: Ediciones Era, 1979), 130.

41. *Ibid.*, 133.

42. NARAW, SD Records, RG 59, 812.062/9-1158, John F. Killea, American Consul General of Monterrey, to the Secretary of State, 11 September 1958.

43. *Ibid.*, 143; Vallejo, *Las luchas*, 39.

44. Cited in Alonso, *El movimiento*, 143.

45. *Ibid.*, 144-45.

46. *Ibid.*, 147.

47. NARAW, SD Records, RG 59, 812. 062/3-759, labor attaché Kramer's telegram to the Secretary of State, 7 March 1959. Also see NARAW, SD Records, RG 59, 812.062/3-1059, telegram from Gray to the Secretary of State, 19 March 1959.

48. *Ibid.*, 812.062/3-2659, telegram from Gray to the Secretary of State, 26 March 1959.

49. *Ibid.*, 812.062/3-2759, telegram from the American Embassy in Mexico City to the Secretary of State, 27 March 1959.

50. *Ibid.*, 812.062/3-3059, telegram from Gray to the Secretary of State, 30 March 1959.

51. *Ibid.*

52. *Ibid.*, 812.062/4-159, Gray to the Secretary of State, 2 April 1959.

53. *Ibid.*

54. *Ibid.*, 812.062/4-359, Gray to the Secretary of State, 3 April 1959.

55. *Ibid.*

56. *Ibid.*, 812.062/4-1459, Terrence Leonhardy, American Consul at Nogales, to the Secretary of State, 14 April 1959.

57. Vallejo, *Las luchas*, 56.

58. NARAW, SD Records, RG 59, 812.062/7-1059, U.S. Embassy assistant labor officer David Simcox to the Secretary of State, 10 July 1959.

59. *Ibid.*

60. *Ibid.*, 812.06/8-2459, David Simcox, assistant labor officer of the American Embassy, and A. Kramer, American Embassy labor attaché in Mexico City, to the Secretary of State, 24 August 1959.

SIX: LEGACY—CHARRISMO AND THE CRISIS OF MEXICAN POLITICAL ECONOMY

1. James M. Cypher, *State and Capital in Mexico: Development Policy Since 1940* (Boulder: Westview Press, 1990), 44-45, 78. Cypher's work is a well-researched interpretation of Mexican development policy since World War II. His explanation of the neo-liberal state's emergence provides an excellent framework for integrating labor relations into the scheme of national economic policy.

2. See Barry Carr, "The Mexican Economic Debacle and the Labor Movement: A new Era or More of the Same?" in Donald L. Wyman, ed., *Mexico's Crisis: Challenges and Opportunities*, Monograph Series, 12 (La Jolla: Center for U.S.-Mexican Studies, University of California at San Diego, 1983), 94-95.

3. For an "official" account of Galván and the DT's activities during the 1970s, see "Homenaje a Rafael Galván," in *Solidaridad*, Numero Extraordinario, 27 September 1980. In the special issue dedicated to Galván, his collaborators during the early 1970s express their accounts of events. Also see Arnoldo Córdova, *La política de masas y el futuro de la izquierda en México* (México: Ediciones Era, 1979) for insight into Galván's movement.

4. *Ibid.*

5. Raúl Trejo Delarbe, "The Mexican Labor Movement: 1917-1975," *Latin American Perspectives* 3 (Winter 1976): 151.

6. Cypher, *State and Capital*, 115.

7. *Ibid.*

8. *Ibid.*

9. *Ibid.*, 167.

10. Cockroft, *Mexico*, 293-94.

11. Cited in Dan La Botz, *Mask of Democracy: Labor Suppression in Mexico Today* (Boston: South End Press, 1992), 162. La Botz culls his information from a December 1990 report issued by the Mexican National Institute of Statistics, Geography and Information (INEGI). La Botz's recent work is probably the best synthesis of current labor- and capital-state relations in Mexico.

12. *Ibid.*, 169.

13. *Ibid.*

14. For information on the Ford LAMOSA strike, I exclusively rely upon Whitney Hoth, "John Gross and the Wildcat Strike at Ford (LAMOSA), Tamaulipas, Mexico: The Rise and Fall of a *Maquiladora* Manager" (Unpublished Paper: Southwest Council of Latin American Studies Meeting, Mérida, Mexico, March 1992). Hoth, a former employee of the Ford Motor Company in Detroit, Michigan, received a guided tour given by John Gross and John Uman, former plant managers of the LAMOSA plant in Nuevo Laredo.

15. *Ibid.*

16. *Mexican Labor News and Analysis*, 1 August 1997.

17. *La Jornada*, 9 July 1997.

18. Andrews, *Shoulder to Shoulder?*, 169-70. Chapter seven provides a provocative interpretation of the interplay between U.S. corporate leaders, American policy makers and the AFL as to how a consensus between these groups developed and how U.S. policy was shaped during the Wilson and Harding administrations toward the Mexican Revolution and Third World nationalism. Andrews also carries the discussion forward to demonstrate how this tripartite alliance has held together until recently.

19. *La Jornada*, 17 July 1997.

20. Richard Roman and Edur Velasco Arregui, "Zapatismo and the Workers Movement in Mexico at the end of the Century," *Monthly Review* (July-August 1997), 103.

21. For a discussion of Hernández Juárez and criticism of his practices and motives for the creation of a new federation see *Mexican Labor News and Analysis*, 5 December 1997.

22. *Mexican Labor News and Analysis*, 16 October 1997.

23. *Ibid.*

24. *Ibid.*

25. *Ibid.*, 5 December 1997.

26. *Ibid.*

27. *Ibid.*, 16 October 1997.

28. *Ibid.*, 22 July 1997.

29. *Ibid.*, 5 December 1997.

30. *Ibid.*, 16 October 1997.

31. *Ibid.*, 5 December 1997; the quote is from Marianne Hart, General Executive Board member of the United Electrical, Radio and Machine Workers' Union (UE), who along with other labor union representatives from the U.S. attended the Frente Auténtico's eleventh annual convention in Oaxtepec, Morelos, 28-30 November 1997.

32. *Ibid.*

33. *Ibid.*

34. *Ibid.*

35. *San Diego Union-Tribune*, 7 December 1997.

BIBLIOGRAPHY

DOCUMENTARY SOURCES AND GOVERNMENT REPORTS

National Archives and Records Administration, Washington, D.C., Records Relating to the Internal Affairs of Mexico, 1910-1910, State Department Records, Record Group 59: Microcopy 274; Rolls 162; 163; and 164.

National Archives and Records Administration, Washington, D.C., Military Intelligence Division, Record Group 165, 1917-1941.

National Archives and Records Administration, Washington, D.C., Records Relating to the Internal Affairs of Mexico, State Department Records, Record Group 59: 1940-1944; 1945-1949; 1950-1955; 1956-1959.

National Archives and Records Administration, Washington, D.C., U.S. Department of State Central Files, 800 Series.

National Archives and Records Administration, Washington, D.C., Department of Justice Investigative Files, Record Group 60.

Investigation of Mexican Affairs: Preliminary Report on the Hearings of the Committee on Foreign Relations, United States Senate, 1919-1920. Washington, D.C.: Government Printing Office, 1920.

Archivo General de la Nación, Mexico City, Ramo de Presidentes: Archivo de Alvaro Obregón; Plutarco Elías Calles; Abelardo Rodríguez; Avila Camacho; Miguel Alemán; Adolfo Ruíz Cortines; and Adolfo López Mateos.

Archivo General de la Nación, Mexico City, Departamento de Trabajo.

Universidad Nacional Autónoma de México, Instituto de Investigaciones Bibliográficas, Centro de Estudios sobre la universidad.

NEWSPAPERS

1906 (Cananea, Mexico) 25 marzo 1943
American Federationist (Washington D.C.)
Ceteme (Mexico City)
CIO News (Indianapolis)
CTAL News (Mexico City)
El Demócrata (Mexico City)
El Diario (Chihuahua, Mexico)
El Imparcial (Mexico City)
El Intruso (Agua Prieta, Mexico)
El Norte (Monterrey)
El Obrero Industrial (Mexico City)
El Popular (Mexico City)
El Porvenir (Monterrey)
El Rebelde (Los Angeles)
El Trabajador (Mexico City)
El Universal (Mexico City)
Excélsior (Mexico City)
Futuro (Mexico City)
Industrial Pioneer (Chicago)

Industrial Solidarity (Chicago)
Juventud Mundial (Mexico City)
La Bandera Roja (Mexico City)
La Nueva Solidaridad (Chicago)
La Prensa (Mexico City)
La Voz de México (Mexico City)
Latin American Weekly Report (London)
Luz (Mexico City)
Mexican Labor News (Mexico City)
Mexican Labor News and Analysis (Mexico City)
Miners' Magazine (Denver)
One Big Union Monthly (Chicago)
Pro-Paria (Orizaba, Mexico)
San Diego Union-Tribune
Solidarity (Cleveland)
Solidaridad (Chicago)
Solidaridad (Veracruz, Mexico)
Solidaridad (Mexico City)
Ultimas Noticias (Mexico City)
Vida Nueva (Mexico City)

PUBLISHED BOOKS, PAMPHLETS AND DISSERTATIONS

Acuña, Rodolfo. *Occupied America: A History of Chicanos.* 3rd ed. New York: Harper & Row, 1988, Third Edition.

Albro, Ward S. *Always a Rebel: Ricardo Flores Magón and the Mexican Revolution.* Fort Worth: Texas Christian University Press, 1992.

_____. *To Die on Your Feet: The Life, Times, and Writings of Práxedis G. Guerrero.* Fort Worth: Texas Christian University Press, 1996.

Aguilar, Javier, ed. *Petroleros: Los sindicatos nacionales en el México contemporaneo.* vol. 1. Mexico: G.V. Editores, 1986.

Alba, Victor. *Politics and the Labor Movement in Latin America.* Stanford: Stanford University Press, 1968.

Alexander, Robert J. *Communism in Latin America.* New Brunswick: University of New Jersey Press, 1957.

Alonso, Antonio. *El movimiento ferrocarilero en México, 1958-1959.* 3rd. ed. Mexico City: Ediciones Era, 1979.

Anderson, Rodney D. *Outcasts In Their Own Land.* DeKalb: Northern Illinois University Press, 1976.

Andrews, Gregg. *Shoulder to Shoulder? The American Federation of Labor, the United States, and the Mexican Revolution, 1910-1924.* Berkeley: University of California Press, 1991.

Anguiano, Arturo. *El estado y la política obrera del cardenismo.* Mexico City: Ediciones Era, 1975.

Aparicio, López. *El movimiento obrero en México.* Mexico City: Ediciones Era, 1975.

Araiza, Luis. *Historia del movimiento obrero mexicano.* Tomo 1-5. Mexico City: Ediciones Casa del Obrero Mundial, 1975.

Ashby, Joe C. *Organized Labor and the Mexican Revolution under Lázaro Cárdenas.* Chapel Hill: University of North Carolina Press, 1967.

Basurto, Jorge. *Cárdenas y el poder sindical.* Mexico City: Ediciones Era, 1975.

_____. *El desarrollo del proletario industrial.* Mexico City: Instituto de Investigaciones Sociales, Universidad Nacional Autónoma de México, 1977.

_____. *Del avilacamachismo al alemanismo (1940-1952)*. Vol. 11 of the *La clase obrera en la historia de México*. Pablo González Casanova, ed. Mexico City: Siglo Veintiuno Editores, 1983.

_____. *En el régimen de Echeverría: rebelión e independencia*. Vol. 14 of *La clase obrera en la historia de México*. Pablo González Casanova, ed. Mexico City: Siglo Veintiuno Editores, 1983.

Beezley, William H. *Insurgent Governor: Abraham González and the Mexican Revolution in Chihuahua*. Lincoln: University of Nebraska Press, 1973.

Benjamin, Thomas and William McNellie, eds. *Other Mexicos: Essays on Regional Mexican History, 1876-1911*. Albuquerque: University of New Mexico Press, 1984.

Bergquist, Charles. *Labor in Latin America: Comparative Essays on Chile, Argentina, Venezuela, and Colombia*. Stanford: Stanford University Press, 1987.

Bernstein, Irving. *The Turbulent Years: A History of the American Worker, 1933-1941*. Boston: Houghton & Mifflin, 1971.

Bernstein, Marvin D. *The Mexican Mining Industry, 1890-1950*. Albany: State University of New York, 1964.

Besserer, Federico, Victoria Novelo and Juan Luis Sariego. *El sindicalismo minero en México, 1900-1952*. Mexico City: Ediciones Era, 1983.

Blaisdell, Lowell. *Desert Revolution, Baja California, 1911*. Madison: University of Wisconsin Press, 1962.

Braverman, Harry. *Labor and Monopoly Capital*. New York: Monthly Review Press, 1974.

Brown, Jonathan. *Oil and Revolution in Mexico*. Berkeley: University of California Press, 1993.

Brown, Jonathan and Alan Knight, eds. *The Mexican Petroleum Industry in the Twentieth Century*. Austin: University of Texas Press, 1992.

Burawoy, Michael. *The Politics of Production: Factory Regimes Under Capitalism and Socialism*. London: Verso Press, 1983.

Calderón, Miguel Angel. *El impacto de la crisis en 1929 en México*. Mexico City: SepSentas, 1982.

Cardoso, Ciro F.S. *La política de masas y el futuro de la izquierda en México*. Mexico City: Ediciones Era, 1979.

_____. *La política de masas del cardenismo*. 2d. ed. Mexico: Ediciones Era, 1976.

Cardoso, Ciro F.S., Francisco G. Hermosillo and Salvador Hernández. *La clase obrera en la historia de México: de la dictadura porfirista a los tiempos libertarios*. Mexico City: Siglo Veintiuno Editores, 1980.

Carr, Barry. *El movimiento obrero y la política en México, 1910-1929*. Mexico City: Ediciones Era, 1981.

_____. *Marxism and Communism in Twentieth-Century Mexico*. Lincoln: University of Nebraska Press, 1992.

Carr, Barry and Ricardo Angaldura Montoya, eds. *The Mexican Left, The Popular Movements, and the Politics of Austerity*. Monograph Series, 18. Center for U.S.-Mexican Studies of the University of California at San Diego, 1986.

Chassen de López, Francie. *Lombardo Toledano y el movimiento obrero mexicano, 1917-1940*. Mexico City: Extemporaneous, 1977.

Christopulos, Diana K. "American Radicals and the Mexican Revolution, 1900-1925." Ph.D. diss., State University of New York at Binghampton, 1980.

Clark, Marjorie Ruth. *Organized Labor in Mexico*. Chapel Hill: University of North Carolina Press, 1934.

Clarke, Tom and Laurie Clements. *Trade Unions Under Capitalism*. Glasgow: Fontana Press, 1977.

Coatsworth, John H. *Growth Against Development: The Economic Impact of Railroads in Porfirian Mexico*. DeKalb: Northern Illinois University Press, 1981.

Cockroft, James D. *Mexico: Class Formation, Capital Accumulation, and the State*. New York: Monthly Review Press, 1983.

Colmenares, Francisco. *Petrolero y lucha de clases en México, 1864-1982*. Mexico City: Ediciones El Caballito, S.A., 1982.
Confederación de Trabajadores de México, CTM, 1936-1941. Mexico City: Talleres Tipográficos Modelo, S.A., 1941.
Cook, Maria Lorena. *Organizing Dissent: Unions, the State, and the Democratic Teachers' Movement*. University Park: Penn State University Press, 1996.
Córdova, Arnoldo. *La ideología de la revolución mexicana: la formación del nuevo régimen*. Mexico City: Ediciones Era, 1973.
_____. *La política de masas del cardenismo*. Mexico City: Ediciones Era, 1974.
_____. *En una época de crisis, 1928-1934*. Vol. 9 of *La clase obrera en la historia de México*. Pablo González Casanova, ed. Mexico City: Siglo Veintuno Editores, 1980.
Cypher, James M. *State and Capital in Mexico, Development Policy Since 1940*. Boulder, Colorado: Westview Press, 1990.
DeShazo, Peter. *Urban Workers and Labor Unions in Chile, 1902-1927*. Madison: University of Wisconsin Press, 1983.
Draper, Theodore. *The Roots of American Communism*. New York: Viking Press, 1957.
Dubofsky, Melvyn. *We Shall Be All: A History of the Industrial Workers of the World*. Chicago: Quadrangle Books, 1969.
Epstein, Edward, ed. *Labor Autonomy and the State in Latin America*. Boston: Unwin & Hyman, 1989.
Foner, Philip S. *Labor and World War I, 1914-1918*. Vol. 7 of *The History of the Labor Movement in the United States*. New York: International Publishers, 1973.
_____. *U.S. Labor Movement and Latin America: A History of Workers' Response to Intervention*, Vol. 1, *1846-1919*. South Hadley, Mass.: Bergin & Garvey Publishers, 1988.
Foster, James C., ed. *American Labor in the Southwest: The First One Hundred Years*. Tucson: University of Arizona Press, 1982.
Gill, Mario. *Los ferrocarrileros*. Mexico City: Editorial Extemporaneous, 1971.
_____. *La Huelga de Nueva Rosita*. Mexico City: MAPRI, 1979.
Gilly, Adolfo. *The Mexican Revolution*. London: Verso Press, 1983.
González Casanova, Pablo. *La clase obrera en la historia de México: en el primer gobierno constitucional, 1917-1920*. Vol. 6 of *La clase obrera en la historia de México*. Pablo González Casanova, ed. Mexico City: Siglo Veintiuno Editores, 1980.
Gordon, David M., Richard Edwards, and Michael Reich. *Segmented Work, Divided Workers: The Historical Transformation of Labor in the United States*. Cambridge: Cambridge University Press, 1982.
Gramsci, Antonio. *Selections from the Prison Notebooks*. New York: International Publishers, 1971.
Grayson, George W. *The Politics of Mexican Oil*. Pittsburgh: University of Pittsburgh Press, 1980.
Guadarrama, Rocío. *Los sindicatos y la política en México: la CROM, 1918-1928*. Mexico City: Ediciones Era, 1981.
Guillen Romo, Hector. *Orígenes de la crisis en México: 1940-1982*. Mexico City: Ediciones Era, 1984.
Hamilton, Nora. *The Limits of State Autonomy: Post-Revolutionary Mexico*. Princeton: Princeton University Press, 1982.
Hart, John M. *Anarchism and the Mexican Working Class, 1860-1931*. Austin: University of Texas Press, 1978.
Hart, John Mason. *Revolutionary Mexico: The Coming and the Process of the Mexican Revolution*. Berkeley: University of California Press, 1987.
Hernández Padilla, Salvador. *El magonismo: historia de una pasión libertaria, 1900-1922*. Mexico City: Ediciones Era, 1984.
Hodges, Donald C. *Intellectual Foundations of the Nicaraguan Revolution*. Austin: University of Texas Press, 1986.
_____. *Mexican Anarchism after the Revolution*. Austin: University of Texas Press, 1995.

Holton, Robert. *British Syndicalism, 1900-1914.* London: Pluto Press, 1976.

Huitrón, Jacinto. *Orígenes e historia del movimiento obrero en México.* Mexico City: Editores Mexicanos Unidos, 1975.

Iglesias, Severo. *Sindicalismo y socialismo en México.* Mexico City: Grijalbo Press, 1970.

Joseph, G.M. *Revolution From Without: Yucatán, Mexico, and the United States, 1880-1924.* Cambridge: Cambridge University Press, 1982.

Katz, Friedrich. *The Secret War in Mexico: Europe, the United States, and the Mexican Revolution.* Portions translated by Loren Goldner. Chicago: University of Chicago Press, 1981.

Knight, Alan. *The Mexican Revolution.* 2 vols. Cambridge: Cambridge University Press, 1986.

Kofas, John V. *The Struggle for Legitimacy: Latin American Labor and the United States, 1930-1960.* Tempe: Arizona State University Press, 1992.

Kornhauser, Arthur. *Industrial Conflict.* New York: McGraw Hill, 1954.

LaBotz, Dan. *The Crisis of Mexican Labor.* New York: Praeger Press, 1988.

_____. *Mask of Democracy: Labor Suppression in Mexico Today.* Boston: South End Press, 1992.

LaFrance, David. *The Mexican Revolution in Puebla, 1908-1913: The Maderista Movement and the Failure of Liberal Reform.* Wilmington, Delaware: Scholarly Resources, 1989.

Leal, Juan Felipe. *La burguesía y el estado Mexicano.* Mexico City: Ediciones El Caballito, 1977.

_____. *México: estado, burocracia y sindicatos.* Mexico City: Ediciones El Caballito, 1980.

Leal, Juan Felipe and José Villaseñor. *En la revolución, 1910-1917.* Vol. 5 of *La clase obrera en la historia de México.* Pablo González Casanova, ed. Mexico City: Siglo Veintiuno Editores, 1988.

_____. *Del estado liberal a los inicios de la dictadura porfirista.* Vol. 2 of *La clase obrera en la historia de México.* Pablo González Casanova, ed. Mexico City: Siglo Veintiuno Editores, 1980.

León Samuel González and Ignacio Marván. *En el cardenismo 1934-1940.* Vol. 10 of *La clase obrera en la historia de México.* Pablo González Casanova, ed. Mexico City: Siglo Veintiuno Editores, 1985.

Levin, N. Gordon, Jr. *Woodrow Wilson and World Politics: America's Response to War and Revolution.* London: Oxford University Press, 1968.

Levenstein, Harvey A. *Labor Organizations in the United States and Mexico: A History of Their Relations.* Westport Connecticut: Greenwood Press, 1971.

Lloyd, Peter. *A Third World Proletariat?* London: Allen & Unwin, 1982.

López Villegas-Manjarrez, Virginia. *La CTM vs. las organizaciones obreras.* Mexico City: Ediciones El Caballito, 1983.

Loyo Brambila, Aurora. *El movimiento magisterial de 1958 en Mexico.* 2nd. ed. Mexico City: Ediciones Era, 1980.

MacLachlan, Colin M. *Anarchism and the Mexican Revolution: The Political Trials of Ricardo Flores Magón in the United States.* Berkeley: University of California Press, 1991.

MacLachlan, Colin M. and William H. Beezley. *El Gran Pueblo: A History of Greater Mexico.* Englewood Cliffs, New Jersey: Prentice Hall Publishers, 1994.

Malloy, James, ed. *Authoritarianism and Corporatism in Latin America.* Pittsburgh: University of Pittsburgh Press, 1977.

Mandel, Bernard. *Samuel Gompers: A Biography.* Yellow Springs, Ohio: Antioch Press, 1963.

Martínez Vergugo, Arnoldo. ed. *Historia del comunismo en México.* Mexico City: Grijalbo, 1985.

Meyer, Jean. *El sinarquismo ¿Un fascismo Mexicano? 1937-1947.* Mexico City: Joaquín Mortiz, 1979.

Meyer, Lorenzo. *Mexico and the United States in the Oil Controversey, 1917-1942*. Muriel Vasconcellos, trans. Austin: University of Texas Press, 1977.

Meyer, Michael C. and William Sherman. *The Course of Mexican History*. 4th ed. New York: Oxford University Press, 1990.

Middlebrook, Kevin J. *The Paradox of Revolution: Labor, the State, and Authoritarianism in Mexico*. Baltimore: Johns Hopkins University Press, 1995.

Millon, Robert. *Mexican Marxist: Vicente Lombardo Toledano*. Chapel Hill: University of North Carolina Press, 1966.

Mills, C. Wright. *The New Men of Power: America's Labor Leaders*. New York: Harcourt, Brace, and Company, 1948.

Montgomery, David. *The Fall of the House of Labor: The Workplace, the State, and American Labor Activism, 1865-1925*. Cambridge: Cambridge University Press, 1987.

_____. *Workers' Control in America: Studies in the History of Work, Technology, and Labor Struggles*. Cambridge: Cambridge University Press, 1976.

Moore, Wilbert E. *Industrialization and Labor: Social Aspects of Economic Development*. Ithaca: Cornell University Press, 1951.

Niblo, Stephen R. *War, Diplomacy, and Development: The United States and Mexico, 1938-1954*. Wilmington, Delaware: Scholarly Resources, 1995.

Nuncio, Abraham. *El grupo Monterrey*. Mexico City: Editorial Nueva Imagen, 1982.

O'Brien, Thomas F. *The Revolutionary Mission: American Enterprise in Latin America, 1900-1945*. Cambridge: Cambridge University Press, 1996.

Palaez, Guillermo. *Partido comunista mexicano: 60 Años de historia*. Culiacán: Universidad Autónoma de Sinaloa, 1980.

Peláez, Gerardo. *Historia del sindicato nacional de trabajadores de la educación*. Mexico City: Ediciones de Cultura Popular, 1984.

Poulantzas, Nicos. *State, Power, and Socialism*. London: New Left Books, 1978.

Quirk, Robert E. *The Mexican Revolution and the Catholic Church, 1910-1929*. Bloomington: Indiana University Press, 1973.

Raat, W. Dirk. *Revoltosos: Mexico's Rebels in the United States, 1903-1923*. College Station: Texas A&M University Press, 1981.

Raat, W. Dirk and William H. Beezley, eds. *Twentieth-Century Mexico*. Lincoln: University of Nebraska Press, 1986.

Radosh, Ronald. *American Labor and United States Foreign Policy*. New York: Random House, 1969.

Revueltas, José. *Ensayo sobre un proletariado sin cabeza*. Mexico: Ediciones Ear, 1980.

Reyna, José Luis and Raúl Trejo Delarbe. *De Adolfo Ruíz Cortines a Adolfo López Mateos 1952-1964*. Vol. 12 of *La clase obrera en la historia de México*. Pablo González Casanova, ed. Mexico City: Siglo Veintiuno Editores, 1981.

Richmond, Douglas W. *Venustiano Carranza's Nationalist Struggle, 1893-1920*. Lincoln: University of Nebraska Press, 1983.

Rivera Castro, José. *En la presidencia de Plutarco Elías Calles, 1924-1928*. Vol. 8 of *La clase obrera en la historia de México*. Pablo González Casanova, ed. Mexico City: Siglo Veintiuno Editores, 1983.

Rocker, Rudolph. *Anarcho-Syndicalism: Theory and Practice*. New York: Gordon Press, 1972.

Rodríguez, Miguel. *Los tranvarios y el anarquismo en México, 1920-1925*. Puebla: Universidad Autónoma de Puebla, 1980.

Romauldi, Serafino. *Presidents and Peons: Recollections of a Labor Ambassador in Latin America*. New York: Funk & Wagnalls, 1967.

Roxborough, Ian. *Unions and Politics in Mexico: The Case of the Automobile Industry*. Cambridge: Cambridge University Press, 1984.

Rudé, George. *The Crowd in History, 1730-1848*. New York: Wiley & Sons, 1964.

Ruiz, Ramón Eduardo. *The Great Rebellion: Mexico, 1905-1924*. New York: Norton & Company, 1980.

_____. *Labor and the Ambivalent Revolutionaries: Mexico, 1911-1923*. Baltimore: Johns Hopkins University Press, 1976.

_____. *The People of Sonora and Yankee Capitalists*. Tucson: University of Arizona Press, 1988.

Salazar, Rosendo. *La Casa del Obrero Mundial*. Mexico City: Costa-Amic, 1962.

_____. *La CTM, su historia y su significado*. Mexico City: Ediciones T.C. Modelo, S.C.L., 1956.

_____. *Historia de las luchas proletarias de México, 1930-1936*. Mexico City: N.p.

Salazar, Rosendo and José G. Escobedo. *Las pugnas de la gleba, 1907-1922*. Mexico City: Comisión Nacional Editorial, 1972.

Saragoza, Alex M. *The Monterrey Elite and the Mexican State, 1880-1940*. Austin: University of Texas Press, 1988.

Scott, Jack. *Yankee Unions Go Home! How the AFL Helped the U.S. Build an Empire in Latin America*. Vancouver: New Star Books, 1978.

Smith, Robert Freeman. *The United States and Revolutionary Nationalism in Mexico, 1916-1932*. Chicago: University of Chicago Press, 1972.

Snow, Sinclair. *The Pan-American Federation of Labor*. Durham, North Carolina: Duke University Press, 1964.

Spalding, Hobart A., Jr. *Organized Labor in Latin America: Historical Case Studies of Urban Workers in Dependent Societies*. New York: Harper Torch-Books, 1977.

Taft, Philip. *The A.F. of L. in the Time of Gompers*. New York: Harper and Brothers, 1957.

Taibo, Paco Ignacio, II. *Los bolshevikis: historia narrativa de los orígenes del comunismo en México, 1919-1925*. Mexico City: Editorial Joaquín, 1986.

Taibo, Paco Ignacio, II. and Rogelio Vizcaíno. *Memoria roja: luchas sindicales de los Años 20*. Mexico City: Ediciones LEEGA, JUCAR, 1984.

Valdivieso Castillo, Julio. *Historia del movimento sindical petrolero en Minatitlán, Veracruz*. Imprenta Mexicana, 1963.

Vallejo, Demetrio. *Las luchas ferrocarrileras que conmovieron a México*. Mexico City: Edición del Movimiento Liberación Nacional, 1977.

Vellinga, Menno. *Economic Development and the Dynamics of Class: Industrialization, Power, and Control in Monterrey, Mexico*. Assen, The Netherlands: Van Gorcum Press, 1979.

Wallerstein, Immanuel, ed. *Labor in the World Social Structure*. Beverly Hills, California: Sage Publications, 1983.

Weinstein, James. *The Decline of Socialism in America, 1912-1925*. New York: Monthly Review Press, 1967.

Wilkie, James W. *The Mexican Revolution: Federal Expenditures and Social Change Since 1910*. Berkeley: University of California Press, 1967.

Williams, William Appleman, ed. *From Colony to Empire: Essays in the History of American Foreign Relations*. New York: John Wiley & Sons, 1972.

Wyman, Donald L., ed. *Mexico's Crisis: Challenges and Opportunities*. Monograph Series no. 12. La Jolla: Center for U.S.-Mexican Studies, University of California at San Diego, 1983.

Yañez Reyes, Serio L. *Génesis de la burocracia sindical cetemista*. Mexico City: Ediciones El Caballito, 1984.

Zamora, Emilio. *El movimiento obrero mexicano en el sur de Texas, 1900-1920*. Mexico City: SepSetentas, 1986.

Zieger, Robert. *The CIO, 1935-1955*. Chapel Hill: University of North Carolina Press, 1995

ARTICLES

Adelson, S. Leif. "Casualidad y conciencia: factores convergentes en la fundación de los sindicatos petroleros de Tampico durante la década de los veinte." *El trabajo y los trabajadores en la historia de México—Labor and Laborers Through Mexican*

History, 632-61. Tucson: University of Arizona Press/Mexico City: El Colegio de México, 1979.

_____. "The Cultural Roots of the Oil Workers' Unions in Tampico, 1910-1925." *The Mexican Petroleum Industry in the Twentieth Century*. Jonathan C. Brown and Alan Knight, eds. Austin: University of Texas Press, 1992.

_____. "La adolescencia del poder: La lucha de los obreros de Tampico para definir los derechos del trabajo, 1910-1920." *Historias* 2 (octubre-diciembre 1982): 85-101.

Adler, Ruth. "Worker Participation in the Administration of the Petroleum Industry, 1938-1940." *The Mexican Petroleum Industry in the Twentieth Century*. Jonathan C. Brown and Alan Knight, eds. Austin: University of Texas Press, 1992.

_____. "La administración obrera en los Ferrocarriles Nacionales de México." *Revista Mexicana de Sociología* 50 (3): 97-124.

Andrews, Gregg. "Robert Haberman, Socialist Ideology, and the Politics of National Reconstruction in Mexico, 1920-1925." *Mexican Studies/Estudios Mexicanos* 6 (Summer 1990): 189-211.

Baena Paz, Guillermina. "La Confederación General de Trabajadores, 1921-1931." *Revista Mexicana de Ciencias Políticas y Sociales* 83 (enero-marzo 1976): 113-86.

Barbosa Cano, Fabio. "El charrozo contra el STPRM." In Luis Medina, *Civilismo y modernicazión del autoriarismo*. Vol. 20 of *Historia de la revolución mexicana*. Mexico City: El Colegio de México, 1979.

Berger, Henry W. "Crisis Diplomacy, 1930-1939." *From Colony to Empire: Essays in the History of American Foreign Relations*, 294-336. New York: John Wiley & Sons, 1972.

Buyer, Herbert O. "The Cananea Incident." *New Mexico Historical Review* 13 (October 1938): 387-415.

Caulfield, Norman. "Wobblies and Mexican Workers in Mining and Petroleum, 1905-1924." *International Review of Social History* 40 (1995): 51-76.

_____. "Mexican State Development Policy and Labor Internationalism, 1945-1958." *International Review of Social History* 42 (1997): 45-66.

García, Adolfo. "The Workers Look to Montevideo." *Industrial Pioneer* (January 1925).

Griswold del Castillo, Richard. "The Mexican Revolution and the Spanish Language Press in the Borderlands." *Journalism History* 4 (Summer 1977): 42-47.

Hart, John M. "The Urban Working Class and the Mexican Revolution: The Case of the Casa del Obrero Mundial." *Hispanic American Historical Review* 58 (February 1978): 1-20.

Katz, Friedrich. "Labor Conditions on Haciendas in Porfirian Mexico: Some Trends and Tendencies." *Hispanic American Historical Review* 52 (February 1974): 1-47.

Levenstein, Harvey. "Leninists Undone by Leninism: Communism and Unionism in the United States and Mexico, 1935-1939." *Labor History* (Spring 1981): 237-61.

Mellinger, Phil. "The Men Have Become Organizers": Labor Conflict and Unionization in the Mexican Mining Communities of Arizona, 1900-1915." *Western Historical Quarterly* 3 (August 1992): 323-48.

Miller, Richard Ulric. "American Railroad Unions and the National Railways of Mexico: An exercise in Nineteenth-Century Proletarian Manifest Destiny." *Labor History* 15 (Spring 1974): 239-60.

Myers, William K. "La Comarca Lagunera: Work, Protest, and Popular Mobilization in North Central Mexico." In *Other Mexicos: Essays on Regional Mexican History, 1876-1911*, 243-75. Thomas Benjamin and William McNellie, eds. Albuquerque: University of New Mexico Press, 1984.

Olvera, Alberto J. "The Rise and Fall of Union Democracy in Poza Rica, 1932-1940." *The Mexican Petroleum Industry in the Twentieth Century*. Jonathan C. Brown and Alan Knight, eds. Austin: University of Texas Press, 1992.

Parlee, Lorena. "The Impact of United States Railroads on Organized Labor and Government Policy in Mexico, 1880-1911." *Hispanic American Historical Review* 64 (August 1984): 443-75.

Rivera Castro, José. "Periodización del sindicalismo petrolero." *Los sindicatos nacionales en el México contemporáneo,* 22-28. Javier Aguilar, ed. Mexico City: G.V. Editores, 1986.

Rodríguez Suárez, Armando. "¡Nueva Rosita! drama y ejemplo de hombres dignos." *La huelga de Nueva Rosita,* 67-113. Mario Gill, ed. Mexico City: MAPRI, 1959.

Roman, Richard and Edur Velasco Arregui, "Zapatismo and the Workers Movement in Mexico at the end of the Century." *Monthly Review* 49 (July-August 1997): 98-116.

Sariego, Juan Luis. "Anarquismo e historia social minera en el norte de México, 1906-1918." *Historias.* 6 (enero-junio 1985): 8-123.

Spalding, Hobart A. "The Two Latin American Foreign Policies of the U.S. Labor Movement: The AFL-CIO Top Brass vs. Rank-and-File." *Science and Society* 56 (1993): 421-39.

_____. "Unions Look South." *NACLA Report on the Americas* 22 (May-June 1988): 14-19.

Taft, Philip. "The Bisbee Deportation." *Labor History* 5 (Spring 1972): 3-40.

Taibo, Paco Ignacio, II. "El breve matrimonio rojo: comunistas y anarcosyndicalistas en la CGT en 1921." *Historias.* 7 (octubre-diciembre 1985): 45-71.

Trejo Delarbe, Raúl. "The Mexican Labor Movement: 1917-1975." Aníbal Yañez, trans. *Latin American Perspectives* 3 (Winter 1976): 133-53.

Walker, David. "Porfirian Labor Politics: Working-Class Organizations in Mexico City and Porfirio Díaz, 1876-1902."*The Americas* 37 (January 1981): 257-89.

Weiler, Peter. "The U.S., International Labor, and the Cold War: the Break-Up of the World Federation of Trade Unions." *Diplomatic History* 5 (1981): 1-22.

Welch, Cliff. "Labor Internationalism: U.S. Involvement in Brazilian Unions, 1945-1965." *Latin American Research Review* 30 (1995): 61-89.

Zapata, Francisco. "Labor and Politics: The Mexican Paradox." *Labor Autonomy and the State in Latin America,* 155-71. Edward C. Epstein, ed. Boston: Unwin & Hyman, 1989.

UNPUBLISHED WORKS

Hoth, Whitney. "John Gross and the Wildcat Strike at Ford (LAMOSA), Tamaulipas, Mexico: The Rise and Fall of a Maquiladora Manager." (Southwest Council of Latin American Studies Meeting, Mérida, Mexico [March 1992]).

INDEX

AFL (American Federation of Labor): 4, 17, 20, 23, 28, 31, 33, 35, 50, 54, 93, 143n26; and CROM, 5, 31, 37-38, 44, 48, 73, 146n88; goals and strategy, 4, 72, 143n26; in Latin America, 93, 102, 143n26; and Mexican government, 5, 12, 17, 31, 39, 48, 50, 53, 73, 90, 143n26, 144n29; opposition to, 4, 17, 71, 86, 90, 92; and ORIT, 90, 94; reform unionism, 7, 35-37, 71, 73, 129; and United States government, 36-37, 73, 101, 129. *See also* Haberman, Meany, nationalism, ORIT.

AFL-CIO (American Federation of Labor-Congress of Industrial Organizations), 134-35

Agrupación de Trabajadores Latino Americanos Sindicalistas. See ATLAS.

Aguirre, Rodolfo (transit worker union head), 44

Alemán, Miguel (President), 8-9, 89, 93, 95

Alianza (union), 108

Alien Act, 36

Allen, José (undercover agent U.S. Department Justice), 47

Alliance for Growth. *See* APEC.

Alliance of Workers and Employees of Buses and Streetcars (CROM), 56

alliances of railroad/mining/petroleum union leaders, 94-95

Almazán, Juan Andréu (presidential candidate), 76

American companies, 26, 47, 50, 57, 80, 82, 127, 153n1

American Cultural Institute, 105

American goods: markets for, 72, 143n26

American labor unions: and *charrismo*, 100-01, 104, 120; involvement in Mexico, 1, 5-7, 9, 12, 17, 55, 78, 87, 101, 106, 129; since GATT and NAFTA, 129. *See also* AFL; CIO; IWW.

American Smelting and Refining Company. *See* ASARCO.

Amilpa, Fernando (FSTDF; CTM leader), 59, 89, 91, 93-94

Amparo Miners' Alliance (CROM), 57

anarchism, 1, 11, 14, 47

Anarchist International Association of Workers, 18

anarchosyndicalism, 2-3, 5-6, 12-13, 18-20, 19, 32, 40, 44-45, 50, 52, 56; tenets of, 2, 4-5, 13, 23, 25. *See also* CGT; IWW.

APEC (Alliance for Growth), 132

arbitration and conciliation boards/committees: 6, 8, 32, 42, 57, 59, 64, 66-67, 74, 78; powers, 79, 133; rulings, 66, 68, 80, 82, 96, 99

Ariete (Casa newspaper), 20

Arizona (Mexican laborers in), 15, 23, 26, 32-33

Arizona Copper Company, 34

Arizona Labor Gazette, 42

Army of the South. *See* Zapata, Emiliano.

ASARCO (American Smelting and Refining Company), 51-52, 71, 79, 82, 98, 146n93

assassinations, 57-58

Atl, Dr. (Geraldo Murillo), 19

ATLAS (*Agrupación de Trabajadores Latino Americanos Sindicalistas*), 103

automobile parts manufacturing plants (*maquiladora*), 123, 126

Avila Camacho, Manuel (cabinet member; president), 8, 75-76, 82, 88-89

Azcapotzalco refinery, 69, 74

Azuara, Aurelio (*El Rebelde* editor), 36, 51

Círculo Azul, 85

Círculo Samuel Gompers, 106, 109

classes: industrialists, 77; workers, 12

Clayton Plan (American), 88, 93

Clinton, William (President), 134

closed shop agreements, 49

CNDP (Committee of Proletarian Defense), 63. *See also* Cárdenas, Lázaro.

CNT (National Chamber of Labor), 62

Coahuila, 37, 41-43, 79, 104

Cold War, 86, 95, 101, 104, 108, 129

Colin, José R. (CONCAMIN), 83

collective bargaining, 49, 53, 60, 84, 119, 129

Comité de Lucha y Democratización, 108

Committee of Proletarian Defense *See* CNDP

"Committee to Prevent Strikes" (1945), 83

Communism: 9, 48, 70, 86, 93, 95 100-05, 107, 109, 111, 115, 118; Communist Third International, 46; Federation of Young Communists, 48; PCM (Mexican Communist Party), 41, 44, 90, 111; World Federation of Trade Unions, 90

companies: company stores, 22, 51; look for stable unions, 52; request government intervention in strikes, 51; required to pay workers back pay, 68; towns, 33, 99; unions, 46, 64

Comte, Auguste (positivist philosopher), 2

CONCAMIN (National Chamber of Commerce), 83

conditions, for workers, 1, 4, 9, 18, 24-25, 32, 39-40, 68-69, 77, 81, 108, 110, 120, 141n45

Confederación de Sociedades Ferrocarrileras. See Confederation of Railway Societies.

Confederación de Trabajadores de México. See CTM.

Confederación General de Trabajadores. See CGT.

Confederación Proletario Nacional. See CPN.

Confederación Regional Obrera Mexicana. See CROM.

Confederación Revolucinaria de Obreros y Campesinos. See CROC.

Confederación Trabajadores de América Latina (Latin American Confederation of Workers). *See* CTAL.

Confederación Unica de Trabajadores. See CUT.

Confederación Unica. See CUT.

Confederation of Railway Societies (*Confederación de Sociedades Ferrocarrileras*), 46, 57

"conflict of an economic order," 68, 74

Congreso del Trabajo (Workers' Congress). *See* CT.

Congress of Industrial Organizations. *See* CIO.

Consejo Coordinador Empresarial (Business Advisory Board). *See* CCE.

Constitution of 1917: 3, 10, 12, 29-30, 47, 49, 59, 65, 107, 125; Article 27, 3, 7, 29, 41, 50; Article 123, 3, 6, 29-31, 39, 41-42 44, 49, 59-60, 115

Constitutionalists: 2, 18-20, 140n24; alliance with Casa and Obregon, 3, 12, 18-20. *See also* Carranza.

Conway, R.G. (company manager), 56

co-optation, 10, 12, 31, 52, 124

Coordinadora Intersindical Primero de Mayo. See Intersindical.

Coordinadoria Democrática Nacional de Telefonistas, 125

Copper Queen Mine (Bisbee, Arizona), 33

Coria, Pedro (IWW organizer), 20, 26, 29, 34-35

Corona (oil company), 53

"Corona Thesis," 94-95

CPN (*Confederación Proletario Nacional*), 80-81, 91-92

criminals as strikebreakers, 49

Cristalería factory, 85, 91

El Trabajador (publication), 46

electrical workers' union, 52, 66, 123-24

electronic assembly plants (*maquiladora*), 123, 126

elite: business, 121-22, 124-26, 132-33; of northern Mexico, 1-3, 9, 14, 17; state-building, 3, 6, 12, 30, 77

embargo (International Seamens' Union), 50

Encina, Dionosio (Mexican communist party head), 90-91, 109

Ericcson Telephone Company, 19, 84

Escalante, Adolpho (electrical workers' union president), 91

Espinosa Mireles, Gustavo (governor), 37

Espinoza, Wenceslao (IWW), 46

exports. *See* manufacturing.

expropriation of industries, 6-7, 19, 31, 42-43, 55-56, 65, 68, 70, 73, 79-81, 84-85, 99. *See also* nationalization.

Fabela, Alfredo A. (*charro* union leader), 119

FAT (*Frente Auténtico del Trabajo* [Authentic Labor Front]). *See* Frente Auténtico.

Federal District Workers union. *See* FSTDF.

Federal Labor Code of 1931, 7-8, 55, 59-60, 118, 132-34; Labor Reform Law of 1980, 125

federal workers' union, 105

Federation of Port Workers, 47

Federation of Railway Unions of the Republic of Mexico, 51

Federation of State Workers. *See* FSTSE.

Federation of Unions of Goods and Services. *See* FESEBES.

Federation of Workers' Unions of the Federal District. *See* FSODF.

Federation of Workers' Unions of the Oil and By-Products Industry (Veracruz), 67

Federation of Young Communists, 48

Fernández Oca, José, 47

Ferrocarril del Pacífico, 115

Ferrocarril Mexicano, 115

Ferrocarriles Nacionales de México. *See* Mexican National Railway.

Ferrocarriles Unidos de Yucatán, 115

FESEBES (Federation of Unions of Goods and Services), 131

Fishing Industry Workers' Union. *See* STP.

Flores Magón, Enrique, 14-15, 20. *See also* PLM.

Flores Magón, Ricardo, 1, 10, 14-15, 135. *See also magonistas*, PLM.

Fodor, Albert (IWW organizer), 42

Ford, Henry, 60

Ford-LAMOSA plant (at Nuevo Laredo), 127-28

foreign capital: economic pressures of, 7, 9-10, 73, 139n5; domination of Mexican economy, 3-4, 12, 68, 99; favored over Mexican workers, 14, 22, 59, 128; power of, 9-12, 22-23, 59

foreign-owned enterprises: 1, 3, 11, 16, 18-19, 40-42, 52, 56; export manufacturing operations, 127; independent trade unions in, 6, 56; light and power, 52, 56; *maquiladora* industry, 127; Mexican Supreme Court rulings on, 48; mining, 5-6, 15, 41-42; petroleum, 5-6, 20, 22-25, 48, 52-53; textiles, 16, 20, 40

Foro (*Foro Sindicalismo ante la Nación*), 130-32

freedom of political affiliation, 99, 132

free-market economic philosophy, 125-26

"Frenesí of Developmentalism," 9

Frente Auténtico (*Frente Auténtico del Trabajo*—Authentic Labor Front [FAT]), 123-24, 132-33

Frey, John (AFL delegate), 44

Friedman, Milton (economics professor), 125

FSODF (Federation of Workers' Unions of the Federal District), 61

FSTDF (Federal District Workers), 59

FSTSE (Federation of State Workers), 103-04

52, 99, 110; protection contracts, 133; sabotage, 117; Spanish language press, 20, 23, 32, 35-36, 39, 41, 43; street demonstrations, 18, 20, 22, 40, 46, 51-52, 66, 94, 111-12, 117, 119; strikebreakers, 49, 57, 75, 89; threats and counter-threats, 111, 116-17; torture, 96; troops, 16, 28-29, 39, 42-43, 46-47, 49, 52-53, 57, 74, 80, 115-16, 119, 124; vigilantism, 124; violence, 31, 40, 42, 52-53, 80, 96, 109-10, 117-20; walkouts, 42, 53, 71, 82, 85, 110-11, 115; yellow-dog contracts, 39-40

Leader Grants (USIS), 105-06, 109

Lejia Paz, Felipe (CROM dissident), 46

Lewis, John L. (CIO leader), 71-73

Little, Frank (IWW leader;martyr), 35

Lombardo Toledano, Vicente, 8, 62, 64-65, 72, 79-80, 82-84, 91, 93, 96, 98, 104-05, 109; and Avila Camacho government, 88-90; and CTM, 65, 70, 74, 76, 83; expelled from CTM, 78, 88-91, 93-94

López Malo, José (mining union leader), 94

López Mateos, Adolfo (president), 109-10, 112, 115

López Portillo, José (president), 122, 125

Lord, James (AFL representative), 37-38, 44

Lozcano family, 85

Lucretia Toriz Feminine League (anarchist), 79

Lugo, Alfredo (IWW organizer), 42

maderistas, 2, 18

Madero, Francisco (leader of the Revolution), 2, 17-18; Mexican Revolution

magonistas, 1-2, 10, 14-15; Flores Magón, Ricardo

"Manifesto to the Workers of the World" (1914), 1

manufacturing, export, 121, 125-26

maquiladora industry, 127-34

Marine Transport Workers' Union (MTW) (IWW-affiliate), 23, 26, 45-46

martial law, 22, 29, 100

Martin, Dick (Canadian Labor Congress spokesman, ORIT president), 134

Martínez, Benedicto (Frente Auténtico, STIMAHCS head, UNT vice-president), 132-33

Martínez, Tomás (IWW organizer), 34-36, 51

Martínez Rojas, Ricardo (CCE head), 132

Marxism, 62, 88

Masonic Lodge, 69, 141n44

May Day celebrations, 18, 47

Maya, Florencia (union president), 105

Meany, George (AFL president), 90, 101-02

mediation, 53

Medina, Nicolás (Frente Auténtico founder), 123

Metal, Steel, Iron and Allied Workers' Union. *See* STIMAHCS.

Metal and Mine Workers' Industrial Union (IWW), 33, 51

Mexican Communist Party. *See* PCM.

Mexican government: and American financial interests, 6, 78; and Bucareli Accords, 50, 146n82; business-government alliance, 121; collaboration with foreign companies, 48; control over trade unions, 7, 77, 102; CROM/AFL cooperation, 41, 48; CTM alliance, 7-9, 55, 65, 70, 74-75; debts, 125; diplomatic recognition, 41, 44, 48-50, 146n82; against labor, 49, 96, 98-100, 108; economic independence/self determination, 55-56, 68, 81, 83; economic stabilization program, 125; economic ties to United States, 86, 120, 124; economy, effect of, 40; foreign capital, 3-4, 7, 12, 22, 68, 99; GATT, 126, 128; imposition of *charro* leadership, 78, 94-101; International Bankers Committee on Mexico, 48; International Monetary Fund, 125; intervention in strikes, 42-43, 49, 66, 91, 107; labor policy, 77, 98, 101-02, 119-20; labor relations, 30, 60, 121; Lombardo Toledano expulsion, 78; manufacturing strategy, 127; NAFTA, 10, 121; national companies privatized, 129; economic development policy, 81, 83, 95, 101, 121, 126; "national interest," 69-70; nationalistic consensus, 77; neo-liberal policies/strategy, 121, 130-31, 155n1; post-war economic readjustment policy, 96, 98; private sector subsidies, 125; privatization, 129; pro-business policy, 121; sub-soil rights (Constitution, Article 27), 29; "structural adjustment," 125-26, 130; Suárez-Tellez Agreement, 81; Supreme Court rulings, 48, 56, 68, 81, 94; technocrats, 126; trade union alliance, 22; and World Bank, 126. *See also* Alemán, Avila Camacho, Calles, Cárdenas, CTM, de la Madrid, Díaz, Echeverría, López Mateos, López Portillo, Obregón, Porfirian government, Salinas de Gortari, Zedillo.

Mexican Gulf (oil company), 53

Mexican immigration into U.S., 39

Mexican Institute of Statistics. *See* INEGI.

Mexican Labor Party (*Partido Laborista Mexicano*), 40

Mexican Liberal Party. *See* PLM.

Mexican Light and Power Company, 56, 66

Mexican National Line (railroad), 115

Mexican National Railway (*Ferrocarriles Nacionales de México*), 66, 110-15, 117

Mexican Petroleum Company, 27

Mexican Revolution, 1-5, 10, 17, 19, 124, 138n3, 140n24. *See also* Madero, Francisco.

Mexican Socialist Party, 40

Mexican Street Car Company (Canadian), 84

Mexican Telephone Company. *See* TELMEX.

Mexican Union of Mechanics, 57

Mexican Zinc (ASARCO subsidiary), 99

Mexican/U.S. trade union working relationships established, 105

mexicanismo, 64, 74

Mexicanization of foreign-owned interests. *See* nationalization.

Mexico, as market for American goods, 72, 143n26

Mexico City, 18-19, 29, 37, 39, 59, 93, 108; general strike of 1916, 12, 22; general strike of 1934, 62

Minatitlán, Veracruz, 43, 56-57

miners: blacklisted, 100; and Frente Auténtico, 123; organized, 15, 23, 32, 50; self-management, 70; uprising, 11

Miners' and Metallurgical Workers' Union. *See* SNTMMSRM.

mining industry: 5-6, 15, 123; and trade unions, 6; 52, 147n102; rank and file unrest, 81

mining/railroad/petroleum union leaders' alliance, 94-95

Ministry of Labor's Workers' Advisory Council, 81

Moctezuma Copper Company (Phelps-Dodge), 81

Modesto Flores, Eduardo (IWW), 51

Monterrey: 39, 47, 60, 71, 79, 82, 85, 119; CTM Pro-Congreso, 85, 91; elite, 60, 64; general strike of 1944, 82; industrialists and capitalists, 59, 76, 124; railroad workers strike, 112, 117

Morenci, Arizona, 15, 34

Moreno (Cantinflas), Mario, 83

Morones, Luis (CROM leader; Calles cabinet member), 29, 37-40, 53, 56-59, 61-62, 64, 76, 144n38; corruption, 56; ties to AFL, 38, 44, 73

Mother Earth (anarchist publication), 20

motion picture union, 83

Moyer, Charles H. (Ex-IWW, WFM, AFL), 33

MRM (Teachers' Revolutionary Movement), 109-10

Múgica, Francisco, 75

multinantional employers, 9, 132-33

multiple action vs. direct action, 24, 26, 37, 46, 53, 67

Murillo, Geraldo (alias Dr. Atl), 19

Murray, John (AFL representative), 20, 37-38